PROGRESS AND REVOLUTION

A Study of the Issues of Our Age

Books by Robert Waelder

PSYCHOLOGICAL ASPECTS OF WAR AND PEACE (1939)

THE LIVING THOUGHTS OF SIGMUND FREUD (ed.) (1941)

BASIC THEORY OF PSYCHOANALYSIS (1960)

PSYCHOANALYTIC AVENUES TO ART (1965)

PROGRESS AND REVOLUTION

A Study of the Issues of Our Age

ROBERT WAELDER

INTERNATIONAL UNIVERSITIES PRESS, INC.

New York

To all those who are not irrevocably committed to one of the current oversimplifications

This whole book is but a draft—nay, but the draft of a draft. Oh, Time, Strength, Cash, and Patience!

—HERMAN MELVILLE

Contents

III

In Personal Matters

A few of the points developed in these essays have been discussed previously in about a dozen articles published in various places over more than thirty years. An attempt is now made to sketch a more comprehensive picture—an attempt to keep in step, while panting heavily, with the rapidly proceeding course of events.

The reader will see that in the evaluation of the essence of modern history I have been greatly influenced by Alexis de Tocqueville and Max Weber. The analysis is then carried a step further, beyond the sociopolitical to the psychological level. The tools for the latter have been provided, except for such classics of common-sense psychology as Aristotle and Thomas Hobbes, by Sigmund Freud whose perspectives permeate the analysis even when his name is not mentioned.

Any man dealing with sociological and political subjects is bound to be asked where he "stands" on the "issues" of his day. Perhaps it is best to inform the reader beforehand on this point: I belong neither to the Right nor to the Left, am neither a Conservative nor a Liberal.

Both philosophies, to my mind, contain elements of truth, but both are misleading because they set down partial truths as absolute and all-inclusive. In the course of the following discussion my views will be developed in detail; but if I were to give a rough sketch of them, I would do so with the help of an example taken from the field of education. There is a story of an Edwardian lady who said to the governess: "Miss X, go into the garden, see what the children are doing, and stop them from doing it." This, in essence, is the conservative approach. The liberal approach would be somewhat like this: "See what the children are doing and help them do it."

I believe that both approaches will, in the great majority of cases, lead to unwelcome consequences.

For the purpose of a scientific investigation one may assume a position of superiority to which one is in fact not entitled, as Freud once said. In order to discern a pattern in the web of fate—if that can be done at all—one must try to detach oneself as far as possible from one's inevitable involvement in the passions and the struggles of the day and try to see contemporary events from a distance, the way we look upon the relics of things long past. The attempt, of course, is never fully successful.

But this —relative—detachment required by the search for truth is offensive to the engagé who marches on what appears to him as the road to salvation. For him, truth is secondary to righteousness (as he sees righteousness) and detachment is the sin of selfish aloofness and complacency. The theoretical mind, on the other hand, feels that most crusades have ended in disillusionment or worse.

Here is a basic dichotomy of our civilization: it has two different roots which have never fully merged; the Hellenic search for clarity and the Christian search for charity. To my mind, the latter cannot be effectively pursued without the former.

Introduction

A tidal wave of change has washed over the northwestern corner of the world in the last two hundred years, spreading from there to other parts, and is now about to encompass the entire globe. The world scene is, of course, filled by human events of all kinds; yet some underlying melody is audible beneath it all as though the whole system with all its disparate trends were still subject to a steady pressure in one direction. There seem to be two trends: a continuously increasing ability of men to control their environment, i.e., a shift in the power relation between nature and man in favor of the latter; and a continuous rise of the lower orders in the social and political hierarchy within the nations and between the nations, i.e., a shift, partial or total, in the power relations between the upper and lower echelons of the pecking order of men. The first of these two trends is the essence of progress in the scientific and technological sense of the word; the second is the core of progress in the moral sense as conceived in modern times, and where it proceeds in violent fashion, we speak of revolution.

The two movements, of man against nature and of the humble aganst those better placed, are closely interwoven: more often than not, those who work for, or support, progress in the first sense are also advocates of progress in the second sense; opponents of scientific-technological progress are often defenders of a traditional social order. This relationship is however, not universal; there have been technocrats who favored elitism (their own), like the Nazis, and advocates of rural simplicity who were egalitarians, like Gandhi.

Both movements, the technological and the democratic, have had some consequences that were not intended by their sponsors. Scientific and technological progress has had victims as well as beneficiaries: it continuously requires new, difficult adjustments and it has led to a struggle as to who is to operate the levers of the new inventions, in the name of what interests and ideals—a struggle that is particularly fierce and dangerous when the inventions at stake are tools of coercion, i.e., weapons.

The struggle against the social hierarchy has led to victories, defeats, and counterattacks; there has been bitterness among the vanquished and disillusion among the victors. Expectations have often risen faster than the capabilities of fulfillment. There has been the inevitable cry of betrayal and the search for scapegoats. Men would not be men if the movement were not as often fraudulent as it is genuine, i.e., if the interests of the humble and weak were not often, consciously or unconsciously, a cover for the aspirations of the ambitious.

The ways in which the two trends and the reactions they have provoked are interwoven provide perhaps the basic plot of modern history.

I

An Essay on Progress

Exact science has laid the world conquered at the feet of man. Nothing threatens him any longer in his cosmic loneliness—nothing but he himself. But this threat is bound to stay with him, for the slightest mistake is now magnified into horrible dimensions, and as nothing in nature resists him any longer, all inner sense of proportion also evaporates.

—WOLFRAM VON DEN STEINEN (1949)[1]

1

Changing Views of Progress

The idea of progress in the sense of a continuous, open-ended, upward movement is a modern conception; it belongs to the historical period with which we are here concerned and is at once an inspiration for rapid change and a theoretical reflection of it.

This does not mean, however, that the idea of progress was altogether alien in past ages. The people of those times were often quite aware of a distance that separated them from a primitive and barbarian past, and sometimes also, as in the case of the ancient Egyptians and the ancient Greeks, from primitive or barbarian neighbors. The distance which they thought their ancestors had traversed could well be called progress; but they looked upon progress as a development that had taken place in the past and was fully consummated by their time. They had reached the plateau of earthly perfection.

They saw achievements both in the control of man's environment, distinguishing them from the *primitive* state of distant ancestors and ignorant outsiders; and in moral terms, distinguishing them from *barbarian* forebears and neighbors. Lucretius described the acquisition of knowledge and skill by early men in these words:

5

All were taught gradually by usage and the active mind's experience as men groped their way forward step by step.

But the process was now finished:

> ... each particular development is brought gradually to the fore by the advance of time, and reason lifts it into the light of day. Men saw one notion after another take shape within their minds *until by their arts they scaled the topmost peak.*[1]*

The chorus in Sophocles' *Antigone* sings the praise of man's achievements: man crosses the seas in the winter storm, he plows the earth, yokes the horse and the bull, catches the fish and birds. He masters language and thought, and has learned to build the political community, the city state. He has found remedies against illness. "He can always help himself. . . . There is only death that he can find no escape from."[2] There is no hint that the ascent would continue in the poet's own, or in later, time.

The same picture emerges with regard to progress from barbarism to civilization in a moral sense; it is seen as substituting the reign of law for primeval lawlessness, and a more humane law, tempered by mercy, for the harsh laws of the ancient talion.

The art of the fifth century is full of representations of the struggle of gods or civilized men against primeval monsters, such as the fight of the Olympic gods against the giants on the Treasury of the Siphnians in Delphi, or the fight between men and centaurs who disturbed the wedding party with their unbridled sexual appetites, on the Zeus temple in Olympia.

Aeschylus shows in his *Oresteia* how the ancient law of talion that demanded blood for blood in unending sequence was replaced by more humane practices which lead to reconciliation and peace. In the most recent of a series of abominations in the house of Atreus, with violence begetting ever new

---

* Superior numbers refer to the Notes at the end of this book. Footnotes are indicated by superior letters and will be found at the bottom of the text page.

violence, Orestes had slain his mother, Clytemnestra. Chased by the Furies, the ancient goddesses of revenge, he came to Athens to ask for asylum; the Furies request his extradition. But younger gods are now ruling on Olympus; Zeus has dethroned his father, Cronus, and has chained the giants. The goddess of the city, Pallas Athena, sets up a court of law, the Areopagus, in which Orestes' case is tried; a tie-vote is broken by Athena in favor of the defendant, who leaves the court a free man. Deprived of the prey that was theirs according to laws of unfathomable antiquity, the Furies spit venom at the new gods and swear revenge on the city. But Athena succeeds in changing their hearts. She offers them a permanent home in Athens and the worship of her citizens if they will stay on as the protective spirits of the city[a]; the Furies, after initial contemptuous rejection, finally accept the offer. Out of primeval spirits of revenge, they become the Eumenides, the well-intentioned ones, the guardians of a civilized law tempered by mercy. The play dramatizes the rise of a milder law among men, and Athenians could take pride in the fact that their city had been the place of this marvelous development.

Here, too, the achievements seem to lie wholly in the past, however, and no further improvement is envisaged.

THE CHRISTIAN VIEW

The Christian age held essentially the same view with regard to natural knowledge and skills. However, in moral matters it believed that the Incarnation of God in history had made a higher morality possible; at the same time, there was some devaluation of the importance of earthly, secular, affairs. Men, of course, continued to do what they could to satisfy their appetites, but a certain stigma became attached to these strivings and the interest of the noblest was diverted to

---

[a] One may wonder how often reformers have had the wisdom to seek the cooperation of the representatives of the old, defeated, ways and to make a serious effort to integrate them into the new order. Modern reformers are not even willing to grant defeated opponents a breathing spell—the time that all organisms need to become adjusted to new conditions.

the supernatural. The earthly existence of the body was seen
as a brief episode in an eternal life and of questionable value
except as a preparation for eternity. This shift of perspective
de-emphasized matters of a material nature and opened a new
dimension of human affairs. Progress from the dark past to
an enlightened present had taken place in a religious sense
as a step from the fallen condition of humanity to a condition in which salvation was possible. The transition had taken
place not through human efforts but through an act of con-
descending Divine Grace in a unique and miraculous event.
From the meeting of this Messianic religion with the latter-
day offshoots of Platonic philosophy, there gradually emerged
the Christian world view. It was a view of a closed universe.

Many centuries later, contact with the Islamic East brought
back to Europe works of the Greek thinkers that had gotten
lost in the Western Empire in the storms of the barbarian
invasions but had been preserved in the East. Translators,
about half of them Jews and Jewish converts,[3] made these
works again accessible to the Latin West which, after initial
resistance against the obviously secular import,[4] accepted
them and integrated them into its own world picture.
Thomas Aquinas, the most important of the integrators,
built his all-embracing system of realms of being in which
Divine Grace topped the structure, perfecting nature but not
replacing it.[5] Enlarged though it now was by Aristotelian science, the universe of the Christian still remained a closed
system.

THE BEGINNING STIRRINGS OF THE NEW

With the onset of the Renaissance, men set themselves against
the limits of a closed universe; they were faithful Christians,
but within an area of their special interest they asked questions where a medieval mind would either have abstained
from reasoning or have accepted the explanations of the
Schoolmen.

It is perhaps not without significance that Dante, who gave

a comprehensive picture, in poetic form, of the Universe of the High Middle Ages, also showed in one episode the beginning stirrings against the confines of this finite world view. Ulysses tells Dante in Hell of his years of wandering over the seas, adventures known from Homer; but there is an episode for which there is no Homeric authority. Ulysses' ships reached the straits of Gibraltar or, as Dante calls it, the pillars of Hercules:

> Where Hercules of old set up his marks,
> As signs that man should never venture farther.[6]

His crews want to turn back, but Ulysses appeals to them to carry on—out into the open Atlantic:

> Consider from what noble seed you spring:
> You were created not to live like beasts,
> But for pursuit of virtue and of knowledge.[7]

They follow his appeal, only to be turned back by horrible experiences once they had entered upon the open ocean. The attempt to disregard the limits that had been set to human endeavor is here regarded not as the sin of rebellion but as a sign of virtue worthy of a "noble seed." Their enterprise, on the other hand, was not successful and the story is told in Hell by the condemned sinner Ulysses. All together, it suggests an ambivalent attitude toward research and adventure, but such ambivalence represents progress over the purely negative attitude of the previous eras; it is the beginning of a shift in valuation which continues to this day.

Probably very few people in the fourteenth century shared the view of Ulysses; it was still a stationary world. Almost a century and a half later, the humanist Lorenzo Valla still called contemptible the mariner who sails his ship on an uncharted course, or the doctor who tries out new medicine on the sick.[8]

Yet the pressures kept mounting, and in the later fifteenth century seafarers set out on all sorts of uncharted courses. After the triumphs of Vasco da Gama and Columbus, there

was no holding people back any longer and European explorers, followed by missionaries, adventurers, traders, and
settlers, swarmed all over the globe.

For a while, the Church still held the line. For his doctrine
of a multiplicity of worlds which contradicted the unique and
central position of man in the cosmic myth of Fall and Redemption, Giordano Bruno died on the stake. One generation
later, the Church, in the trial of Galileo, tried to assert her
authority against the teaching of the heliocentric system; but
this trial, which progressives usually see as a monumental testimony to the fearful power of the Church, was actually more
of a rear-guard action, and not a very successful one, for that
matter. Galileo recanted, it is true, but when, according to
canon law, he should have been held in permanent confine-
ment as a recidivous heretic, the Archbishop of Siena, Ascanio
Piccolomini, asked for permission to be his jailor; and
Galileo spent some time in the archiepiscopal palace in
Siena, legally a prisoner, actually an honored guest, and was
later permitted to live on his little farm. He continued to
hold and, in some degree, to express, the condemned heliocentric doctrine without further interference from the
Church.[9] The "climate of opinion" had changed, and ever
since the Church has been reluctant to throw the book in the
way of developing science.

THE MODERN BELIEF

Toward the end of the eighteenth century, belief in the possibility or the inevitability of progress as a continuing movement took a firm hold in the minds of influential thinkers.
Since progress was no longer a development of the past now
fully consummated, as with Lucretius, but an open-ended
journey toward an infinite horizon, it assumed a quasi-reli-
gious character and inspired men with the same devotion and
enthusiasm that religious beliefs had elicited in preceding
centuries. It saw the Absolute no longer, as the Christian age

had done, as a transcendent Being but as immanent Becoming: the unlimited perfectibility of man.[b]

Once again, progress was seen both in terms of man's control of his environment and in moral terms. The dreams about the former were at first somewhat vague, since the Scientific and the Industrial Revolutions were still in their infancy, but they were no less daring and ambitious for that. One of its prophets, Condorcet, thought that it implied an indefinite increase in the human life span:

> The improvement of medical practice which will become more efficacious with the progress of reason and the social order, will mean the end of infections and hereditary diseases and illnesses brought on by climate or working conditions. It is reasonable to hope that *all other diseases will likewise disappear as their distant causes are discovered*. Would it be absurd then to suppose that the perfection of the human species might be capable of indefinite progress; that the day will come when death will be due only to extraordinary accidents or to the decay of the vital forces, and that ultimately the average span between birth and decay will have no assignable value?[11]

The picture of moral progress was more precise: it was to be, in the words of the same enthusiastic author, "the abolition of inequality between nations, the progress of equality within each nation, and the true perfection of mankind." Condorcet lists some more of its characteristics:

[b] I am applying these philosophical categories largely in accordance with Erich Przywara's philosophy of religion.[10] Przywara distinguishes three forms of religiosity—i.e., of concepts, explicit or implied, of, and attitudes to, the Absolute: immanentism, transcendentism, and transcendentalism, according to whether the Absolute is seen as existing *in* man (immanentism), or *outside* of man (transcendentism), or as the infinite goal *toward* which man may move, approaching it asymptotically without ever reaching it (transcendentalism). The first two are, so to say, static; the third is realized in the movement. Thus, the belief in an eternal God, outside of and above all creation, is transcendentism; the belief in the divine spark in man is immanentism; the belief in the infinite perfectibility of man or of society, coupled with an attitude that finds the fulfillment of life in making a "contribution" to this process, is transcendentalism. Przywara allows for mixed forms and further combines this division with the dichotomies of body vs. mind and of individual vs. collective in order to arrive at a comprehensive scheme.

> How consoling for the philosopher who laments the errors,
> the crimes, the injustices which still pollute the earth and of
> which he is often the victim is this view of the human race,
> emancipated from its shackles, released from the empire of
> fate, and from that of the enemies of progress, advancing
> with a firm and sure step along the path of truth, virtue and
> happiness! It is the contemplation of this prospect that re-
> wards him for all his efforts to assist the progress of reason
> and the defense of liberty. He dares to regard these strivings
> as part of the eternal chain of human destiny....[12]

Condorcet did not stop to ask whether all these goals were
mutually compatible; whether, e.g., liberty was always compatible with equality. Nor did he consider the possibility that
progress itself may have its victims, as his own later fate at
the hand of the French Revolution suggests with diabolic
irony.

Faith in progress became universal in the nineteenth century. The expectations of scientific and technological progress became more specific, fed by the constant triumphs of
discovery and invention and their application to the daily
lives of men. There was also belief in steady moral advance.
These two sides of progress were seen not merely as parallel
but as two facets of an advancing civilization. Men would be
naturally humane once the mind had been liberated from
the bondage of ancient superstition and dogma—as Condorcet
had put it: "emancipated from its shackles, released from
the empire of fate, and from the enemies of progress." Evil
was based on prejudice, i.e., on ignorance and error. Once
again, the Platonic doctrine that virtue was knowledge prevailed; the term "enlightenment" covered them both.

Thus, progress meant a better and longer life with less frustration and suffering for the individual in increasing populations, and an ever more complete reign of justice in all human relations.

THREE VERSIONS OF THE THEORY OF PROGRESS

Progress can be seen either as something very desirable that is by no means assured but that can be achieved if men set themselves to work on it, and fight for it indefatigably; or as a trend of human history, a beneficent destiny of mankind. In the latter case, the trend may be conceived either as resulting from the spontaneous, uncoordinated actions of countless men and women, all pursuing their own business, or it can be conceived as metaphysically inherent in the very nature of reality; Being, in the latter case, would be by its very nature Becoming.

The first of these views, which sees Progress as a possible but not inescapable outcome of a perpetual struggle with Reaction, is the view of the fighting Liberal; the second, which sees it as the consequence of man's individual strivings, is the view of those who generalize from natural science and technology to the whole of human experience; the third, which believes in progress as inherent in Being itself, is the Hegelian view of the identity of the Being and the Ought, of the physical and the moral world, and in our time essentially the view of Marxism-Leninism.[13]

The Manichaean View of Progress

In the first view, progress is by no means a foregone conclusion. It has taken place in the past only in the sense that some civilizations have progressed, and only the progressive civilizations have survived or have prevailed in the long run; but there have also been civilizations that have closed themselves against progress, and they have often lasted in a kind of fossilized state for an embarrassingly long time. It all depends on an incessant struggle between the forces of Progress and the forces of Reaction—the latter formed by an alliance between ignorance and vested interest—i.e., a struggle between the forces of Light and the powers of Darkness. It is a modern version of the dualistic creed of Manichaeism or of the philosophy of Zoroastrianism, of which Manichaeism was itself a latter-day offspring, a philosophy which saw the course of the world as a perpetual struggle between Ormuzd and Ahriman, between Good and Evil. Zoroastrianism or *Manichae-*

ism, with the belief in history as an eternal struggle between Good and Evil, is probably *the secret religion of modern man,* who likes to think of himself as an atheist or an agnostic.[e]

Progress Seen as Due to the Accumulation of Experience

According to the second view, history is a story of progress because the specifically human dimensions of symbolic speech and abstract thought permit upward development to occur through a process that is faster by many orders of magnitude than the slow-moving process of organic evolution through natural selection to which development seems confined in subhuman nature. This human dimension makes possible progress through the accumulation of experience beyond the individual life span. Progress, then, rests on the fact that each generation can hand its knowledge and skills down to its successors, who can start their own efforts on a higher level than their predecessors did; every generation turns matters over to the next in what Ralph Barton Perry called the advancing crest of civilization. This does not mean that mankind is believed to progress in a straight line; there are defeats, relapses, retrogressions, but they are temporary and they never quite wipe out the achievements of the past. This view was clearly expressed by the prehistorian Gordon Childe in the concluding passage of his bird's-eye view of history:

> Progress is real if discontinuous. The upward curve resolves itself into a series of troughs and crests. But in those domains that archaeology as well as written history can survey, no trough ever declines to the low level of the preceding one; each crest out-tops its last precursor.[14]

Progress Seen as Due to an Immanent Trend of Self-perfection

The third view is provided by the Hegelian philosophy.

[e] The belief that human actions can be morally good, bad or indifferent, and that good is opposed by bad, is not in itself religious. However, the belief that all life is a constant struggle between the forces of Good and the forces of Evil, i.e., that all actions have moral significance, and that both individual life and the history of mankind receive meaning and vast significance from the role they play in this struggle, may well be called religious.

The upward movement of history is due not simply to the cumulative effect of knowledge and skills transmitted from generation to generation but rather to a quality intrinsic in all Being, a kind of inherent necessity of self-perfection. Nature is subject to a dialectic law of development in time. Each condition generates its "opposite" and the subsequent struggle leads to a "synthesis." Once quantitative changes have accumulated beyond a certain limit, they become qualitative; differences in degree become, by a sort of quantum jump, differences in kind and the new is born out of the womb of the old. In this way, matter itself is bound to "develop" by its immanent tensions to ever higher forms. It is the ancient doctrine of Heraclitus that everything is in permanent flux and that strife is the father of all things, with a built-in arrow of time. In this way, the dialectic philosophy, either in its idealistic version (Hegel) or in its incomparably more influential materialistic version (Marx-Engels), postulates the existence of, and claims to have explained, a perpetual creative evolution which occurs without an outside creator, but comes about by virtue of a *creativity inherent in matter itself*, and operates through the mechanism of dialectic.

Through a peculiar twist of thought, or sophistry, this deterministic doctrine of progress still holds open the possibility that its course can be influenced, to a degree, by deliberate human action. Those who understand the inextricable laws of history and who diagnose correctly the present situation of society in the scheme of dialectic ascendancy can accelerate the course of events by "correct" action and so hasten the hour of consummation, while incorrect action may delay it for a long time. In this way, this school of thought believes in *inexorable* historical laws, the actualization of which still *depends*, in a measure, on the actions of living men.

This is a strange result. Laws of nature, such as the law of gravitation or the laws of thermodynamics, do not need human hands to make them valid. But the Marxist-Leninist feels that just as the knowledge of the laws of nature has made it possible to influence nature, so must the knowledge of the laws of history—the "science of Marxism-Leninism"—make it possible to influence history. The famous dictum of Francis Bacon—"nature, to be commanded, must first be obeyed"—might thus be extended to include history: history, to be commanded, must first be obeyed; so, approximately, the Marxist of Leninist persuasion seems to think.

This reasoning is seductive, but it has a serious flaw. "To apply the laws of nature" is actually a paradox. "Law" implies an inherent regularity of nature, with the same circumstances always bringing about the same results; "to apply" assumes a free agent, who stands outside of the causal chain and intelligently chooses adequate means to realize his purposes. The former comes from the world of determinism, the latter from the world of freedom; the combination of both suggests a world of necessity, with the speaker himself hovering as a free agent above it.

This paradox is not really disturbing as long as one deals with limited systems. In the applications of physics and chemistry to technology or of physiology and pharmacology to medicine, he who does the applying actually stands outside of the determinism of the system with which he deals. True, his body and his mind may also be determined—in fact, they are conceived as determined in the postulates of science—but their determinateness does not lie in, or at least is not exhausted by, the laws of the physical system which he studies. From the point of view of the natural laws under study, the engineer's mind, however determined in itself, can be looked upon as a free agent.

However, this is no longer true when it comes to applying laws of history in order to influence history. The leaders and the political movements that do the influencing are themselves part of history; and if we take determinism seriously, we must assume that they are themselves determined, a part of the causal chain of events. How can they, then, at the same time stand outside of the events, applying, by operations of reason, the insights gained to the steering of the course of history?

A deterministic outlook like the one adopted by modern science—the guiding postulate of its research, reinforced by the results so gained—might have led to a fatalistic acceptance of destiny, as did the ancient deterministic philosophies of Stoicism and Epicureanism. As will soon be discussed in more detail, however, the attitude of modern man to the world has been active rather than receptive, and its sustaining impulse has been the impulse to mastery rather than that of wonderment and submission. Whereas most modern thinkers have shied away from the ultimate paradox by not expanding the deterministic concept beyond limited systems under study and not making it all-embracing, one offshoot of the modern movement, Marxism-Leninism, has done just this while at the same time adding to determinism a peculiar twist: man, determined by the laws of history, still somehow retains a measure of freedom. He can still steer his capsule, as it were, within the predetermined orbit; he can give history a boost.

One of the results of this paradox is an ambiguity in the concept of "laws" in Marxism-Leninism. The word "law" seems to be used at one moment in the sense of the laws of nature—like the law of gravitation or the law of the conservation of energy—and in the next moment in the sense of the laws that are passed by legislatures to regulate human conduct. Thus, we hear that conflicts within society, e.g., between employer and worker or between ethnic groups— "contradictions," in Marxist-Leninist terminology—are the consequence of the "class structure" of society and must therefore disappear with the disappearance of the private ownership of the means of production in which the class structure is rooted. This is a *law of history*. But when private ownership of the means of production has disappeared and conflicts still continue—e.g., discontent of workers with their wages and working conditions or nationalist sentiments—the Marxists do not draw the conclusion that their theory was wrong and that there are factors other than private property that can produce such tensions; they merely make a *law, in the second sense of the word,* which forbids strikes in industry or the expression of hostility toward ethnic groups, with

heavy penalities attached, on the ground that after the disappearance of capitalism these conflicts have no longer any
right to exist. *The man-made law supported by the mailed
fist of an omnipotent state has now to bring about what the
alleged law of history has failed to deliver.*

So we read in Stalin's *Problems of Leninism:*

> A party is a part of a class, its most advanced part. Several
> parties and, consequently, freedom for parties, can exist only
> in a society in which there are antagonistic classes whose in-
> terests are mutually hostile and irreconcilable—in which
> there are, say, capitalists and workers, landlords and peas-
> ants, kulaks and poor peasants, etc. But in the U.S.S.R. there
> are no longer such classes as the capitalists, the landlords, the
> kulaks, etc. In the U.S.S.R. there are only two classes: workers
> and peasants, whose interests—far from being mutually hos-
> tile—are, on the contrary, friendly. Hence, there is *no ground*
> in the U.S.S.R. for the *existence* of several parties and, con-
> sequently, *no freedom* for these parties.[15]

The twist lies in the double meaning of the word "ground."
In one moment it means ground in nature, ground for existence (as in: there is no ground for the existence of life on
the moon) and in the next moment it means moral or legal
ground, justification (as in: there are no grounds for divorce
in this case). Where there is no ground for existence in the
first sense, no preventive government action is needed; no
prohibitions are needed to prevent prisoners from escaping
through keyholes.

It is as if someone had made the "scientific" discovery that
loose sexual morals are due to the existence of comfortable
furniture such as couches, and on the basis of this theory laws
had been enacted which ordered all such furniture destroyed
and forebade its further production. If thereafter loose sexual
morals still continue, severe penalties would now be decreed
for extramarital sex relations, on the rationale that now, with
the causes for such behavior—the couches—eliminated, there
are no longer any "grounds" for such behavior and "conse-
quently" no freedom to indulge in it.

This possibility of switching back and forth between the two meanings of law—law as a regular pattern of reality and law as a man-made and man-enforced regulation—seems to be essential to Marxism, particularly in its Leninist version. The equation of the factual and the moral has made it possible for the Marxists to keep their theories and actions immune from criticism because they can shift from a factual to a moral position and back again any number of times. Whenever they are criticized on moral grounds—e.g., for the cruelty of their actions—they assume the position of cool "scientific" objectivity; they have only acted in accordance with objective laws. "Don't blame me," said the Cuban Communist leader Che Guevara on such an occasion, "I have only carried out the laws of Marx the scientist."[16] (As though the laws of science needed the services of men to "carry them out.") If, however, they are criticized on factual grounds—e.g., on the ground that capitalism has not actually developed in the way it had been predicted, that workers in capitalist countries have not been sinking into ever greater misery but have seen their fortunes steadily rise—the Marxists assume the position of the outraged moralist; capitalism is simply immoral.[a]

Communist political writing shifts back and forth between these two positions according to the needs of the argument. The tremendous appeal of the ideology to intellectuals whose ambitions or pretensions outrun their capacities is probably due in no small degree to this feature which makes it possible for the adherent of the ideology to be "right," to his own satisfaction at least, in every argument. Some such device that makes a line of reasoning inaccessible to adverse criticism—heads I win, tails you lose—is probably essential if an ideology is to conquer the earth.

[a] The seesaw between the factual and the moral has been described by various authors. Michael Polanyi, for instance, stated: "Any criticism of its [Marxism's] scientific part is rebutted by the moral passions for which its science stands, while any moral objections to it are coldly brushed aside by invoking the inexorable verdict of its scientific findings."[17]

It should be noted, however, that Marxism is not the only offender in this respect. The confusion between "is" and "ought" is quite common; in any case, it is a distinctive characteristic of ideological thinking. William Thomas remarked recently: "The nineteenth-century English historian believed with his scientific contemporaries that he was tracing causes and with his eighteenth-century predecessors that he was also distributing praise and blame. He could slip unphilosophically from laws of behavior to rules of conduct without noticing the difference."[18]

According to this view, the world is so constructed that the good is also the necessary, the law of nature and the moral law coincide, if not necessarily in today's event, at least in the consummation of time which is now close at hand. This Hegelian twist which in its materialistic, Marxian, version has fired the enthusiasm of millions of intellectuals, may have its ultimate roots in the Hebrew concept of Monotheism, i.e., in the concept of a single God, at once the source of all Being and all morality, at once the creator of the Universe and the lawgiver of men.

This concept of Divinity, at once omnipotent and infinitely good, has created the problem of the Theodicy: Why does an omnipotent God permit Evil to exist in the world? "Wherefore do the wicked live, become old, yea, are mighty in power?" (Job, 21:7). The problem does not exist in paganism since the pagan gods, for the most part mythical personifications of natural and social forces, are conceived of neither as omnipotent nor as morally good. With the union of cosmology and morality in Judaism (and the religions with a Judaic basis), however, the questions are inescapable. The answer in the book of Job was to the effect that mortal men cannot comprehend the ways of God: "Whence then comes wisdom and where is the place of understanding? Seeing it is hid from the eyes of the living..." (Job, 28: 20-21).

This has probably always been the feeling of simple piety, but not all people were satisfied with it and numerous other solutions to the question were worked out. One is the transcendentalist solution, which finds the unity of the Being and the Ought in the future: this is an imperfect world in which Evil exists, i.e., in which there are many things that should not be, but it is moving toward a condition in which fact and moral standards will coincide and what should not be will not be.

DISSENTING VOICES

The doctrine of progress, in all these manifestations, held a wide but not unchallenged sway over the minds of nineteenth-century men. The triumphal march of scientific and technological progress in Western civilization was accompanied by a chorus of prophets and critics, of whom more will be said later; but up to World War I at least, belief in the beneficial nature of scientific progress and in the actuality of progress of human kindness was part of the tacit assumptions, of the "unwritten philosophy,"[19] of Western men. In our days, the first of these beliefs has seeped down the pyramid of education and is finally beginning to spread through the illiterate masses of unhistoric peoples. At the same time, the avantgarde of progress, the educated strata of the most advanced nations, is beginning to show signs of disillusionment. A ranking contemporary scientist, the microbiologist René Dubos, wondered whether men would have embarked on the Industrial Revolution if they had realized all its consequences,[20] and the writer Evelyn Waugh was reported to have said that he who would arrest the so-called progress of mankind deserved a monument.[21]

Belief in the reality of humanitarian progress suffered its first heavy blow on the Continent of Europe through the senseless massacres of World War I. In the years following the war, European intellectuals embraced various illiberal—conservative, relativistic, or existentialist—philosophies, and belief in the value of scientific, or the reality of humanitarian, progress was distinctly disreputable. "To continue to believe in progress," said Denis de Rougemont with reference to Europe west of the Russian border, "was an immediate disqualification of the intelligence and the idea quickly emigrated to the U.S.A. and the U.S.S.R."[22]

In the latter countries the philosophy of progress held complete sway. In the United States it took the form of a firm belief in the perpetual increase of wealth and of human welfare and the expansion of democratic institutions—a concept that combined the material goal of abundance with the moral ideal of justice. In Russia the new rulers were utterly convinced of the historical unavoidability of progress as well as of the possibility of consciously directing and accelerating

it through the possession of Marxist-Leninist "science." As
Raymond Aron has said, Leninism is "the ultimate form of
European rationalist progressivism."[23]

After the defeat of Hitler and the renewal of their prosperity, Central and Western Europe seemed to recover from
the shock which they had suffered and to emerge from their
existentialist redoubt into a renewed faith in progress in the
Western sense. The emancipation of the colonial empires—
in itself probably an unavoidable consequence of the colonial
elite coming into contact with Western ideas on the one hand,
and of the weakening of the West's belief in its own right on
the other—was accelerated through the collapse of Western
prestige in the Second World War, and immensely accelerated in addition by Communist support and encouragement of the most radically anti-Western solution of all issues.
All these nations, while rejecting even the faintest trace of
Western dominance, demand the introduction of Western
technology at breakneck speed. They believe in the desirability
of progress in the restricted sense of technical modernization.[24]

2

The Modern Spirit

. . . ye shall be like God.

—GENESIS

From time immemorial, men seem to have felt themselves as part of an enduring whole—the family, the tribe, the cosmos—with which they were identified and to which they had shifted part of their self-concern; and to the degree that they felt themselves as individuals, they felt dependent on superior powers.

The ancient Greeks believed men to be dependent on the will or the whim of immortal gods, who, for the most part, were mythical personifications of the forces of nature and the forces of society, and on an inscrutable fate to which the gods themselves were subject. Gods could be appeased and won over by obedience and sacrifice, and the help of one god might be solicited against another. But such help is not a solid rock on which man can rely in an emergency. His enemy may have stronger Olympian support. Moreover, Artemis explains in Euripides' *Hippolytus* the solidarity between the Olympian gods: if a god is out to destroy a mortal man, the latter's patron among the gods will not interfere; he will revenge himself on the offending god on the day when the latter in turn becomes infatuated with a mortal man and will destroy the rival's protegé in retribution. It is like the principle attributed to the princes of the Renaissance and the Baroque: if you hit my Jew, I hit your Jew.

Furthermore, once the dice of Fate have fallen and the

mortal's day of doom has arrived, his protector god deserts
him so as not to be polluted by contact with human suffering
and human perdition. When Hector flees before the wrath of
Achilles around the walls of Troy,

> ... the father lifted on high his golden scales, and set therein
> two fates of grievous death, one for Achilles, and one for
> horse-taming Hector; then he grasped the balance by the
> midst and raised it; and down sank the day of doom of Hec-
> tor, and departed into Hades; and *Phoebus Apollo left him*.[1]

Moreover, the gods envy the mortal man who has risen too
high and destroy him—a steady motif of Greek thought.
Hubris leads to destruction.

Jew, Christian, and Moslem saw himself in the hand of the
omnipotent Lord God of History. The Jew could influence
God's will by obedience to His laws and a righteous conduct
of life; the Christian hoped that divine grace would make up
for human failings; it was the Moslem's duty to accept Allah's
will without demur.

There has been a progressive change in human attitudes
in the West during the last centuries; a process has taken
place which is characterized by demythification, secularization, and rationalization. Supranatural aspects in the thinking of men have progressively shrunk and supranatural beliefs have declined; traditions have ceased to be accepted
without question. At the same time a systematic self-perpetuating science of nature has come into being and all affairs of
life have been approached in an increasingly rationalist manner. The rise of science is the expression and the consequence
of a new philosophical orientation toward the world; its results seemed to vindicate this philosophy and have thus reinforced it and made it spread around the globe.

THE SHIFT OF INTEREST FROM METAPHYSICS TO PHYSICS

The rise of natural science was, first of all, a consequence of
a radical shift in man's interest.[2] In the Middle Ages, the best
minds devoted their intellectual powers to the solution of

ultimate questions such as these: What was the *origin* of the world? *Why* was the world the way it was rather than different as it might also be imagined? What was the *purpose* of the world in general and of human life in particular?

Generations of able and learned men had struggled with these questions without coming up with universally satisfactory answers—without, as Hume might have put it, reaching a point where the mind comes to rest. As when an army lifts the siege of a city it has long and vainly tried to conquer and turns its attention in another direction where there are better returns for its efforts, so we are witnessing in the beginning of the modern age a decline of interest in these fundamental but apparently unanswerable problems and a corresponding dedication to other, more answerable, questions: *what does actually happen when and how?* It was an act of renunciation or, perhaps, of resignation and, as is often the case when man gives up his naïve aspirations, renunciation was richly rewarded by the enormous harvest of knowledge about worldly things and the consequent possibility of influencing them.[a] In this way, the origin of science can be said to be related to the decline of supranaturalistic and metaphysical interest, and to a concentration on matters secular.

ANCIENT AND MODERN SCIENCE

Science per se was not altogether new; men have tried to understand the world around them and scientific discoveries have been made since the dawn of history, but there are significant differences between ancient and modern science.

Ancient science is largely separated from technology; the former is a matter for the men of thought, the "philosophers," the latter, for practical men like architects and craftsmen; the former proceeds by pure thought; the latter, by the pure

---

[a] For instance: when men gave up trying to build a perpetual motion machine, whether in the absolute sense of creating energy out of nothing or in the sense of a machine that would win energy from cooling the environment, and recognized the fact that these fantasies could not be realized, they had the two fundamental laws of thermodynamics in their hands.

empiricism of trial and error. There is no contact between the two; the roads of the ancient natural philosopher and the ancient artisan and engineer were separate and rarely met. The former became involved in often sterile speculation, for thought alone may get lost in the inexhaustible possibilities in the realm of ideas; while practice alone depends on chance or on trial and error and so can advance only slowly. One may say in a paraphrase of a famous Kantian dictum: ideas without facts are empty, facts without ideas are blind.

It is precisely the most intimate interaction between practical engineering and abstract thought that is characteristic of *modern* science and accounts for its enormous dynamism and rapid progress. In this constant interaction between theory and observation in modern science, philosophical thought abstracts from a wealth of observation a few drops of essence, some hidden Gestalten, which permit one to formulate fruitful questions with which to return to observation.

Ancient science was thus based only on observation of events as they naturally occurred (as in astronomy) or on trial-and-error empiricism (as in ancient medicine). It did not know the genuine experiment in which nature is forced to give an unambiguous answer to questions about basic facts; yet it is to the experiment that modern science owes its rapid advance.

Without experiments, the student of nature could discover only conspicuous and relatively simple regularities, such as those of the planetary movements or of the life cycle of plants and animals; but more hidden and more complex patterns would escape detection by mere observation for a long time, perhaps indefinitely. In particular, it is difficult for the mere observer to establish cause-and-effect relationships conclusively; so many things occur at the same time that one cannot be sure what are necessary conditions of an event, and what is merely accidental. One would have to observe for a long time—sometimes for hundreds and thousands of years— before the answer, purely on observational grounds, could approach conclusiveness.

The experiment permits one to shorten immensely this time of study. In the experiment, the scientist varies only one of the many factors of reality at a time, keeping the others at a constant level, and he registers the consequences. In this way, he presents nature with a precise question and forces her to give an unambiguous answer. In the study of nature, the experiment represents a progress similar to, and as great as, the progress *from food-gathering to food-producing* in neolithic times; it is *information-producing instead of mere information-gathering*.

The experiment, to be sure, is not universally applicable. It requires that the things which we study occur before our eyes, i.e., that they are not a matter of the past; that things can be manipulated by us and are not beyond our reach, as e.g., the stars; that one can vary one factor without simultaneously varying a host of others, i.e., that the various parameters are loosely coupled; and, practically, it also requires that the events run their course within such time limits as is possible for man to plan for. That still leaves many disciplines outside the scope of the experiment. Within the area of its applicability, however, the experiment has immeasurably accelerated the progress of science.

One has often wondered why experiments were so little used in earlier times. Many ancient philosophers of nature made claims that could easily have been tested by experiment but apparently never were. F. M. Cornford cites the doctrine of Anaximenes, according to which "differences of heat and cold can be reduced to difference in density"; this implies, for instance, that water is denser than steam and ice denser than water. As Cornford points out, Anaximenes could easily have tested this hypothesis; he had only to fill a pottery jar full of water and leave it outdoors at freezing temperatures. According to his thesis, the water had to contract in freezing; the simple experiment would have taught him differently.[3]

The absence of systematic experimentation seems to be due to the fatal separation of philosophical thought and practical action. For without philosophical thought, experimentation is limited to trial and error, such as the trying out of various diets in different illnesses suggested by Hippocrates. Philosophical, theoretical thought is necessary to abstract simple essences from the chaos of observation and so to formulate the kind of question that has a chance of producing unambiguous answers.

Galileo, said C. F. von Weizsäcker, "is probably the first to embody that unity which is no longer either philosophy or handicraft because it encompasses both; each of his manipulations is guided by thought, each of his thoughts by experimental evidence."[4]

Another interesting hypothesis regarding the lack of experimentation in ancient science was advanced by the philosopher of science, Samuel Sambursky. He suggested that a kind of inner resistance had to be overcome before experiments could become possible. Experiments force nature to give an unambiguous answer to our questioning; they put nature into a strait jacket. It is about the opposite of the darkness and ambiguity of the answers of the Delphic Pythia. While in the mere observation of nature the human mind is purely passive and receptive, man in experimental research takes an active role toward nature. Perhaps primeval awe of the cosmos had first to be overcome, the world had no longer to be the seat of gods and demigods, or the handiwork of God still somehow participating in His sanctity, before men could adopt this attitude.[5]

It seems to me that Sambursky's hypothesis receives support from an episode that happened so close to our time that we have detailed information about it, viz., Goethe's passionate fight against Newton's optical theories and, in particular, against Newton's demonstration that ordinary light is composed of the colors of the spectrum. Goethe thought that nature must be approached in a contemplative attitude only; he had to his credit a discovery in the field of morphology which could be made by Gestalt perception alone, but he did not understand the experimental method. The following passage is characteristic:

To make the light come into appearance, Newton imposes many a condition upon light—transparent bodies which divert the light from its course, opaque bodies which reflect it and others which it passes; but these conditions do not suffice for him. He gives all kind of forms to the refracting media, arranges the room in which he operates in manifold ways, restricts the light through small openings, through tiny slots and embarrasses it [*bringt es in die Enge*] in a hundred ways. And with all this he claims that all these conditions have no other influence than that of activating the characteristics, the "fits" of light, so that its innermost nature is exposed and what is in it is revealed.[6]

Goethe, apparently, recoiled from what he called "embarrassing nature" (which is the essence of experiment); he wanted men to let nature impress itself upon their minds. He reacted to nature in the way Sambursky thought that the ancients did. It is not without significance that Goethe was fundamentally a pantheist—as were the ancient Greeks.

In a similar way and as part of the same process, the dissection of human corpses, which had been considered sacrilegious since ancient times, became possible in the Renaissance. In antiquity, Galen built his anatomical theories on his dissection of apes, while Alexandrian scholars like Erisimachus had allegedly done anatomical research on living men. Strange as it may seem to us, an age that had little or no inhibition to inflicting torture on the living shrank from the dissection of the dead as a sacrilege. In the fifteenth century a few artists began anatomical studies on human corpses as part of their study of the human body. In the sixteenth century anatomy won its place in medical education; but the anatomical lectures in the Archiginasio Antico in Bologna were still overheard, through a little opening in the wall, by a papal delegate ready to interfere when he deemed it appropriate.

After experiments in physics and chemistry had been well established, there followed in the nineteenth century, not without a great deal of opposition, the biological experiment, which still appears as sacrilegious to many.

In addition to the differences between ancient and modern science which flow from the interaction of theory and practice and the role of experimentation in modern science, there is also a vastly different attitude toward technological applications.

The results of modern science are speedily applied in the service of human purposes. While the main trend goes from pure science through applied science to factory, store, and hospital, there is also a kind of feedback: human "needs" become demands on the technologist which sometimes stimulate progress in pure science.

Science in antiquity, on the other hand, was largely looked upon as a part of contemplation and wisdom; the knowledge of nature gave serenity to the mind. As Virgil said, "Happy is he who could *understand the nature of things* and who has conquered all fear, the inexorable destiny and the noise of the voracious Acheron."[7]

Practical applications were rare. They were not altogether absent, though. Thales used the method of isosceles triangles to measure the distance of a ship from the shore. Archimedes used his discovery of the principle of the lever for the construction of machines to incapacitate Roman ships during the siege of Syracuse. However, there do not seem to have been many such cases in antiquity.

Science, in our day, is still a source of aesthetic delight to its modern devotees, and the pure scientist is more likely to be attracted by its beauty than by its practical applications.[8] But there is always a man of more practical proclivities nearby to take on the job of application. Moreover, the aesthetic delight which the pure scientist finds in the hidden and majestic harmonies of nature has a quality somewhat different from the pleasure described by Virgil. There is in the modern's joy something like a triumph of conquest that existed only in a much more rudimentary fashion in the contemplative pleasures of the ancients, and a kind of self-aggrandizement through the continuous opening of new horizons which in turn wait for their conqueror—an element which was absent in the outlook of the ancients.

Some kind of activity is inherent in any attempt to grasp the nature of things and to develop skills. There are hints, in myth and poetry, that the quest for knowledge and skills had long been felt to be an act of impiety, a trespass upon the precincts of the gods. Lucretius spoke in these words of the discovery of the "nature of things" which he ascribes to Epicurus:

> When human life lay grovelling ... crushed to the earth under the dead weight of superstition ... a man of Greece was first to raise mortal eyes *in defiance*, first *to stand erect and brace the challenge.* Fables of the gods did not crush him nor the lightning flash and the growling menace of the sky. Rather, they quickened his manhood, so that he, first of all men, longed to *smash the constraining locks of nature's doors.*[9]

Much has been written about the barrier which the established Churches with their revealed dogma had set up to scientific progress at a later age, but we can only vaguely sense the primeval curse of sacrilege that once adhered to the search of the unknown.

It was the same with skill; here, too, man invaded the preserves of the gods. Prometheus, according to the myth, taught men many skills and, above all, brought them the fire: for this, he was chained to the rock by order of Zeus and tortured for eons. It is as though certain kinds of knowledge, and certain activities, are the exclusive monopoly of the gods, as they are in the family the prerogative of the parents, and men, like children, fall in sin if they extend their curiosity beyond the borders that have been set for them.

Thus, science in general, and modern science in particular, is the consequence of an act of rebellion against God and of emancipation from traditional inhibitions of thought upheld by fear; and the success of science further reinforces this attitude and brings about further steps of emancipation.

THE DECLINE OF SUPRANATURALISM

Two events in the history of science, in particular, are landmarks of this development: the Galilean conception of inertia which eliminated God as the mover of the stars; and the Darwinian conception of evolution through natural selection which eliminated God as the creator of living organisms marvelously fitted for tasks of high complexity.

For thousands of years, the existence of superhuman powers seemed to be obvious to man. He had only to look at the heavens, at the sun or the moon wandering each day over the firmament before his eyes. He knew from daily experience that when he saw a cart moving along the road or over the fields, he could be sure that a man or an animal was pulling it; he felt sure that somebody must move the sun, the moon, and the planets in their orbits.[10] It was obviously beyond the power of a being like himself to do this; it had to be the work of a superhuman Being, a Being far more powerful than himself. Whoever ventured to deny the existence of God, or gods, would have had to face the question: who is moving the sun and the stars? To this question there was no answer.

It was Galileo who first grasped the fact that motion does not necessarily require a mover, despite the evidence of everyday life here on earth; that objects moving on the surface of the earth need the constant pull or push only because they have to overcome the surface friction, but that without such friction, in a vacuum, a movement once started would continue indefinitely. He thus rejected the Aristotelian theory that force was needed to keep an object in motion, and he substituted for it the theory that every body, without external influence, continues in its motion and that force is required only for a *change of speed*.

Hence, the heavenly bodies traveling in their orbits did not need any force to keep them there; once started on their course, they would keep moving indefinitely. God was no longer needed to explain the daily events in inanimate nature.[b] "I was never in need of that hypothesis," was Laplace's answer to Napoleon's question about the place of God in the Universe.

There remained the question of how the heavenly bodies were *first started* on their course, and that might still point to a divine architect. The concept of God resulting from this was that of the "watchmaker God," the God who had created the cosmos in all its intricacies but had then left it to run for itself, by its own devices, and interfered no longer.

However, there was still a vast area in which the elimination of God was far less easy, viz., the realm of the living. There is organic nature with its many forms of adaptation, filled to the brim with meaning in the teleological sense; in its description, words with supranatural connotations such as wondrous, miraculous, mysterious, come easily to our mind. They appear on all levels of organic life.

There are highly intricate plant and animal organs, well equipped for the task of survival; the cooperation of cells and organs in the maintenance and expansion of life as in homeostasis, or of organisms as in symbiosis or in sexual propagation; there are complex forms of inherited behavior which serve the survival of the individual or, even more wondrous, of the species. How has this all come into being unless through elaborate design? Even though in the inanimate world no supranatural interference was any longer needed for the explanation of things—at least as long as one did not ask the question of origin—the world of the living still seemed to testify in myriad ways to the existence of a creator God.

In the nineteenth century many minds were at work on the problem of making God altogether expendable in the cosmos,

[b] It is characteristic of the extent of human foresight that the Church fought against the heliocentric doctrine which, while difficult to reconcile with the literal interpretation of a passage in the book of Joshua, does not contradict any fundamental tenet of the Faith; but the Church did not react at all to the earlier work of Galileo, his theory of inertia, which had far more revolutionary implications for religion because it removed what had been the most immediately convincing evidence for the existence of higher Powers.

i.e., of making goal-adequate organic structure comprehensible without the design of a supranatural architect. Eventually the question seemed to be solved with the theory of evolution through natural selection, commonly associated with the name of Charles Darwin.

In simplest terms, and in the contemporary, revised, form, the theory holds that the characteristics of the organism are transmitted to the offspring through the genes, the atoms of heredity. Sometimes, albeit rarely, spontaneous mutations appear at random which lead to a slight change in the organism. Some of these random changes are favorable to the survival of the species, others are not; i.e., some mutants survive while others do not. In this way, the species changes in the direction toward increased adaptation, measured in terms of successful procreation. Given eons of time, the development of the most intricate structures, right up to the human brain, can be explained through this mechanism of evolution.

The theory of evolution was one of the greatest events in the history of human thought. It brought to many the sensation of the final emancipation of the human spirit. Now for the first time the whole of the cosmos seemed to be comprehensible in purely naturalistic terms. Men triumphantly proclaimed that they had examined everything and found no evidence of the hand of God.

Whether Darwinian theory is actually an adequate explanation of evolution from the lowest forms of life to man is another question which I am not competent to answer. The aggressive stance of many writers on genetics, the dogmatism with which they rule out any possibility of doubt, the immoderate claims that are made on behalf of the theory—it has been called the greatest achievement of the human mind[11]—do not inspire confidence.

Viewed from the outside, it seems questionable whether the problem of creative innovation in nature has actually been solved by genuine explanation or, as happens so often, been merely hidden behind a convenient word; the word in this case would be "chance." The theory can show why certain organisms survive and others do not: why, e.g., penicillin-resistant microorganisms can take the place of the ordinary, nonresistant, brand. It can show how life "selects" from among the vast offerings of nature those types that survive. But how do new and, in particular, more highly structured forms of life come into being in the first place? It is all well and good to understand why some of the entrants pass the examination and others do not, but how do we explain the emergence of these entrants? This, we hear, is due to "chance mutations"; but is this really an explanation, or has the whole problem of creative evolution been merely hidden behind the word "chance" rather than been explained by it?

Moreover, one can distinguish between micromutations, macromutations, and megamutations. The theory is well established for micromutations; there is daily evidence, in hospitals and in agriculture, that once we have introduced new drugs which kill certain organisms, a variant that is immune to the effects of the drug, or may even thrive on it, is likely to appear. Parasite-killers and pesticides are likely to be effective for some time only. However, there is as yet no evidence for the existence of macromutations and megamutations. One may wonder whether the theory offers a plausible explanation for the ascent of life from amoeba to man. The biochemist and Nobel Laureate Albert Szent-Györgyi recently expressed some doubt in these words:

> If you look at the symbol of a molecule, say riboflavin, . . . you will see some simple geometric figures and the symbols, C, N and H placed at regular intervals. . . . If you look up riboflavin in the Pullman papers you will find the same figure but you will find a series of numbers written alongside every atom and bond. These are indices giving information about certain features of the electronic qualities. These numbers have been obtained at the price of much work and ingenuity. At the measure at which our methods improve, these numbers will become more precise and there will be more and more of them, which means that the whole molecule is not a crude structure built of elementary building blocks but a most refined and complex machine of excessive subtlety, built with a precision which far surpasses the precision of any machinery built by man. If we are ever able to find out all the qualities of the molecule, we will probably find that this is the only molecule which can fulfill the specific function of riboflavin. This molecule has to interact with other

molecules built with the same precision. *What frightens me is the enormous complexity and precision of the system,* which has now been thrown into relief for the first time by quantum mechanics. *I find it difficult to believe that such an enormously complex system could have been built by blind random mutation.* My feeling is that living matter carries in itself a hitherto undefined principle, a tendency for perfecting itself. Whether this principle can be expressed in terms of quantum mechanics, I do not know. It is possible that we have to wait for new physical principles to be discovered.[12]

That would leave us about where we were before the Darwinian theory of evolution.

Szent-Györgyi's last suggestion, incidentally, brings him into the philosophical neighborhood of dialectics; but, of course, a theory of the kind that Szent-Györgyi has in mind would be no closer to Hegelian or Marxian dialectics than modern atomic theory is to the crude ideas of Democritus.

MAN THE CREATOR

The process of human emancipation from subservience to higher powers has not stopped here, and men are beginning to dream of, and to plan for, taking over, or remodeling, the universe.

A recent letter to the editor of a New York daily, written by a professor of physics, is illuminating in this respect. An editorial in the paper had deplored the fact that great works of art and fiction were not produced in America today. The correspondent pointed out that beauty could be found not only in art and literature but also in science, and that it is there that we have to look for it in our time. He then stated:

Creative minds are no longer interested in becoming the type of artist whose work you can understand. Why make daubs on canvas or spread words on paper when you can change the very environment about you? The earth, and ultimately the universe itself, is our marble block to shape as we can.[13]

Man is no longer merely emancipated from divine guidance; he is himself becoming God.

This attitude is not restricted to the control of inanimate nature. Biologists interfere in ever new ways with the ways of nature. They implant organs from one animal to another; they make artificial freaks. In our time, even the process of procreation is no longer left alone: there is artificial insemination. Semen can be kept active under refrigeration and a woman can thus be impregnated by the sperm of a man long dead. A prominent geneticist has called for the setting up of a "sperm bank" in which semen deemed to carry the most desirable genes can be preserved for a long time for purposes of planned breeding. It may soon be possible for one woman to borrow the womb of another woman to carry her baby if pregnancy, for her, is dangerous or just bothersome. It may be possible to change the relative part which the parental organisms have in the genetic equipment of their offspring, to produce, e.g., children who have two thirds of the genetic inheritance from their mothers and only one third from their fathers.[14] The end cannot even be dimly fathomed.

Such developments that we have witnessed in recent times or that we can see on the rising horizon of a not too far distant future are further steps along the road of rationalization and secularization. With these steps, man *sets himself up in the business of creation.* Many a man who considers himself an atheist or an agnostic shrinks back from these ultimate consequences. He shrinks from what he feels to be a sacrilege, though he would not call it so as the word does not exist in his vocabulary. The biologist, Jean Rostand, asks: "Is man not going too far, in this domain as in others?"[15] Yet who is to say what is far enough and what is too far? For Dante, Hercules had set the posts at the straits of Gibraltar as signs that men should never venture farther.

Rostand continues:

One would like to be sure that man will always be able to accept himself, bear himself, be responsible for himself in the new forms he would take. One would like to be sure that he will be able to *adapt himself to all he adds;* that his innovations will not finally offend what might be called the internal sensibility, the awareness of bodily existence of the species. Just as there are thresholds of radioactivity which must not be crossed, so, in the spiritual domain, there may be mysterious barriers which should not be let down, or else the human animal will fall into a state of confusion.

As our horizons expand, there still reappears, on new levels, the old question of the limits of humanity; Rostand is at pains to formulate them in naturalistic terms and to emphasize their naturalistic character by comparing them to the limits of permissible radioactivity, which are now so much in the public eye. But is there really a *basic* difference between the awe that Lucretius told us once stood in the way of a search for truth and the awe that lets men like Rostand—or the present writer, for that matter—shrink back from the prospects of "planning" which biologists hold out? Where is there a borderline that is not merely relative to time? And are the "mysterious barriers" of which Rostand speaks and which he tries to see, naturalistically, in terms of adaptation, fundamentally different from the barriers felt in more ancient times and frankly conceived as religious?

3

The Moral Impulses

Liberty, equality, fraternity.

—THE SLOGAN OF THE FRENCH REVOLUTION

HUMANITARIAN TENDENCIES

Together with the development discussed in the preceding chapter, there has been a continuous rise of compassion for human suffering. Throughout most of history, callousness toward the suffering of others was widespread. Men have been largely indifferent to mass misery. There is little evidence of much compassion for, and hardly any for a revulsion against, the suffering of the vagrant surplus population, the outcast, the slaves, the serfs, the victims of war and pestilence, right into the nineteenth century.

There is unmistakable evidence that, in addition to callous indifference, there was much sadistic delight in the suffering of others, particularly when it could be rationalized in moral terms, as in the case of criminals. Executions, often involving severe tortures, were public spectacles and a major source of popular entertainment. One town might purchase a doomed criminal from another town so as to be able to offer a spectacle to its citizens. At the time of Columbus' discovery of America, some citizens of the economically and artistically highly developed city of Bruges were executed for political activities. When the prescribed tortures had been completed and the executioner was about to administer the *coup de grâce,* some spectators protested that they had not been able to see because the scaffold was too high; the tortures were repeated to accommodate this part of the audience.

Close to our own time, in the early nineteenth century, the lash was a frequent punishment in the British army; the strokes were administered on the bare back by the cat-o'-nine-tails, executed by a relay so that fatigue would not detract from the severity of the blows. Their number often ran into many hundreds, and a fatal outcome was not infrequent. The Duke of York set an upper limit of 360 strokes, but his order was honored more often in the breach than the observance.

Richard Wagner remembered that in his youth, i.e., at approximately the same time, he was once pushed off the sidewalk by a young man in a hurry to get to an execution where a man was broken on the wheel.[1][a]

The idea of eternal torment in Hell is a reflection of the cruelty of the age and served in turn to justify cruelties on earth. It is perhaps characteristic of the temper of the times that St. Thomas Aquinas, the *doctor angelicus*, thought, as had Augustine before him, that the souls in paradise could see the tortures of the damned because their bliss would not be perfect otherwise.[2]

The historian, D. P. Walker, recently studied the decline of the belief in hell during the seventeenth and eighteenth centuries on the basis of the discussion of this subject in the writings of that time.[3] He came to the conclusion that a rising feeling of compassion, alien to preceding generations, made people doubt, and finally refuse to believe, that God could condemn His creatures to such eternal torment.

Humanitarian compassion with suffering and revulsion from cruelty began very slowly. Isolated individuals stand out against a background of callousness and cruelty, e.g., the Jesuit father Friedrich von Spee, who, circumventing the prohibition of his superior, published the first plea in favor of those wantonly condemned for witchcraft (1635).[4] The

---

[a] Perhaps if those who passionately castigate "our culture" for the popular entertainment offered by the "mass media" had any knowledge of popular entertainments in the past, they might take a different view of the matter.

eighteenth century brought the abolition of torture as a legal means of criminal investigation. The sentiment gained momentum and became widespread in the nineteenth century. In some parts of the world, compassion with the "underprivileged"—the poor (individuals or nations), the sick, the retarded, those who have fallen afoul of the law—is the dominant sentiment of the age.

The picture is far from uniform, though. Cruelties as great as any reported from the past have been committed in our time on a larger scale than ever before. However, this has happened mainly not as a matter of frank individual expression but under the flag of an ideology, i.e., for a presumed higher future good. Moreover, such outrages have provoked worldwide reactions, albeit expressed less in efforts at saving the unfortunate victims than in aggression against the perpetrators of these outrages and their (willing or unwilling) cooperators.[b]

POLITICALLY QUALIFIED HUMANITARIANISM

In many cases, humanitarian sentiments are highly discriminating. Men are aroused by the tribulations, real or imaginary, of some and remain indifferent toward those of others. In an essay on the battle of Navarino (1827) in the Greek War of Independence, the historian, Robert Fedden, stated: "Though atrocities were equally and dishonorably divided, liberals in Europe attributed them only to the Turks."[5] It would seem that the peasant lad from Anatolia who was

[b] A case in point is the world reaction to the German war on the Jews. The Soviet Union, most vocal in denouncing the crimes of "Fascism," was the only country which refused to accept any quota of Jewish refugees when League of Nations Commissioner James Macdonald tried to relocate as many German Jews as possible. The United States Government, which admitted and thereby saved a larger number of Jews than any other country, stretched the letter of the immigration laws, but nobody dared suggest that the law be changed or even temporarily suspended in the face of the supreme emergency. The proposal, made by some Jewish representatives, that somewhere temporary shelters be set up to which Jews could freely migrate and where they could stay until they could be relocated—a procedure that might have saved the largest number of Jews—was never considered in any country.

brutally mutilated and slain by Greeks had as much claim to the humanitarian's sympathy as the Greek lad who suffered the same fate at the hand of Turks.

In our time, humanitarian sympathies have been aroused by the condition of the workers, who were seen as victims of exploitation; but there was widespread indifference toward, if not connivance at, the suffering of the Russian peasants, who had to foot most of the bill of industrialization and who were deliberately starved when they resorted to passive resistance. Yet, the peasants, most of whose income was confiscated through the "scissors" of token prices for agricultural deliveries and very high prices for industrial goods, were at least as exploited as industrial workers could ever have been said to be.

In our own days, "progressives" feel compassion with the lot of the poor peasants in prerevolutionary Cuba and in other Latin countries but show little sympathy for the plight of refugees from the present Cuban dictatorship and from revolutionary dictatorships in general. Yet, men and women have waited for months for a chance to leave their native country, and with it every security, economic and emotional, and have had to go, without funds, into an uncertain future—not to speak of those who cross vast stretches of sea on rafts. They must be desperate and should, on purely humanitarian grounds, have as much claim to sympathy as the *campesinos* who, whatever their grievances, have not been driven to such acts of desperation.

This difference in reaction is obviously due to a *political* rather than a humanitarian sentiment. The liberals of 1827 sided with the Greeks because the latter fought to liberate themselves from alien rule. The existence of Greek atrocities threatened to produce a conflict within their hearts; as professed humanitarians, they would have been compelled to protest against such acts and so to weaken the side to which they wished to give their unqualified allegiance. They escaped this conflict by closing their eyes to Greek atrocities and so bought peace of mind and simplicity of outlook at the expense of reality testing.

The progressives of the late 1920s and early 1930s sympathized with the workers—or, more precisely, with the "working class"—and with the party which seemed to represent their interests. The peasant, clinging tenaciously to his small holding and showing little enthusiasm for surrendering voluntarily the product of his toil, stood in the way of what was deemed a political ideal; one either closed one's eyes to his suffering, or claimed that reports were vastly exaggerated by hostile propaganda, or else that his tribulations, however deplorable in themselves, were necessary for the attainment of a higher good. Often enough, one did all these things at the same time.

Progressives in our days feel compassion for the poor peasants of Latin America, but they have hardened their hearts to the suffering of Cuban refugees because the latter come largely from the middle classes; and if some of them turn out to belong to the lower class, the very fact that they have left revolutionary Cuba proves in the eyes of progressives that they are unworthy of sympathy.

Similarly, there were many who rose in moral indignation at the plight of Russian revolutionaries imprisoned or deported to Siberia under the Czar but who were indifferent to or apologetic about the mass executions of oppositionists— real, alleged or merely future prospects—during the first thirty years of Soviet history, including the show trials with the enforced self-denunciation of the victims; who have been indignant at Western colonialism but indifferent to or apologetic about the oppressions and atrocities committed by non-Westerners; indignant at apartheid in South Africa but indifferent to or apologetic about the kind of rule in the German Democratic Republic that made virtually the entire younger generation flee across the border with nothing but the clothes on their backs, so that it became necessary for the authorities to build a wall to keep their people in.

In these and countless similar cases, we have to do with a humanitarianism that is highly selective—a humanitarianism that is politically and ideologically qualified for the sake of an alleged future good. The qualifying political idea was, in the case of the Greek War of Independence, *liberty*; the Greeks fought for liberation from foreign rule, and so they could do no wrong. In the case of the Russian workers and peasants of 1930 or the Cuban peasants and refugees of the early 1960s, the politically qualifying idea is *equality*; the Russian and Cuban Revolutions were aiming at, or were believed to be aiming at, an egalitarian society, and so they could do no wrong. Hence, the purely humanitarian impulse is in many cases diverted and distorted into a *libertarian* or an *egalitarian* impulse. Both are claims made in the name of justice and the rights of man.

THE CONCEPT OF JUSTICE

On a high level of abstraction, agreement about the nature of justice is easy. It is the principle of *suum cuique*—to each his due. The *Institutiones* of Justinian formulated it in these words:

> Justice is the constant and earnest will to render to every man his due.
>
> The precepts of the law are these: to live honorably, to injure no other man, to render every man his due.[6]

Throughout the ages there has been agreement that an order is just if it gives to everybody his due. But the statement is tautological; the question is precisely *what* a man's due is.

For Aristotle, justice meant treating unequal things unequally: "It is thought that justice is equality, and so it is, but not for everybody but only for those who are equals; and it is thought that inequality is just, for so indeed it is, though not for everybody, but for those who are unequal."[7] That could justify any degree of social inequality; Aristotle did, in fact, justify slavery on the ground that some people were born to no better lot.

We moderns, on the other hand, are more inclined to think that justice means treating all people alike, regardless of how unequal they may be in their natural endowment and the conditions of their early lives; and some of us go farther still and think that justice demands to treat unequal things unequally in a sense exactly opposite to that intended by Aristotle, viz., to give special odds to those not favored by nature and early environment and so to compensate for the inequalities of nature and chance.

Does social justice consist of accepting, disregarding, or actively correcting the inequalities of nature, chance, or past history?

Justice, in a social context, faces the fact of the *stratification* of society and has to deal with it. All human societies known to us have been stratified, not excluding those that were founded on egalitarian principles. Stratification also appears on the subhuman level, in animal groups. If we are to understand the general character of social stratification, we should perhaps look first at its manifestations on the subhuman level.

STRATIFICATION IN THE ANIMAL KINGDOM

In 1922, the zoologist Schjelderup-Ebbe discovered the social hierarchy among birds and called it the pecking order.[8] He found some pattern in the well-known pecking behavior: one hen hits another with her beak, sometimes slightly and sometimes very hard, in a way that would be painful even to a human, but the recipient of this treatment usually accepts it without resistance and without trying to retaliate. Schjelderup-Ebbe concluded that the right to peck another bird with impunity constitutes what may be called social rank among the birds. It turned out that among hens the social order so defined is largely linear, i.e., that there is a bird at the top of the flock that pecks everyone else and is pecked by no one; a bird second in rank is pecked by the top-bird but pecks all the others; and so on, down to the "buck private" of the flock that is pecked by everyone else and pecks no one. Sometimes, there is the complication of a circular pecking order where A pecks B, B pecks C, and C pecks A.

While the possibility of expressing one's aggressiveness at the expense of someone else remains a criterion of social rank in the animal kingdom, further investigations among animals have shown that it is not the only one. Dominance is not merely a matter of interpersonal relations, as it were, but also a matter of differential relationship to third objects, persons or things. In a group of two or more animals, one animal is likely to have preferred access to food; the other animals do not touch the food until the first one is fully satisfied. When supplies are short, they may actually starve. Furthermore, some males have preferred access to females in the group; other males, who are sexually active when alone with the females, are discouraged by the presence of a dominant male. A few successful males may actually impose celibacy upon the great majority of the males, who in this way are, so to say, socially castrated. Finally, one animal may be ahead of another in escaping from situations of discomfort or danger when only one can escape at a time.

On the whole, these criteria seem to coincide: the animal that qualifies as dominant according to one criterion is likely to qualify according to the other criteria as well. Social rank in the animal kingdom is then measured by *preferred access to incentives*—food, the sexual object, and safety—*and by the possibility of abusing others with impunity*. This seems quite similar to the way in which privilege manifests itself among men.

The pecking order, in some species, is rigidly tyrannical, as is the case with the species in which Schjelderup-Ebbe made his original discovery. In other species, the social distance, so to speak, between the upper and the lower ranks may be smaller; all members of the group may peck everyone else and be pecked by everyone else in the group, and dominance is merely a matter of the relative frequency with which the one and the other occur.

The following factors, expressed with a minimum of anthropomorphism, seem to make for dominance: superior health, seniority, size, physical strength, courage, pugnacity, fighting ability, ability to bluff, prestige (i.e., the memory of past victories), and closeness to home territory; in females, also the time of oestrus.

Dominance as manifested in preferred access to desirable things and as the right to abuse the others with impunity serves the interests of the dominant animal; the interests of the submissive one are, in the case of preferred access to goals, merely disregarded; while in the second case of permitted abuse, the submissive one is actively exploited by the dominant animal and has to suffer pain, perhaps death, for the satisfaction of its master.

This is, however, not the whole picture. Sometimes, the dominant animal also exercises leadership in pursuits that are in the interests of the whole flock, and so promotes the interest of all. There seems to be no regular relationship between dominance and leadership among animals. Of this, more will be said later in a different context.

Some authors of Rightist inclination—Schjelderup-Ebbe among them—have claimed on the basis of these observations that despotism is a universal law of nature and should therefore be considered necessary and unalterable.[9] Authors of the Left, on the other hand, in particular Marxists, maintain for that very reason that the social life of animals has no relevance for the social life of man, which follows an entirely different kind of law. Both sides, it seems to me, overshoot the mark. What we know about the social hierarchy among animals does not prove that despotism among men is inescapable. For one thing, not all animal pecking orders are clearly linear; it so happened that Schjelderup-Ebbe had hit upon an animal society whose structure may be called despotic. Even if this condition were universal, however, it would not prove that man cannot alter it; for man, though rooted in nature, can transcend it to a large degree. As Denis de Rougemont put it: *"Man's nature is to pass beyond nature."*[10]

On the other hand, the laws of animal societies are not irrelevant for human societies. For while man has risen above
his animal relations, he still shares with them some core in
his nature, a kind of substratum of his being. Thus, the uni-
versality of stratification in animal groups suggests not that
man is unalterably bound to the same pattern, but that the
condition is deeply rooted and can probably not be overcome
by such relatively superficial environmental changes as the
abolition of private property.

HUMAN STRATIFICATION

The various features of animal stratification have their anal-
ogies in the social life of humans. The human world, to be
sure, is much richer. Man may belong to many social hierarchies at the same time and rank differently in each: he may
rank high as an athlete and low in social status, high as a lover
and low in his work, high in the economic scale and low in
military service. Above all, the social order is often influenced
by ideas, and that is specifically human.

Moreover, human stratification has an important hereditary element. Men are born into their social place; and in
some instances, as in the Indian caste system or in European
feudalism, birth determines social rank unalterably. In other
instances, as in capitalist society, the inborn rank is not unalterable, since the property on which it essentially depends
is not unchangeable but subject to the fluctuations of the market; but it still makes for great differences of opportunity.
It takes more than the proverbial three generations to dissi-
pate a really great fortune, particularly if it is legally protected against dissipation by heirs.

In bureaucratic societies without much income-yielding
private property, hereditary privileges are further reduced
though not altogether eliminated. It is inevitable that the
sons and daughters of high officials in the centers of administration have better opportunities for advancement than the

sons and daughters of semi-literate collective farmers in a culturally remote corner of the country.

THE MODERN VIEW OF SOCIAL JUSTICE

Moderns reject inborn inequalities as clearly unjust; there is little disagreement on this score. But once hereditary privileges have been wholly or largely eliminated, an alternative presents itself: one can aim at equality of opportunity, i.e., at liberty for all to rise as they may, or at equality of station, i.e., actual equality of life circumstances. In the latter condition, some theorists still make allowance for differences of function (as between factory worker and factory manager) while insisting that they must have no bearing on income and human dignity; others, Marx and Lenin among them, went further and even expected functional differences to disappear in the socialist dispensation: every man will fulfill every function part of his time, including the function of governing, somewhat the way it is believed to have been among Athenian citizens of the classic age.

Under conditions of *equality of opportunity*, life is a race which is conducted under equal conditions. All start from where they are and arrive at very different places. A pecking order establishes itself.

Some feel, however, that there is no real equality of opportunity as long as the starting points differ with regard to past history such as education and early childhood conditions; equality of opportunity thus seems to require arrangements that would guarantee to everybody equal starting conditions in this broader sense: and until the latter can be assured, a system of compensatory advantages and handicaps seems indicated. Others go still further and request that not only inequalities due to past history but also inequalities due to nature be eliminated.

In this way, equality of opportunity approaches *equality of status*; people should not start at the same point and arrive at different points, but everybody should arrive at the same point at the same time.

If that is to be achieved, there must be a permanent system of odds, as in games of chess between players of vastly different strength. Such odds may consist in different starting conditions or in handicaps along the road which prevent the frontrunners from taking full advantage of their talents or their opportunities.

Hence, an egalitarian order requires constant interference from the outside to forestall the establishment of a pecking order.

LIBERTY AND EQUALITY

Liberty and equality were coupled together in the slogan of the French Revolution and have remained closely associated in public consciousness ever since. Yet, they are actually compatible only in a specific context and become contradictory outside of it.

They are reconcilable and may be identical as long as liberty means liberation from restraints imposed by a common master; for slaves, liberty and equality (with the free) mean the same thing. But they become opposites once liberty is applied not only to the relations of the members of a group to their superiors but also to their relations *among themselves*; for where there is liberty in interpersonal relations, a pecking order quickly emerges, whereas equality means the absence of such a hierarchy.

If a group of children at a party is left to themselves, without adult supervision, some children may get more ice cream than others and some may get none at all; some will determine what games are to be played, while others will have to go along; some will allocate the more desirable roles in the games to themselves and their friends, while others will have to take what is left. If we want all children to get an equal share of the refreshments and all to take their turn in the games, somebody with authority has to supervise the proceedings.

If men are free to pursue gainful activities, the result will be that some people will be more affluent than others; if equality of income and wealth is to prevail, activities that may lead to personal enrichment must be forbidden. If people are free to practice polygamy, some men will have several wives while others will have none; if every man is to have a fairly even chance of finding a mate, nobody must be permitted to have more than one. If people are free to choose their place of abode, there will be more and less desirable neighborhoods; if housing discrimination is to be prevented, the freedom of living where one wants must be curtailed.

These facts have their roots in the unequal distribution of abilities and in the inclination, natural to all living beings, of looking out first for their interests and the interests of those closest to them, a condition that education can modify in humans but not altogether undo.

Native endowment varies in a wide spectrum with regard to many characteristics that are relevant for social dominance; experience may increase or diminish these inborn inequalities. The product of native endowment and early life history, the adult person, shows wide differences in qualities such as physical strength, physical and mental health, endurance, initiative, perseverance, aggressiveness, frustration tolerance, self-control, morale, judgment, and creativity. Whenever people are left to themselves, these differences will become manifest in differences of social rank; if the latter is to be forestalled, authority must constantly intervene.

It may well be held that interference with liberty is a characteristic which the request of equality shares with *all* moral imperatives; the rules of the Decalogue—thou shalt not kill, thou shalt not steal, thou shalt not commit adultery, for instance—may be said to interfere with the freedom to kill, to steal, and to commit adultery. Yet, these rules can be implanted by education in the individual consciences; once this has been done, and men have made them their own, the respective prohibitions are no longer felt as restrictions of liberty because the particular liberty is no longer appreciated

This is true, but a few points must be added. First, the internalization of moral commands is never universal, as is shown by the continued existence of criminal codes, police and law courts in all political systems. Moreover, the internalization has been conspicuously less successful in some areas than in others; the prohibition of adultery, for instance, is less generally accepted than that of homicide; and the less internal acceptance there is, the greater is the dependence on external enforcement if the rule is to be obeyed at all. Finally, the demand for equality, seen as a moral principle, requires the sharing of all desirable things; i.e., it is in essence a prohibition of selfishness and that is a far more sweeping demand than any of the previously cited rules which restrict liberty only with regard to particular activities. Particularly if the required renunciation of self-concern is not limited to a special aspect of it, e.g., material goods, but extends to all things desirable, including, e.g., power, influence, and status, the renunciation asked for is on so vast a scale that it seems doubtful to me that the result could ever be achieved, in a majority of people, by educational indoctrination alone; it is more likely that realization would require the constant threat of external force. Perhaps, some people may be able to forgo concern for self all the time, and most of the people will be able to do so some of the time, under the impact of a strong collective emotion, but one cannot expect it to be done by all the people all the time.

To sum up: while liberty in relation to a master is compatible with equality within a group, intragroup liberty and equality are *complementary goods,* i.e., the one can be advanced only at the expense of the other.[11]

It seems strange that these simple relationships have rarely been understood. Goethe saw it quite early; he wrote: "Lawgivers or legislators who promise both equality and liberty are either utopian dreamers or charlatans."[12] George Santayana said in our century that in social democracy—which is Santayana's term for an egalitarian society—"the only free man would be the one whose ideal was to be an average man."[13] But these are isolated voices.

The libertarian impulse was dominant in the late eighteenth and nineteenth centuries; the egalitarian impulse grew noticeably in the latter part of the nineteenth century and has been gaining great momentum in the last generation.[c]

At the present time, pure, undiluted libertarianism has a somewhat sectarian character. The world is divided between a West which seeks a balance, or compromise, between libertarian and egalitarian tendencies, and the rest of the world which seems to be committed to an egalitarian philosophy (though not necessarily to an egalitarian practice).

---

[c] However, the fact of a dominant egalitarian sentiment does not necessarily mean that we are actually moving toward greater equality. It may well be that the egalitarian moral sentiment provides a climate in which a new elite of intellectuals, a kind of secular priesthood, which persistently challenges the authorities in the name of egalitarian morality, can rise to power, just as in ancient Israel the priesthood challenged the kings in the name of the law of God and so established its own power. We now see clearly how the incessant cry for liberty in the eighteenth century made it possible for a patriciate of wealth to form itself and to oust a nobility of birth from the seats of power. Perhaps a later age will find that in our time the cry for equality made it possible that this patriciate of wealth was in turn ousted by a rising mandarinate operating the tools of indoctrination.

4

Assets and Liabilities of the Modern Movement

Everything that is perfect in one direction is harmful in another.

—CHUANG TZU (4th c. B.C.)[1]

In history ... one value must always give way for another to emerge, and only those who are happily—or wantonly—prejudiced believe in absolute progress.

—ROMANO GUARDINI (1945)[2]

GENERAL CONSIDERATIONS REGARDING SCIENTIFIC AND TECHNOLOGICAL PROGRESS

The assets of scientific and technological progress as they appear at this point of the unfolding story are plain for everyone to see. They are manifested, above all, in biological terms, as a proliferation of human life both through the increase of the population of the earth and the simultaneous rise in individual life expectancy. The universal experience of archaic societies collapsing in contact with advanced Western societies and the present, impetuous demand of the educated strata of these societies for the immediate and rapid introduction of the technological aspects of Western civilization testify to its superiority, so far, in terms of worldly success. The case was well put by C. H. Waddington:

> The major political force which is shaping in our time is the conviction of these people [i.e., in India or China] that to

die at eighty after a healthy life using inanimate sources of
power is, in some real and undeniable sense, better than to
die at forty after a life of backbreaking labor, hunger and
sickness.[3]

At this point of the unfolding events, there can be no doubt
that progress in this sense has been real and very great.
Whether its achievements will grow further, or even be
maintained, is still hidden in the future. On the moral side,
we can say that humane sentiments have grown stronger, but
the width of their distribution and, in many cases, their solid-
ity under pressure are open to question. There is also vast inhumanity in the name of ideals.

There remain some questions regarding progress which
only history can answer: its possible range, its continuation
over prolonged time, its costs, and its built-in contradictions.
In their enthusiasm for progress and their desire to reap its
benefits, the devotees of progress, a still increasing host, have
failed to ask any of these questions.

There are simple reasons why progress must have a price.
One rests on the fact that some of the things men cherish are
mutually contradictory so that one can be achieved only at
some cost to another. They are what economists call complementary goods. Sometimes, aspirations are clearly mutually
exclusive and form true *logical* antinomies; sometimes, it is
more a matter of *psychological* incompatibility.

Among the former are the antinomies of change and stability or of progress and security. Every change does away with
stability. There are values in stability, particularly if an order
of things has already taken root and life has fallen in line
around it; among these values are economy of adjustment,
peace, predictability of responses, and the rule of law. Even
the most beneficial change exacts a price on these scores.

There is no guarantee that change will always be beneficial. Measures adopted by men to answer their needs are
likely to have many consequences, not all of which are readily
foreseeable and not all of which will always be advantageous.

This situation is dramatically illustrated by the so-called toxic side effects of therapeutically effective drugs; they are called *side* effects not because they are always less important than the curative ones but because they have not been intended; man takes his purposes as the standard of what he considers central or peripheral. It is precisely because of these unpredictable "side" effects that change carries with it a measure of insecurity.

In this way, the full realization of one value interferes with the realization of the opposite one, and any partial realization of one permits only a partial realization of the other.

While there are clear cases of antinomy, there are other instances in which the simultaneous fulfillment of different aspirations, while perhaps not logically impossible, is psychologically highly improbable. The most outstanding antinomy of this kind appears between adjustment to reality by means of changing oneself so as to fit in with reality and adjustment by means of changing reality to make it fit one's needs (called autoplastic and alloplastic adjustment by Ferenczi[4]). The great civilizations of the East and the antiquity of our own civilization were largely autoplastically oriented, while the post-Renaissance civilization of Europe has been characterized to an ever-increasing degree by an alloplastic attitude. The famous prayer of Alcoholics Anonymous—"God grant me the serenity to accept the things I cannot change, the courage to change the things I can, and the wisdom to know the difference"[5]—is a request for the ability to practice alloplasticism to the limit of its possibilities and autoplasticism beyond it. This prayer does not ask for anything *logically* unthinkable, but the two approaches require such radically different attitudes of mind that it is not likely that they will be equally developed in a person. One person is not likely to combine the analytic mind, the initiative, and the skill of the engineer with the wisdom of the sage.

Rudyard Kipling, a Westerner who was exposed to Indian culture, drew a fictional picture of a man who had mastered both attitudes. Sir Purun Dass, the Prime Minister of a princely Indian

State, had been a powerful, successful statesman who had inaugurated many beneficial reforms. At one point, he suddenly resigned his post and disappeared from the eyes of the public. He had followed the ancient Indian rule that a man should be twenty years of his life a youth, twenty years a fighter, twenty years the head of a household, and should then withdraw from the world to devote his remaining time to the search for the Absolute. He took to the road, barefoot, with his begging-bowl. After some time of wandering he stayed in a deserted shrine of Kali on the slope of a mountain. The villagers in the valley, happy that a holy man had settled in their midst, saw to it that his bowl was filled, and the animals of the mountain became friends of the motionless contemplating ascetic. Many years passed. One night, during the torrential rains, Purun Dass was wakened by his animals and pushed by them to the door. There he saw the signs of a landslide coming down. For himself he was ready to welcome death in any form, but he remembered the villagers who had taken care of his needs all these years. With all the strength left to him, he rushed down the hill, leaning on a stag, awoke the villagers, and, once again the man who used to command thousands, he led their speedy exodus from the village up a hill to safe higher ground. The villagers were rescued in the nick of time; Purun Dass fell dead of exposure and exertion.[6]

Finally, the balance of assets and liabilities, of achievements and costs of progress, can be drawn only if we look at a whole population over a period of time as though it were a single living organism that pays the costs and reaps the benefits, while in fact those who do the sowing or are being used as seeds are rarely those who bring in the harvest. We then see that even when the price of an achievement seems cheap on the collective balance sheet, for many individuals it has meant a disproportionate price in their own personal accounts and often the sacrifice of all they had and all they were.

These aspects will now be considered in greater detail.

1. CHANGE AND STABILITY

Whenever a way of life has become stabilized and has endured for a considerable length of time (measured in terms of the individual life span), its change, no matter how beneficial, exacts a price because previous adjustments are rendered worthless and new adjustments become necessary. However, the ability of living organisms to meet the challenge of circumstance, that marvelous characteristic of life, is not unlimited. The organism loses its elasticity with advancing age. The time needed for the regeneration of lost or damaged tissue increases rapidly with age; eventually, wounds no longer heal. In the end, when the homeostasis of the body no longer works, the organism dies.

This does not mean that stress is always detrimental. Just as there are physical exercises that develop the fitness of the body and are conducive to good health, there also exist certain kinds of mental stress that are conducive to the realization of man's potentialities. There is no guarantee, however, and indeed little likelihood, that the stress imposed by the changing conditions of a progressing society will always, for all people, be of the latter variety.

This is particularly important in older age when adjustments to new conditions involve great personal suffering, become increasingly difficult, and may not be possible at all. In the early days of industrialization, the workers were keenly aware of the misery that machines were likely to bring to them. The skills on which their livelihood, their social status, and their personal feeling of achievement rested became irrelevant, and they were left stranded by the onward march of progress. The advocates of progress have always pointed out that the use of machines, in the end, results in a greater demand for work rather than less. This is true as far as it goes, but the new work is probably different from that which has become expendable, demands different skills, and usually is needed in a different place. At best, people are retrained and given new jobs in new environments. They must then start afresh at the bottom or at a lower rung of the occupational ladder; the experience of the previous working life is made largely worthless; and status, income, and the feeling of personal achievement that go with it are lost. Legislation may, in some degree, protect a man against the loss or the diminution of his income, but nothing can protect him from the loss of status and of personal satisfaction. Radical technological innovations often wipe out the achievements of decades.

Moreover, relocation means the separation from a familiar neighborhood, from friends, from the club of which one was an esteemed member, from many things that have given warmth and security to life.

For many people, particularly those of more advanced age, retraining and transplantation are no longer possible, and premature retirement, often with economic distress, becomes their lot. It is characteristic of the immense victory of the ideologies of the Left, i.e., of the ideologies of progress, that "vested interest" has become a pejorative term; vested interests are considered to be evil and the source of evil. Yet, the only people who have no vested interests are youths, who are not only without responsibilities but also without occupational training. As soon as a youth has started on a vocational training, he has a vested interest in the expectation that the skills he is about to acquire will remain in demand during his lifetime; and as soon as he starts a family, he has a vested interest in being able to earn his livelihood in the place where he has built his nest. A man who has learned to do work connected with railroads has a vested interest in railroads not being supplanted by air or motor transport; and the more he has achieved in his work, the greater becomes this interest.

All this takes on a more sinister aspect as progress gains in speed. It is one thing if there is a considerable chance for a man in his middle or old age to find that his skills are no longer in demand; it is another thing if this complete mental retooling is required every few years. We may not be far from the time when a man, at the end of his occupational training, will find things to have changed to such a degree that the knowledge and the skill he has just acquired are no longer in demand. A point may well be reached, in the not too distant

future, when the speed of technological and social change
will be such as to overtax man's adaptive capacities. Biological processes in the living organism, after all, require a certain
period of time, and the biological tempo shows little sign of
being accelerated like the speed of production or transportation. Gestation still takes the same time it took in the ice age;
and man still needs, on the average, a year or two until he can
accept the loss of a beloved one.

However, change involves more than stress. It makes reactions to events less predictable, and so makes rational action,
i.e., the weighing of alternatives in the light of their consequences, more difficult and more ambiguous.

Above all, change undermines the legal order. Law is *necessarily* the power of the dead hand of the past over the present. Law reflects the power relations and the views prevalent
at the time of its adoption, and it demands that future situations, which occur in a different and often unforeseen reality,
be treated according to the old prescription. This is particularly true in the case of constitutional law, which sets limits
to possible future changes of the law. In more recent times, a
school of thought has advocated a minimalistic interpretation
of these constitutional prohibitions and a larger freedom of
action for the legislator. Yet, no matter how cautious the interpretation of constitutional (or legal) restraints may be,
the rule of law acts as a brake to change.[a] Change and the law
are natural antagonists; and fast-moving radical change is
bound to impair the rule of law or to bring about frequent
readjustments of the law, which are likely to weaken its authority and to detract from its role as a guarantor of predictability.

These costs of change have as yet scarcely been realized,

---

[a] In the United States there is also, more recently, a school of "judicial ac-
tivism" which holds that the courts must take the initiative and order the
Legislature and the Executive to take such measures as are necessary to realize
the ideals of social democracy said to be implicit in the Constitution. Law, so
conceived, is of course no longer a brake but a spur to action; but it has been
questioned whether it is still Law.

and many people take it for granted without further inquiry that the faster we are progressing, the better it will be. Arthur I. Waskow and Stanley L. Newman, after demanding the immediate dismantling of the major part of the American military establishment, make the following request:

> Turn the engineers, secretaries, administrators, airmen, and private supporting companies behind the SAC and missile systems into inventing and carrying out new techniques for extremely fast economic development.... Put most of RAND, MITRE, and other USAF think factories behind this effort.[7]

One must wonder whether the authors have tried to assess the influence of "extremely fast development" on various areas of life such as, among others, economic stability or mental health. The rate of obsolescence of technical equipment and technical procedures, which not too long ago was measured in terms of centuries and which in my childhood was still measured in terms of generations, is at the present time somewhere around a decade or less. As the demand for faster and ever-faster progress—"extremely fast economic development"—is realized, this rate of obsolescence will have to be counted in terms of two or three years, in months, perhaps in weeks, eventually to end in a spin, with unimaginable consequences.

The speeding up of the rate of progress also increases the likelihood and the severity of economic fluctuations and vastly increases the difficulties of economic adjustment. Fast progress means that new inventions are immediately put into practice on a large scale. This requires very fast retooling. Once this retooling has been accomplished, the demand for such tools must sink to the maintenance and replacement level, which of necessity is lower and which in all likelihood will be lowered further by virtue of the fact that fast technological progress probably will soon make the whole production system obsolete. Hence, an immense demand for a particular kind of capital goods is soon followed by a rapid decline in demand for the same kind of goods; the consequences are quick and heavy fluctuations of demand for capital goods.

There is also the problem of emotional roots. In the most advanced country, the United States, a house is practically never acquired as a family home, for generations to live there through all the stages of their lives and to acquire the sense of being a mortal link in an immortal chain. Moreover, it is hardly ever a possession for life. Rather, it is a transient abode to serve for a number of years and then to be exchanged for another place, larger or smaller as the case may be, or in another location when the breadwinner is "transferred" by his company. However, if and when the ideal of "extremely fast progress" is realized, there will hardly be any homes at all, and people will perhaps live in hotels or trailer camps or other temporary establishments. One must wonder about the children's schooling: will they change school every year or even more often, or will they leave the family to go to boarding schools, or will all instruction be conducted in the homes by means of prerecordings and television and methods yet to be invented? In any case, one is left wondering how children can acquire those stable and deep personal relations which so far appear to be a prerequisite of healthy personality development. They may turn out to be people with whom nothing endures but change.

Some advocates of speedier acceleration of progress would perhaps reply that this is just one of the questions which the scientists, released by the closing down of the military research centers, will be called upon to solve. There is a widespread, almost universal, conviction that *everything* can be done provided government is determined to do it and has the necessary power.

2. TECHNOLOGICAL PROGRESS

Autoplasticism and Alloplasticism

These two terms, as indicated before, refer to two types of

adjustment. In the former type, man changes himself so as to fit in with his environment; in the latter, he changes the environment so as to make it respond to his desires. Many of the ancient systems of thought, e.g., Buddhism, Stoicism, Epicureanism, were mental disciplines through which men trained themselves to bear suffering with equanimity. Western civilization, on the other hand, is largely alloplastically oriented, toward an ever-increasing control of the outside world.

The difference in orientation is shown, e.g., in the attitude toward pain. Under primitive conditions, children were naturally exposed to pain and so acquired a certain amount of tolerance for it; in some cultures, the adults deliberately inflicted pain on children in order to harden them. Modern men protect their children from pain, and anesthetics or analgesics are on hand whenever pain strikes nevertheless.

It is hard to realize how complete a change has taken place with the shift from autoplastic to alloplastic orientation; the reasoning of the ancients is sometimes the exact opposite of what the reasoning of moderns would be. Marcus Aurelius, emperor and Stoic philosopher, said in his *Meditations:* "Do away with opinion and gone will be all complaining; and if complaining is gone, gone will also be all harm."[8] Contemporary man, with his exclusive alloplastic orientation, starts at the other end and reasons in the opposite direction: if the grievance is redressed, the sense of grievance will disappear, and once the sense of grievance will have disappeared, the outlook on life will change as well. The ancient Stoic started with the outlook on life, proceeded from there to the individual complaint, and ended up with denying the significance of reality.

We are daily instructed by our political commentators that we must not expect the people of Asia, Africa, or South America to show much interest in free institutions; they are too poor to care for such luxuries, we are told. If we do not want them to follow the call of revolutionary leaders who will not satisfy their economic aspirations, to be sure, but will offer them an outlet for their resentment (against us, of course), we had better see to it that their economic desires are satisfied, and satisfied quickly; they will not wait any longer. However, once they have ample and good food, decent housing with modern conveniences, and some luxuries, we are told, they will begin to care for their liberty too. Seneca's argument was exactly the opposite: a large part of liberty, he said, is a well-trained stomach that can patiently endure insult.[9] That is to say, he told the people that if they wanted to be free, they had better learn first how to get along with miserable food, and with little of it.

The former United States Ambassador to the United Nations, Henry Cabot Lodge, has been quoted as having said that a hungry man is more interested in four sandwiches than in the four freedoms;[10] Seneca would probably have thought that if a man is interested in freedom, he must learn to get along without sandwiches.

Man, it seems, prefers freedom from pain to tolerance for pain; the autoplastic training for the latter is probably entered into only as a second best when there is no way of controlling reality. Epicurus, in agony due to a urinary obstruction, tried to persuade himself, philosophically, of the ultimate insignificance and transience of all physical suffering. He would probably have preferred the alloplastic possibilities of modern medicine had they been open to him.

Be that as it may, the fact remains that a genuine antinomy exists. People who have always been effectively protected against pain do not acquire any tolerance for pain, just as animals brought up in the sterile building at Notre Dame University do not acquire any immunity to infectious diseases. These animals die when they are brought out of their artificial, sterile environment, and men who have been brought up without acquiring a measure of tolerance for pain suffer grievously when they are exposed to it—a possibility that has been made less and less likely in recent times but that cannot be entirely ruled out in human life. And even if it were possible to eliminate pain altogether, it remains to be considered whether a human being who is always entirely dependent on props for his survival and well-being is not in some significant sense something less than his technologically less proficient but more independent forebears.[b]

Suffering can probably not be considered an unmitigated evil in all circumstances; it is through suffering that men reach maturity and depth. The man who has not been chastised has not been educated, said Sophocles.

Human character is formed against, and hardened by, resistance. Americans often appear as immature or shallow to European eyes, and all Westerners, both European and American, appear in this light to Asians; in both cases, the impression is due to the fact that the people from the alloplastically more efficient countries have encountered suffering more rarely than the people from "less happier lands."[12]

René Dubos, a prominent scientist and thus a protagonist of the modern world, considers it an open question whether this road or the autoplastic way will turn out to be more beneficial for mankind:

> The urge to control nature is probably the most characteristic aspect of Western civilization. It has not yet been proven, however, that this ideal is the best for human life. After all, great civilizations have been created in the past, and much profound happiness has been experienced, based on the philosophy that man must strive for harmony with the rest of nature instead of behaving towards it as dominating lord and as exploiting master. It is much too early to be sure that Galileo, Watt and Edison have contributed more lastingly to human advancement and happiness than have Socrates, Lao-tse and Francis of Assisi.[13]

Thus, change from the outlook of a Seneca or a Marcus

---

[b] The point was tragically and ominously illustrated by a sarcastic remark attributed to Ho Chi Minh: "If you wound one American soldier," he said, "you have put three out of action because it takes two others to carry him from the battlefield."[11]

The Asian jungle war may in one respect actually be called a contest of strength between alloplastic and autoplastic capabilities, between men with superior machines and men with superior adaptability to extreme conditions.

Aurelius to the modern outlook is hardly only a change for the better. Rather it seems to be progress in some ways and retrogression in others. Both autoplastic and alloplastic adjustments contain values, and the exclusive pursuit of either exacts a price in terms of the other. The progress of our age is progress in alloplastic adjustment, and it has exacted a price in terms of autoplastic capabilities.

The "Side" Effects of Remedies and the Danger of the Unknown

One can adduce many examples of undesirable "side effects" of measures which at first seemed to be entirely beneficial.

Whenever man influences the course of human, animal, and plant life, he interferes with the balance of nature. There are self-regulatory mechanisms in nature, a kind of homeostasis through which balance is restored after each disturbance; they operate somewhat in a wholesale fashion: the procedure is often cruel to individuals, but it is effective. In this way animal populations are kept in ecological equilibrium with their environment.

Man disturbs this balance continuously and thus prevents the natural self-regulatory mechanisms from operation; he is then often confronted with dangerous situations which demand new interferences. A simple example is the so-called population explosion in the poor countries of the earth. It is largely the consequence of the introduction of insecticides and antibiotics. The increase of population threatens to frustrate the demand for higher standards of living which arose simultaneously, another consequence of the contact with the technologically more highly developed West, and it may actually lead to starvation; it may also bring about large-scale violence. Perhaps it will be possible to forestall such calamities through birth control or by other means; but whatever means are employed to this end, they are likely to cause new troubles. Thus, human intervention into nature's automatisms can bring about dangers which can be averted only by new interventions. This has of course been going on for most of known history, but it has only recently assumed dimensions which dwarf everything done in past ages. It is generally assumed that man will always be able to deal with the consequences of his actions—an assumption that may or may not be correct.

Most of us, particularly in the higher age brackets, rejoice at the fact that life expectancy has been raised to the level of the Biblical life span; but this has also resulted in an enormous rise in the average age of the population, with "senior citizens" forming an increasingly large segment of it. The consequences of this change in the age composition of a population are not yet visible. Perhaps there will be much psychological misery among old people who can find no satisfactory niche in the social order; perhaps young men will have to wait longer before they can assume responsibilities for which they are ready; perhaps a frustrated youth will be radicalized. All of these things have happened in the last generation. We do not know which way things will go in the long run, but it does not seem likely that all consequences of the increased life span will turn out to be beneficial.

Medicine has made it possible to cure, or compensate for, many illnesses which have been the curse of mankind, an achievement most eagerly welcomed. Yet one of its consequences is to keep alive the bearers of defective genes, thereby increasing the number of defectives in the population. Perhaps it will be felt that defects do not matter if medicine can compensate for them. This may be a strong line of reasoning as long as one is dealing with mild and easily correctable defects, e.g., myopia, but one hesitates to accept it with regard to more fundamental defects; it is not a matter of indifference that a large number and perhaps a majority of people might depend all their lives on artifacts for their survival or their functioning.

Countless similar examples could be provided; and much of the public discussion of proposed policies concerns their possible side effects. It does not facilitate matters that they are usually not all known in advance.

The fact that a new and apparently beneficial invention may also have severe, sometimes catastrophic, disadvantages which are revealed only in actual practice, was recently dramatically demonstrated by the thalidomide disaster. A new drug had proved to be effective in controlling pain and nausea and had shown two important advantages over other preparations with similar effects: it could be taken in any quantity without ill effect (hence could not be used for suicide) and it was not habit forming. The animal experiments had failed to disclose any toxic effects. In some countries, it became widely used and was sold without a physician's prescription. It then turned out, after some time, that when taken by pregnant women the drug led to terrible deformations of the embryo. There ensued a wide demand for enacting laws which would more tightly control the introduction of new drugs, a demand that caused anxiety among scientists who feared a slowing down of scientific research. In some quarters, the disaster was blamed on the greed of the pharmaceutical producers.

With reference to the latter point, one may consider that it is not only the prospect of material gain that can blur a man's vision for the disadvantages of his product. Whenever new products are being developed—regardless of the political system of the country—those who have had a hand in their development will be interested in seeing them succeed. Such interest may be rooted, apart from the promise of monetary returns, in the prospect of honor, fame, increased influence, or the satisfaction of creative achievement. One should also remember, however, that this interest, whether of the monetary or the nonmonetary varieties, may not only make a man enthusiastic but may also make him cautious; it is not a trifling thing for a pharmaceutical producer to have his name associated with grave damage—a situation that could easily spell financial ruin.

However that may be, arguments of this kind do not come to grips with the essentials of the problem; for the crucial point is that as long as new drugs are introduced, there is no sure way of avoiding damage. The animal experiment is sometimes an indicator of what one can expect in humans, but it is not always, and it was not in this case. There is no sure way of finding out whether a drug causes damage to the unborn except by actually administering it to an expectant mother; and that is no longer merely a test, a trial run with samples that can cause no serious harm, but a procedure involving full risk for mother and child. It could well be said that new drugs should first be tried on very few and that the range of application should be enlarged only slowly; had this been done in the case of thalidomide, there would be fewer victims—but victims there still would be. And if this policy of careful, gradual advance is generally adopted, it would cut down the number of victims at the price of cutting down the rate of progress; if the new is introduced rapidly, progress is accelerated at the price of multiplying its victims.

The simple fact is that there is *unavoidable risk* in the application of the new, as yet untried. Perhaps it is possible to stay safely at home, but *one cannot pioneer safely*. The risks can be cut down (at the price of slowing down the advance), but they cannot be eliminated. The thalidomide story provides an instructive example of what current enthusiastic calls for technological progress imply: the people demand continuous progress, ever faster progress, but at the same time they demand that the new inventions should be perfectly safe. The ship should go at lightning speed to ever new pursuits, but with full safety guaranteed.

Who should perform this miracle? The government, of course, because "the government," in the present climate of opinion, is believed to be capable of achieving anything; for it, there are no limits, not even the limits of logic.

A situation such as this may help us understand why today so many expect to have their aspirations fulfilled as a result not of their own activities, individually or in groups, but those of the State, the government; and why the modern reformer has contempt for the initiative of individuals and groups, but conceives of his reform plans as part of a government policy. This line of thinking is usually attributed to the wide scope of the reformers' aspirations. That is probably true, but the attitude may also be due in part to the fact that if these aspirations were advanced by individuals or voluntary associations, one would see that they are unrealizable because of their inner contradictions. The State, the government, however, has for many a magical quality, something of the omnipotence which we attributed to our parents when we were very young; and by bringing the government as the acting agent into the picture the impossible becomes possible in the imagination.

The thalidomide story has often been called the "thalidomide tragedy" in the press. I have called it a disaster because it is not a tragedy in the Aristotelian sense. Disaster, for Aristotle, is tragic only if it overcomes a man in consequence of his own actions and if these actions flow from character traits which, on the whole, are not without nobility and which therefore deserve our sympathy.

Misfortunes, however great, that befall the innocent are merely pathetic. The colossal misfortune of children born with severe malformations is pathetic rather than tragic. But *if we speak of society as though it were one organism*, these events can well be called a tragedy because they are an outgrowth of the impatient demand for progress, and thus of a trait not unworthy in itself.

It seems to have happened more than once in history that a great catastrophe was preceded by an event of the same kind, but on a much smaller scale, which in retrospect looks like a warning and might have served as such if the people had been willing to be warned. The "necklace affair" before the French Revolution showed that it was possible for a courtier to believe that the favors of the Queen of France could be had for a diamond necklace, and it thereby revealed how low the prestige of the monarchy had fallen. The "unsinkable" *Titanic,* going to sea with an inadequate number of lifeboats and racing through the iceberg-infested waters of the North Atlantic in disregard of repeated warnings, showed, on the eve of the First World War, the dangerous complacency and recklessness of a generation that considered European civilization to be "unsinkable." In another affair that happened at the same time, the "Captain of Köpenick," an embezzler, just discharged from prison, needed only a captain's uniform, purchased from a secondhand clothes dealer, to improvise a military platoon from soldiers passing by on the street and to enter the Mayor's office and order him to hand over the city's cash; the successful coup revealed the fatal stupidity of German militarism. Perhaps the thalidomide tragedy can be viewed as a similar warning of the dangers inherent in the rapid race into the unknown.

The Janus Face of Science

A particularly important aspect of the ambiguity of remedies rests on the fact that science has potentialities for both good and evil. The liberal philosophy and its predecessor, humanistic thought, have held that science is the instrument of man's redemption.

Science, however, can be used for all purposes. Knowledge is a morally neutral tool that serves any master. This fact was dramatically brought home to contemporary man by the invention of atomic weapons, one of which can wipe out a major city, and of the means of their delivery to distant lands. A universal demand has arisen for this curse to be lifted from the brows of mankind.

Yet the knowledge of how to produce such tools of wholesale destruction can probably not be abolished by any means —except, perhaps, by an enormous catastrophe on a worldwide scale that would wipe out the knowledge of nuclear physics and technology by killing all men who have such knowledge and by destroying all books in which it can be found, i.e., by the fullest apocalyptic consummation. As long as this knowledge exists, the danger that nuclear arms may be produced and used will hang over men, even if all existing arms should be dismantled and their component parts be dropped into the ocean. There is even no guarantee that a fully denuclearized world, if it were somehow to come about, would not be just as unsafe as, or perhaps even more unsafe than, the world in which we are living at present. Wars could still break out—wars were, in fact, fought long before the invention of nuclear weapons—and they might break out even more easily than now if statesmen were no longer restrained by the danger of immediate destruction. Once war between major powers in a denuclearized world had started, a race would be on for the speediest conversion of industry to the production of nuclear explosives and the means of their delivery. The country that was a few days ahead in the rebuilding of nuclear power would have the world at its mercy.

The concern of those responsible for national security would therefore be concentrated on keeping their own industry geared to the speediest possible conversion to the production of nuclear weapons, and they would watch their presumptive antagonists with anxiety. Continuous efforts at cutting down one's own reconversion time and nightmarish fears that the opponent was about to succeed in doing so—a race in *conversion potential* which would replace the present race in nuclear armament—could keep international tensions as high as the current arms race does, and the absence of the restraints imposed by the possibility of *immediate* supreme penalties might make the climate even more perilous.

Man, it seems, will not escape the Hobbesian fear of imminent violent death, which civilization seemed to have all but removed, by trying to put the technological clock back. It is conceivable, though by no means assured, that this fear may be greatly reduced or lifted by further, not yet foreseeable scientific advances which would open the way to an effective defense against nuclear weapons.

The problem which the bomb created was neither entirely new nor altogether unforeseeable; the bomb merely highlighted a predicament in its most menacing form; yet this dilemma has been inherent in technological progress from the beginning. Scientists and the ever-increasing number of devotees of scientific and technological progress, however, have either not seen it or have evaded it. They could evade this dilemma by assuming either that the perils of scientific discoveries can always be neatly separated from their benefits and controlled (like the application of drugs with toxic "side" effects), or that "in the end"—whatever that may mean—the beneficial effects of science would always outweigh its destructive potentialities. In either case it is an act of faith.

Still, at the very beginning of the scientific age, Leonardo da Vinci, sharing the expansiveness of the spirit of the new age though not yet its moral optimism, deliberately kept his notebooks only for himself because he feared that his mechanical inventions might be used for purposes of war. And as early as the fifth century B.C., Sophocles seems to have foreseen something of our present predicament when he said of man:

> Clever beyond all dreams,
> the inventive craft that he has,
> which may drive him one time or another to
> well or ill. . . .[14]

3. THE MORAL ADVANCES

Pitfalls of Humanitarianism

Humanitarian tendencies can be carried to the point where they become a hazard to survival; the field may then be left to the bullies, and humanitarianism itself may be eliminated through something akin to the evolutionary mechanism. Saint-John Perse once remarked that pacifism, unfortunately, often means in practice giving the green light to aggressors. At the time when Hitler became German Chancellor, the Oxford students swore their famous oath never again to fight for king and country; they were probably motivated as much by humanitarian as by self-preservative impulses. The oath convinced many hitherto skeptical men in Germany that the time was propitious for a new bid for the domination of Europe.

Yet, in all but a few individuals, these sentiments are not likely to survive a clear and immediate challenge. Less than seven years after the oath, these students and their like-minded contemporaries manned the defenses of Britain. Albert Einstein, a lifelong pacifist, urged President Roosevelt to start an atomic program when he feared that Hitler Germany might produce a nuclear bomb.

We are now prepared to turn to the discussion of the off-shoots of humanitarianism, i.e., of the various trends toward the abolition of privilege; all have their liabilities.

The Abolition of Hereditary Privilege

However much people may differ about the relative merits of liberty and equality, there is nearly unanimous agreement about the proposition that hereditary privileges are an un-mitigated evil, at once stupid and unjust. Yet, even in this case, the situation is ambiguous.

A plausible case can be made in favor of the proposition that a class of men who are secure in their status and have nothing to gain from participating in the competitive melee may be an asset to a community because they may be more inclined than others to identify themselves with the interests of the whole and to consider long-term interests rather than merely short-term advantages. The class may breed men of honor and taste and may thus function as a model of conduct and taste, setting standards for those who rise in the social ladder and counteracting trends toward atomization and dis-integration.

Furthermore, the existence of privilege may serve an important function by providing an alibi for the losers in the competitive struggle. A society in which all rank is determined by merit alone—a "meritocracy" as it is sometimes called—is not free of faults of its own. It would be a cruel place to live in for those who have not been well endowed by nature. In a society like ours, in which position depends on many factors, of which merit is but one, those who have failed to fulfill their ambitions can find comfort in the thought that their failure may be due less to their own deficiencies than to social injustices; in a perfectly just order they might have fared better. In a true meritocracy, however, there is no alibi. They stand in the limelight, exposed before themselves and others as inferior specimens of man, and may be broken in their spirit.

This is not as far-fetched as it may seem; a renowned educator, John W. Gardner, reports:

> In the course of World War II, a military commander told me about a situation he had encountered in the small unit under his command. This unit had been organized for special work, and had an unusual number of highly intelligent enlisted men. An opportunity arose to send men to officers' candidate school and the commander set it as his high-minded goal to recommend every one of his enlisted men who was properly qualified. He screened them, identified those of officer caliber, and everyone that he recommended was accepted for officers' candidate school.
>
> What were the consequences? The morale of the remaining enlisted men disintegrated. Investigation revealed that the screening process had left them without a shred of self-esteem. They were relatively happy as long as they could say to themselves that they were enlisted men because this is an unjust world, or because the military services do not value ability. But the commanding officer's scrupulous search for talent had deprived them of those comfortable defenses. They had no place to hide. It was now clear to all concerned that they were enlisted men because that was where they belonged.[15]

The idea of a society in which all rank is exclusively determined by ability is probably a typical case of an ideology rationalizing personal interests; it is in the interest of those whose I.Q. is above 130 and who can confidently expect that in such an order they would monopolize all higher positions.

The Perils and Injustices of Liberty

Liberty is absence of restraints, and that has both creative and destructive potentialities. Liberty tends to weaken authority, without which no community can long survive; in the extreme case, it turns into anarchy which, as James Madison remarked, always leads to despotism.[16] Liberty also leads to the questioning and undermining of the moral aspects of authority, the ethos of the community, which is no less indispensable for its survival, and thus to moral relativism, the breeding ground both of private protest (delinquency) and of ideological protest (revolution).

Thucydides presented the case in simple terms, which, on the whole, still seem valid. Liberty brought forth, in the Periclean age, an enormous outburst of creativity; later, in the times of Cleon and Alcibiades, it led to unrestrained mass passions, to confusion, to treason, and thus to disaster. Whether it is creative or destructive depends, in Thucydides' analysis, on whether or not there is wise, politically effective, and personally disinterested leadership. Thucydides did not suggest by what means such leadership could be secured.

On the moral side, liberty within a peer group leads to great inequalities and therefore unavoidably also to exploitation, material, emotional, and otherwise. Where there is success there is conceit, and the latter is likely to express itself in ways that are offensive to others; and where there is power there is temptation to use it, and regard for the interests of others is likely to be gradually corroded. These consequences have been vividly described by countless critics of capitalist society.

The Perils and Injustices of Equality

From the point of view of expediency, equality may be an obstacle to the effective organization of the community.

Stratification in the social group is not merely a matter of who gets what, when, how;[17] it is also a question of expert judgment and of guidance in matters of common interest. The former is *dominance,* the latter *leadership.* The two are related, but their relationship is not simple.

There is a vast difference between the bully and the leader. The bully satisfies his own urges—active and, in particular, sadistic urges—at the expense of others; the archetype of the leader, on the other hand, is the individual who marches ahead of the others in the face of danger, exposing his own body first and so permitting the others to take cover behind his back.[18] While the bully is characterized by strong active and sadistic drives, which are not restrained by love, pity, or a sense of social obligation, the earmark of the leader is his superior ability to bear anxiety.

In practice, the two are often found in the same person: the bully may be a leader, too. There have been great political leaders whom their co-workers and subordinates saw as overbearing tyrants. The connection is easily understood psychologically because the pleasure in protecting others which the leader feels may be a civilized transformation and modification of the pleasure in bullying; and both forms, the undomesticated and the domesticated, may well coexist in the same person. But the two do not *necessarily occur* together; there are leaders who are not bullies—e.g., Gandhi— and bullies who are not leaders, since they are not the first to meet danger but rather the first to take cover.

As might be expected, there is vast disagreement on whether the role of each upper class or group in history was that of leadership or of dominance; and to what degree it was the one, to what degree the other. As a rule, every ruling class sees itself as the leader of its people, at least during the halcyon days of its rule, and is so seen by some of the contemporaries and of posterity, while others see the same group as exploiters in one sense or another.

The capitalist entrepreneur, e.g., saw himself as a leader, i.e., as an innovator who opened up new or improved ways of production or distribution and thereby provided work and livelihood for others who lacked the ability to do it for themselves. He saw himself—and was widely seen by others, particularly in the nineteenth century—as a benefactor of his workers and of mankind. The basis for his leadership did not lie only or even predominantly in intellectual abilities—these might even have been supplied by hired executives and advisors—but in the ability to carry responsibility for himself and others, the willingness to take risks, i.e., in psychological terms, the *ability to bear anxiety*.

On the other hand, however, the entrepreneur was seen by men like Proudhon or Marx, and is seen by most intellectuals today, as an exploiter, a man who knows how to appropriate the products of the toil of others.

In the first view, management supplied leadership; in the second, it was merely dominant. In the first view, it was creative; in the second, parasitic.

The same divergence of opinion exists with regard to the upper stratum of Communist society, the Party. The Party men, in their view and that of their friends, are the leaders in constructing a new, better society; in the view of their opponents, the Party men are the collective owners of the country and, notwithstanding the perils of their internal strife, one of the most privileged groups in history.

Victorians regarded European colonialism in Asia and Africa as leadership in the interest of all, including the Asians and Africans themselves ("white man's burden"); while later generations of liberals and European-trained native elites regarded it as imperialism, i.e., as exploitation pure and simple.

Egalitarianism may threaten the selection, the development, and the functioning of the leadership elites which the community needs. Contrary to their original intentions, Soviet leaders were forced by experience to allow great inequalities of income and status; these differences are supposed to be only temporary, but so far they have shown no more sign of withering away than the State itself.

The egalitarian trend in education which gives priority to the interests of the majority over those of the highly gifted few is probably not conducive to the best development of the latter. Equality of station is opposed to differential valuation, and unless equality is strictly confined to particular aspects of life, e.g., income, it becomes opposed to quality. In this way, egalitarianism tends to substitute *quantity for quality*.

Moreover, the postulate that all *men* are equal can easily lead to the consequence that their *ideas* are looked upon as equally true (or equally untrue) and their *ideals* as equally valid (or equally invalid); every man's opinion is as good as any other man's opinion. Romano Guardini once remarked that our time cannot create a culture because it lacks a hierarchy of values. Some will challenge his implication that the latter is a prerequisite of "culture"; it clearly is part and parcel of structured cultures.

Egalitarianism can also be criticized on *moral* grounds. It promotes the interests of those who take the lower places in the pecking order which emerges from open contest; but the case of the higher echelons is within wide limits as defensible as that of the lower.[e]

A good case can be made in favor of putting schoolchildren of average, or less than average, ability in the same classes with more highly endowed children, so that the former can profit from contact with the latter and are not stigmatized in their own eyes and those of others by separation. It seems to me, however, that an equally good case can be made in favor of giving abler children a separate curriculum adapted to their capabilities so that they are not slowed down in their development by instruction attuned to the needs of the majority.

The problem turns up in all spheres of life. The currently prevailing climate of opinion always seems to favor those who, unaided, would take the lower place in the pecking order: the sick, the aged, the unemployables, the lawbreakers, thus putting heavier responsibilities on the shoulders of the healthy, the young, the producing, or the law-abiding. However, the other side of the case is just as arguable.

One can feel sympathetic understanding for the desire of parents living in slums who want their children to get out and to attend school together with children from more advanced environments in what would presumably be a better learning experience; but one can also feel sympathetic understanding for parents in more favorable social and cultural

[e] It is characteristic that the word "to discriminate," which originally merely meant "to note the difference of," has more and more assumed the meaning of *unjust* discrimination.

conditions who resist arrangements which they fear would depress the educational and behavioral level of their children.

It is, in essence, the eternal conflict between two siblings of different, though not too widely different, ages. If children are far apart in age, they go different ways; but if the difference is small—say two or three years—the younger brother often wants to be included in the activities of the older one; as he sees it, he is old enough to join in with his brother's gang. But the older brother takes a different view and resents the intrusion; in his eyes, the baby brother does not fit in and merely ruins the fun. It is a kind of obtuseness to look upon such conflicts as contests between right and wrong; they are merely conflicts of interest which become unavoidable once a stable status order, in a family or in a society, has broken down and is replaced by social mobility.

In its most radical excrescences, egalitarianism turns the traditional value system and the social pyramid around and puts them on their top. In Nazi Germany, pseudo-scientific theories propagated by semi-literates (such as, e.g., Hörbiger's glacial cosmology) were officially promoted; and, in concentration camps, educated men were put at the mercy of foremen ("Kapos") selected from the scum of society; in communist China, scientists and scholars had to take courses from semi-literate hacks; stone-throwing and looting mobs were recently hailed as the "politically most advanced part of the American people."

4. THE INDUSTRIALIZATION

All the problems discussed are involved in the great process of rising standards of living. Technical applications of scientific discoveries and social practices appropriate for their adaptation to mass consumption have made possible, in the industrially most advanced nations, the practical elimination of destitution as the word was understood fifty years ago. The enormous increase in output which has made this possible depends on certain conditions: on mechanization of the production process, i.e., on mass production methods, and an ever farther-going division of labor; on the breakdown of all social structures that resist change, such as tribal custom or caste; on the establishment of utmost mobility; and on the willingness of the people to accept the mass-produced goods and demand no others. All these conditions, however, have their implications and their consequences.

Division of labor means that men can no longer get much creative enjoyment out of their work because they can no longer look upon something and feel: this I have made—be it a field they have cleared, a house they have built, a piece of furniture they have made. Instead, they have made a tiny *contribution* to a vast collective enterprise. Their relation to their work becomes abstract; without joy in what they are doing, they become *alienated* from their work, and to the degree that the sense of belonging depends on the sense of contributing, they are alienated from society as well. They are, of course, compensated for their loss by the higher standards of living which mass production makes possible for them; i.e., they get back as consumers what they had to sacrifice as producers, and they probably would not want to have it otherwise; but the sacrifice is nonetheless real.

A mass-producing society must be a society without caste barriers. The rigid caste system of India was a serious obstacle to industrialization because it severely restricted the kind of men with whom a man could work together in a factory. In effective and expanding mass production it must be possible to use all primary resources, both goods and manpower, in the most rational way, and as far as men are concerned, that implies a high mobility of place, function, and social position. Where men have to keep themselves ready to go to some other place at short notice when the market conditions make it advisable or, in the case of employees, when they are transferred by their companies, they cannot put their roots deep down in the soil. They must be ready to make friends quickly, in a shallow sort of way, and they must be able to keep their human relationships on a superficial level if they are not to be hurt deeply whenever they have to break up tents.

At the same time, the breaking down of all fixed patterns of life—social mobility—also breaks down the security of stable adjustment. Where social position is highly insecure and transient, people are necessarily afraid lest they lose what they have; there is also the lure of an improvement of their station which this very mobility makes possible, hence a high degree of competitiveness.

Finally, when goods are being mass-produced, with a tremendous investment of national resources, there must be some reasonable expectation that what has been produced will also be accepted by the consumers. This implies a willingness on the part of the people to live in the same kind of homes, with the same kind of furniture, appliances or cars, and wear the same kind of clothes as their neighbors. It means a certain conformity in taste. Persuasion must be used toward this end; thus, a necessary companion of mass production is advertising, one of the features of modern industrial society that is most offensive to the moralists. Advertising is by no means a feature limited to a capitalist market economy; it appears in a socialist economy as well, as propaganda for the goods put out by the nationalized economy, though not for a variety of competing brands. There are cases in a market economy in which a monopoly advertises its goods or services —as when the Bell Telephone Company recommends its newest devices and services—and we rightly consider this as advertising, even though there are not several telephone companies trying to attract the people by their competitive offers.

Industrialization means, indeed, the liquidation of poverty, the freedom from want for ever more people; but this success entails the loss of a sense of creative achievement for the worker, alienation from his work and, at least partially, from his society, a certain kind of rootlessness, a high degree of competitiveness, and a considerable degree of conformity of habits and tastes. *The end of poverty requires mass production and mass production requires, or produces, a kind of mass man.*

It does not follow from the considerations presented in this chapter that progress, scientific-technological, libertarian or egalitarian, is not worth while. I do wish to suggest, however, that progress, on whatever line, is more complex than its devotees seem to assume. Progress has *its costs, its dangers, and its victims.*

5

The Conservative Criticism of Modernity

. . . this present hour of pure chaos when life and art are evidence of centuries of aimlessness.

—ANANDA K. COOMARASWAMY[1]

It is not surprising that the modern development was accompanied by criticism and warnings resembling those of a Greek chorus. Conservative[a] criticism attacked the modern development as a whole and considered it an aberration from the right way.

The various critics do not agree on the point at which mankind became derailed from its proper course. Most critics put the date in the second half of the eighteenth century, with the appearance of both the Industrial Revolution and the germinal ideas of the French Revolution. Others would see the point of departure earlier, with the beginning of the so-called Scientific Revolution, around 1600, or with the Reformation, or, still earlier, with the waning of the cosmos of the

[a] The word "conservative" is used here in the European rather than the American sense. A conservative in the European sense is someone who wants to preserve, or to restore, a fairly stable, hierarchical order; a conservative in the American sense is an advocate of free enterprise, i.e., of one method of change (through the market mechanism) rather than another (through government action).

As a rule, political terms coined in Europe assume a different meaning in the United States; the realities to which they referred do not to any appreciable extent exist in the United States and the terms then are applied to different American realities. This is a source of never-ending misunderstandings between Europeans and Americans.

Middle Ages and the rise of humanism. Some go back even farther.

The following statement made by George Santayana is a characteristic example of conservative criticism in its most mature form:

> The natural state of mankind ... is full of incidental evils; prophets have ample cause for special denunciations and warnings; yet there is, as in all animal economy, a certain nucleus of self-preserving instincts and habits, a normal constitution of society.... They know what is for their good and by what arts it might be secured.... and when a quarrel arises among them, or with strangers, they battle to preserve or to restore their free life, without more ambitious intentions.... Civilisation had become more enterprising, plastic, and irresponsible.... Intellectual chaos and political folly could thus come to co-exist strangely with an irresistible dominance of mechanical industry. The science that served this industrial progress by no means brought moral enlightenment.... At first it was expected that science would make all mankind both rich and free from material cares (two contradictory hopes) and would at the same time enlighten them at last about the nature of things, including their own nature, so that adequate practical wisdom would be secured together with fabulous material well-being.
>
> This is the dream of the moderns.... This society lacked altogether that essential trait of rational living, to have a clear, sanctioned, ultimate aim. The cry was for vacant freedom and indeterminate progress. *Vorwärts! Avanti! Onward! Full speed ahead!* without asking whether directly before you was not a bottomless pit.[2]

In these words, Santayana directed his attack against the absence of a stable norm and an effective homeostasis that would bring life back to equilibrium after each crisis, against the ills of perpetual change, against the centrifugal potentialities of liberty.

The instability of modern civilization was emphasized by Paul Valéry:

The mind has transformed the world, and the world is repaying it in kind. The mind has led man where he had no notion of going. It has given us a taste for life and the means of living; it has conferred on us a power of action enormously surpassing the individual's powers of adaptation and even his capacity for understanding; it has aroused desires and produced results from them greatly exceeding what is useful to life. Hence we have moved farther and farther away from the primitive conditions of all life, borne along as we are at a speed now growing so great as to be terrifying, toward a state of things whose complexity, instability, and inherent disorder bewilder us, allowing us not the least foresight, taking away our ability to reason about the future or to make out any of the lessons we used to expect from the past, and dissolving in their violence and fluctuation all effort at founding and building, whether intellectually or socially, just as quicksands absorb the strength of an animal that ventures upon them.[3]

These lines were written in 1937; one suspects that the author would state them even more strongly today.

Other favorite targets of conservative criticism have been: the emphasis on material welfare (particularly among the masses); the stimulation of appetites which either cannot be fully satisfied or set life on the road of an endless race between rising satisfactions and rising aspirations; the progressive division of labor and mechanization of production which deprive workers of the sense of creative achievement; the reliance on reasoning over instinct and tradition, and the emphasis on the mechanistic rather than the organic, on things that can be made rather than on those that grow—on the approach of the engineer rather than that of the gardener;[4] and the trend toward equality which threatens quality and promotes mediocrity. These critics see the modern world as a desolate "wasteland" (T. S. Eliot), peopled by men of "irrelevant abilities and fatal incompetence" (Arnold Toynbee).[5] This picture of decadence is often drawn against the background of a past in which life is believed to have been a meaningful whole. Stefan George, the poet who was worshiped as a seer by a small circle of intellectuals in late Wilhelmine and Weimar Germany, castigated modern men time and again for their alleged emptiness:

> What you have termed the dark and savage age
> In days that boast of freedom, knowledge, mercy:
> That strove at least through torture, murder, dread,
> Through grimace, error, madness, on to god.
> You felons are the first to down the god,
> Carve out an idol not resembling Him,
> Hailed by sweet names and gruesome as no other,
> And hurl the best you have into its jaws.
> You call it YOUR approach and will not rest
> In torrid frenzy running, till all venal
> And base alike, instead of God's red blood,
> The pus of idols courses in your veins.[6]

George turns against the democratic concept of science as a knowledge that is, in principle, accessible to all: "A knowledge equal for all is a fraud."[7] There are three levels of knowledge and the boundaries between them cannot be simply leaped over; the first lies in our inherited organic equipment; the second, in learning; "the third knows only with whom the god cohabited." Such views are reflected in T. S. Eliot's elegiac question: "Where is the wisdom that was lost in knowledge? Where is the knowledge that was lost in information?"[8]

The core of these charges is age-old and antedates the Industrial Revolution by many centuries. The expectation that the machine will lead to a withering of man's natural abilities was expressed thousands of years ago. Archidamus, king of Sparta at the time of the Peloponnesian war, was shown a catapult that could throw stones at some distance, and said sadly: "The days of courage are gone." Chuang Tzu, a contemporary of Aristotle, saw on one of his wanderings an old man working in his garden. The man had dug ditches for irrigation and he climbed down in the ditch with his pail, filled it with water, and carried it up again to water his garden. Naturally, he made little progress. Chuang Tzu explained to him how with the help of a pump he could bring up many times the amount of water with little effort. But the old man laughed and said that he had learned this from his teacher: once one begins using machines, one will soon do all one's business in a machinelike way; and once one does that, one will get a mechanical heart. But once one has a mechanical heart, one loses the simplicity of thinking, becomes uncertain in one's impulses, and loses good sense. His teacher had told him so; it must have been an old story even in the days of Chuang Tzu.[9]

There is something comforting in the fact that such fears were felt and such warnings voiced so long ago, and that the warnings have not, to our minds, been borne out by subsequent developments. It would be rash to conclude, however, that these fears will be equally unsubstantiated in all future time. It is possible that those who sounded the warnings were right in principle, but that they vastly underestimated the threshold of the untoward consequences which they foresaw, i.e., that they underestimated the possibility of satisfactory adjustments to the machine while still preserving the essential virtues or beauties of an earlier existence. The fact that so far the limit of such adjustments has not been reached does not necessarily prove that such limits do not exist, nor even that may not be right around the corner.

The idea that scientific and technological progress means *moral* progress as well has also come in for heavy criticism. Biologists have questioned the belief that man's superiority over the animal world implies moral ascendancy—a belief so deep-rooted that it is reflected in language itself in such words as "brutal," "bestial" or "humane." The zoologist Adolf Portmann points out:

> One of the worst [illusions] is the idea of a slow but inescapable improvement of human nature. Very slowly, so many people thought, must the base and mean be left behind in

the gradual upward development from animal to man. A superficial way of thinking has thus successfully attempted to explain the evil that we find so powerful in man, as a survival from an earlier animal stage that is slowly but certainly overcome in continuous progress. And when terrible things, cruelties hardly conceivable, occur among men, many speak thoughtlessly of "brutality," of bestialism, of a return to animal levels.... As if there were animals which inflict on their own kind what men can do to men. Just at this point the zoologist has to draw a line; these evil, horrible things are no animal survival that happened to be carried along in the imperceptible transition from animal to man; this evil belongs entirely on this side of the dividing line and is purely human.[10]

Conservative critics have pointed out that the progress of *ratio* does not imply moral progress. Reinhold Niebuhr formulated this kind of criticism from a Christian point of view:

The Christian analysis of life leads to conclusions which will seem morbidly pessimistic to moderns, still steeped as they are in their evolutionary optimism. The conclusion most abhorrent to the modern mood is that the possibilities of evil grow with the possibilities of good, and that human history is therefore not so much a chronicle of the progressive victory of good over evil, of cosmos over chaos, as the story of an ever increasing cosmos creating ever increasing possibilities of chaos.[11]

Much of the essence of the conservative criticism, mitigated by skepticism, was recently expressed epigramatically, in archetypical terms, by a contemporary philosopher who belongs to a branch of European civilization which has followed the modern trend only with much hesitation and at a great distance. "Spaniards," says Luis Diez del Corral, "with their national myth, more Christian, idealistic and generous, and less technical, still see in the super-Promethean Faust the features of the knight of the sorrowful countenance."[12]

6

The Scapegoat Movements

We complain about the shoes but the trouble is with the foot.

—Samuel Beckett[1]

When the old man in Chuang Tzu's story refused to use a pump to bring water up from a lower to a higher terrace in his garden, he knew what he was doing. He knew that he could make his work at once easier and more effective by the use of such a device, but he refused to do so because he wanted to avoid what he believed to be the evil influence of machines on the soul of man. With his eyes open, he preferred hunger and backbreaking labor to more ample food and easier work at the price of the mechanization, however small, of life. Our choice would be different, but we must feel respect for this man's decision.

In more modern times, such readiness to see, and willingness to take, the consequences of one's actions is rare. Many people who derive benefits from some aspects of modernization and are frustrated by others do not see that one is but the reverse side of the other. They live in centrally heated apartments, travel in automobiles and airplanes, and have the decay of their bodies slowed down by modern medicine, but they are indignant at the way new developments ruin the quiet of the countryside and automobile traffic clutters up modern cities and makes their air a health hazard. They would like the sweetness which life had in the *ancien régime* (for the wealthy) together with the advantages of industrial-

90

ism.[a] They request more and ever faster progress along the lines of rationalization, while accusing some institutions of its less desirable consequences.

CONFIDENCE IN INSTITUTIONAL REMEDIES

We are easily inclined to overestimate what can be done by institutional change and to expect relief from changed arrangements in matters which have deeper roots in less tractable circumstances. We are all the more inclined to do so the stronger the desires are. J. D. B. Miller, a political scientist, gave a list of such ideas common to political planning:

> ... ideas about a second chamber which will always be wise, a court which will banish industrial disputes, a constitution which can be interpreted without argument, a parliament in which there will be no parties. Men in studies have spent a good deal of time elaborating these ideas. So have practical politicians and officials. The function of a Utopia is to suggest that things can be made right by institutional changes, which will not make anyone worse off but will eliminate friction and improve the general welfare. Schemes for consultation, advice, regulation, etc., put forward by particular interests, are usually of this type. In practice they often improve the position of the interest in question without improving anybody else's.[2][b]

[a] To some degree, this is actually possible *in some well-sheltered places,* remote from the centers of the great decisions, where people can participate in the modern world with limited liability, as it were. In Switzerland, for instance, one can enjoy the charm of an old, in some ways almost medieval, order and the amenities of modern technology.

[b] A similar phenomenon is the belief that the abolition of certain institutions that are experienced as repressive would release the most marvelous potentialities in man. Socialists harbored tremendous expectations for the abolition of capitalism. Many thought that all crime would disappear, for, as August Bebel put it, "who should seek joy and satisfaction in it once society has removed all possibility of hatred?"[3] Leon Trotsky believed that the abolition of capitalism would lead to the rise of a much higher species of man: "Man will be incomparably stronger, more intelligent, more subtle. His body will be more harmonious, his movements more rhythmical, his voice more musical; his style of life will acquire a dynamic beauty. *The average type of man will rise to the level of an Aristotle, Goethe, Marx.* From this mountain crest, the new peaks will rise."[4]

We have also seen time and again that people, aggrieved by one or another aspect of their current situation, expect the redress of their grievances from a transfer of power to some other authority which, it is tacitly assumed, will always be just and wise. During the later Middle Ages, many people suffering at the hands of feudal lords or the Church, or blaming Church or lords for their suffering, expected the redress of their grievances from a strong central authority—the king or, in Italy, the emperor—who would set things right. Generations of propaganda had thus prepared the ground, and when the development of weapons technology—the introduction of the cannon—shifted the balance of power from barons to larger sovereign units, absolute monarchy was actually established: as the rule of Henry VIII in England, and Louis XIV in France.

The new dispensation failed to impress itself universally as just and wise. People felt aggrieved by the despotism of monarchs and asked for liberty, which was sometimes viewed as the right of all individuals to work out their own destiny, and sometimes as the right of majorities to impose their will on minorities. Again, it was taken for granted that justice and wisdom would reside in the new order; individuals would be the best judges of their interest and a free play of forces would bring about a natural order of mankind, or majorities would be right and wise by virtue of their numbers. Generations of propaganda prepared the ground, and once technological development—the invention of the rifle—had shifted the balance of power from organized government to citizens, democracy was really established.

Once again, the new reality failed to convince all people of its justice and wisdom. Those who felt aggrieved believed that redress of their grievances would come from transferring power from individuals and from electoral majorities to an omnipotent State that would act in the interest of all and set things right. Why the State should always be just and wise was not explained but, as in the former examples, simply taken as true by definition. Generations of propaganda had prepared the ground and once weapons technology had again shifted the balance of power to totalitarian government (or to totalitarian insurgent groups within a nontotalitarian state) the new order was established over half the globe.

Once again, the hopes for justice and wisdom have not been fulfilled through the reshuffling of power. At the present moment, totalitarian states can hold power regardless of the feelings of their citizens and thus can make most of their citizens accept their values and their philosophy as a matter of adjustment.

In more recent times, the new idea has developed that all things will be set right by putting them under an international authority, like "turning them over to the U.N.," again without the slightest reason to believe that this will improve matters, and indeed in the face of considerable evidence to the contrary. Thus, the political scientist Ernest B. Haas discusses the possibility, now dramatized by the nuclear bomb, that technological progress need not always be beneficial and demands that an international agency be set up for the licensure of permissible technological progress:

> From an initial basis of field-by-field *ad hoc* consultations, there may emerge a modest international brain trust for the general planning of innovation. Composed of eminent scientists and philosophers and representing East, West, and neutrals, it would take as its task the review of all technical and scientific inventions in order to assess their probable impact on society. When persuaded that, if used properly, a given invention would conduce to orderly progress, this panel of reviewers could then license the invention for general application; the unlicensed utilization of inventions would become punishable. I can live with the idea of new drugs capable of controlling heredity and able to shape individual motivation only if their use is subjected to this kind of scrutiny; I am emboldened to think that adherents of mutually antagonistic ideologies would feel the same if they suspected that the enemy might otherwise possess a weapon favorable to himself.[5]

Full circle in a little more than three centuries! The control of innovations which the Church had to abandon after Galileo is to be reintroduced, with the College of Cardinals, who had at least a common ideology, replaced by a committee representing a variety of ideologies, most of them intensely anti-Western.

The dangers which worry Professor Haas and the rest of us are inherent in the very fact of progress into the unknown; the unknown is the unknown and does not become known through the vote of a committee—least of all a committee which, in effect, would be composed of agents of political power.

To my mind, the adoption of Professor Haas's plan would most likely have the following consequences for the industrially developed Western nations: if in this committee, in which presumably the Latins and Afro-Asians would be in the majority, the moderates should prevail, the West would have to pay heavy tribute to them in return for permission to put its technical inventions into practice; if the radicals should prevail, such permission would simply be withheld with a view to destroying the West. It would be a most effective weapon, because continuous and, in fact, accelerating growth is a necessity for an industrial society and any stop or substantial slowdown of growth must lead to a major depression. The West would simply put its head on the block.

The demand by aggrieved, discontented or worried men to cure or forestall ills by transfering authority to someone else who will set things right is apparently one of the most enduring features of history. Only in brief historical moments—e.g., at the time of the founding of the American Republic—did a sufficient number of men realize that exclusive or predominant concern for self and lack of foresight and wisdom are characteristics of men, not of specific rulers, groups, classes or institutions, and that man's best hope for a tolerable conduct of affairs lies in a wide distribution and balance of power.

FOCUSING ON SCAPEGOATS

All these are illusions about easy solutions. These attitudes take on a pointedly hostile aspect once the blame is laid at the door of specific culprits like "society," "our culture," the "Establishment," "the bourgeoisie," "World Jewry," or "Western Imperialism."

The basic pattern appears, for instance, in these words of Lenin (1913): "In progressive Europe, the bourgeoisie which supports every reaction is ruling. *Europe is not progressive because of, but in spite of, the bourgeoisie.*"[6]

One wonders how he could be so sure. True, the success of a group or institution—a nation, a political system, a church, an army, a business enterprise, a political party, a theater, orchestra or whatever—does *not necessarily* testify to the quality of its leadership. Perhaps, the British fleet defeated Napoleon not because of, but in spite of, Nelson; Britain emerged victoriously from the Second World War not because of, but in spite of, Churchill's leadership; and Paris has been the world's art capital for 150 years not because of, but in spite of, her famous painters from Ingres to Picasso. The cases are arguable; but argued they must be. Experiments which would lay all doubts to rest are not possible, but alternate hypotheses must be weighed in the light of all available facts, in the manner of historical criticism. There is no indication that Lenin's peremptory statement was based on any such dispassionate analysis; it seems to have been based on the will to believe, which comes from the emotions of love or of hatred—in his case, of hatred.

Lenin's was but one example of a widespread attitude. Bertrand de Jouvenel remarked:

> The intellectual is really of two minds about the general economic process. On the one side, he takes pride in the achievement of technique and rejoices that men get more of the things which they want. On the other hand, he feels that the conquering army of industry destroys values and that the discipline reigning there is a harsh one. These two views are

conveniently reconciled by attributing to the "force" of
"progress" everything he likes about the process and to the
"force" of "capitalism" everything he dislikes.[7]

Here is the origin of the various scapegoat theories which
have been the most potent political dynamite of modern
times. Three groups or institutions, in particular, have been
singled out for the role of culprits and public enemies: the
"capitalists" (or the institution of private property); the Jews
(or the alleged conspiracy of "World Jewry"); and "Western Imperialism," in particular, at present, the United
States of America.

What these groups have in common is that they have been
in the vanguard of the modern movement; that their members have had a considerable share in bringing it about or
have profited from its growth; and that they, or a conspicuous
part of them, occupy higher places in the social (or international) hierarchy. Much as these movements may differ from
each other, they have in common a savage hatred of a group
which, for better or worse, had a substantial share in making
the modern world what it is.

The "capitalists," the "bourgeoisie," have taken the initiative in the process of industrialization; they own and operate the machinery of production and the media of communication. There has been a shift in actual power from owners
to salaried executives in more recent times, but this shift has
changed little or nothing in the attitude of the protest movement, partly because the change has not yet been generally
recognized, and partly because the executive group is not
sharply separated from that of the shareholders but gradually
shades over into it.

The Jews have also been leaders along the road of the modern development, quite beyond their proportionate share in
the population. They had already been largely instrumental
in the revival of ancient Greek learning in medieval Europe,
as was noted in Chapter 1. Jews were moneylenders in early
times, and they have had a considerable share in industry and

commerce since the onset of the industrial era. They have launched or sponsored all kinds of new ideas and have actively participated in the criticism of established creeds. They have a traditional appetite for learning, and a considerable number of them have had the ability to absorb it. Whenever competition in a field was halfway open, Jews quickly rose on the social ladder and took a share of the leading positions in science, education, art, banking, industry, commerce or the press, a share that far exceeded their numbers in the general population.

A few examples may illustrate the situation. Around the turn of the century, a statistic of property holdings of Protestants, Catholics, and Jews in the Southern German State of Baden revealed that the per capita property of German Protestants was almost twice as high as that of Catholics, while the per capita property of Jews was four times as high as that of Protestants and about seven times as high as that of Catholics.[8] In November, 1938, after five years and nine months of Nazi rule in which expropriations of Jews had gone on incessantly, the Nazi government ordered all Jews to submit complete statements of their holdings. It turned out that after years of spoliation the Jewish assets were still considerably higher than their percentage of the population at large—a fact that Marshall Goering scornfully announced to discredit the reports in the world press about persecution of Jews.

The share of Jews in the modern scientific development has been entirely out of proportion to their numbers. When the Hitler policies drove German scientists to emigration—not all, though most of them, Jews—the German universities lost half of their physicists and two thirds of their physical chemists; yet only about 1 per cent of the population of pre-Hitler Germany was Jewish. Charles Singer, one of the founding fathers of the history of science, opened a chapter on the Jewish contributions to science in Central Europe in the course of a century with the words: "The role of the Jews in the drama of modern scientific progress has been noteworthy in several Western countries. *In Central Europe it was over-whelming....*"[9]

Jews have shown themselves able to absorb, without much visible harm, a considerable measure of job discrimination, as in the Habsburg and Hohenzollern monarchies. These Jewish propensities have been the more conspicuous, the more "backward," in terms of the modern orientation, the host communities have been, as, e.g., in Eastern and much of Central Europe.

It may seem surprising to many that the Jews who were despised in many parts of the world throughout most of the period in question—a "pariah nation," in Max Weber's term—should here be counted among the leaders of the modern world, the "top dogs." However, the unfavorable social position of the Jews was not the outcome of a free play of forces in which each finds the place in the social hierarchy that is appropriate to his make-up, as in the pecking order of animals; it was rather due to an artifact of legislation and social convention among the host peoples in whose midst the Jews lived; and the latter was often a response to the very fact that, without such artificial impediments, a disproportionate number of Jews would rise to the top.

The *Western world*, finally, is clearly superior in wealth and power to the nations of Asia and Africa and, to a lesser degree, of Latin America, whose social and economic systems and cultural attitudes resemble those of Europe before the advent of the modern movement or at an earlier stage of it. It varies in degree from country to country, according to the great differences in their respective stages of modernization.

Among the countries of the West itself, the United States has been the most advanced along the road of modernization, and it has been the target of similar resentments on the part of a Europe moving in the same direction but trailing the United States at some distance, as was the entire West on the part of the "underdeveloped" world.

The flourishing of such theories is not too surprising. For

one thing, there is the very real difficulty of determining cause-and-effect relations within the stream of historical events. One cannot isolate individual factors in laboratory experiments and study the consequences one at a time. Short of the experiment, however, one can only attempt to assess, in the bundle of natural events, the relevance and importance of various factors, and this is a matter of interpretation, of judgment. Experience is deceptive and judgment is difficult, as Hippocrates said. The reliability of such judgments increases with experience, but a great deal of experience is needed before judgment can compel conviction.

Leopold Schwarzschild, the German-Jewish journalist who published an anti-Nazi periodical during the Hitler era, used the following comparison to illustrate a particular kind of reasoning frequent in political arguments: a man rents a three-room apartment and sits down to a meal of scrambled eggs; thereupon, he has a heart attack. From this the conclu-assumptions of the three-room-apartment-and-scrambled-eggs type.

The example was, of course, meant as a caricature; there is no danger that this conclusion would actually be drawn in this case because many thousands of people suffer heart attacks every year, and most of them under quite different circumstances; but if heart attacks were very rare events and had happened only two or three times within men's memory, such a theory might seem plausible.

However, this is just about the case with historical phenomena. There were not many cases of industrialization on record when Karl Marx or Houston Stewart Chamberlain, the founding fathers of Socialism and National Socialism, formed their theories. There are more cases at hand today, and we can hope that with time they may lead to a revision of older assumptions of the three-room-apartment-and-scrambled-eggs type.

In the eighteenth century, when people began to look upon wars as part neither of the natural nor of the moral order, i.e., as avoidable evils, they thought that wars were due to dynastic rivalries, and that they would disappear once the monarchical system had everywhere been replaced by popular governments. The wars of which they knew most were those that had been fought in their own lifetime or in that of their parents and grandparents, and those were the wars of the Spanish and the Austrian succession and their aftermath—wars about the occupancy of thrones and the seizure of provinces. Since all governments in those days were weak, government had little impact upon the lives of the people, the upper classes as well as the common people, and it mattered little to them under whose rule they were living.

The theory of wars as a by-product of the monarchical system appeared convincing for a long time; as late as 1918, President Wilson demanded, in the exchange of notes following the German request for an armistice, that the "King of Prussia" be deprived of the power to declare war. President Wilson should not be blamed too much for having believed in the theory of the dynastic origin of wars because, as late as 1914, the Emperor of Austria and King of Hungary had said it himself in the proclamation which set forth the reasons for the declaration of war against Serbia: "The Serbs want to destroy me and my house."

When it then turned out that wars were still fought after most dynasties had disappeared from their thrones and those that remained had a symbolic and representative rather than governmental function, the theory exploded. One could then see clearly that the monarchic system may have determined, in some degree, the *form* of international conflicts and perhaps the *course* which they had taken, but hardly the fact that conflicts there were.

It must be added, however, that unless the new facts are of the most unambiguous kind, the revision of old theories in the light of new facts is neither as complete nor as fast as one might expect. Beliefs are a function of experience, it is true, but, as we already have had occasion to note, this is only one half of the truth. We must add the other half of the truth, viz., that strongly held opinions often determine what kind of facts people are able or willing to perceive.

The difficulty of judgment of which Hippocrates speaks, is vastly increased if available experience is short; it is further greatly increased if strong human passions are involved; and in the movements under discussion, violent passions are rampant. Even in the relatively peaceful, detoxified, atmosphere of the old democracies, each party, as a rule, attributes whatever good has happened during its term of office to its own actions in running the government; and whatever ills have shown themselves, to the bad inheritance it had to accept when taking office, to difficulties caused by the opposition, and to events beyond human control; and each party attributes everything good that has happened during their opponents' term of office to the excellent condition in which the opponents were fortunate enough to find the ship of state upon taking office, to their own actions as a watchful opposition, and to acts of God, while attributing all ills to the sins and mistakes of the party in power.

Yet, an analysis of the cases according to their merits offers little to support the theories that, on the whole, capitalism is responsible for the frustrations of the working class, or Jewry for the frustrations of that part of the middle class which was sandwiched between the two parties of industrial class warfare, or "Western imperialism" for the frustrations of Asians, Africans, and Latin Americans. On the other hand, there is much to support the view that the causes of these frustrations are deeper, inherent in the process of industrialization itself and sometimes even in the human situation itself, and that capitalism, or Jewry, or Western imperialism are convenient *scapegoats*.

THE ANTICAPITALIST CASE

The social costs of capitalism cannot be measured by the total profits of all successful enterprises and not even by the balance of all profits and losses, because a large part of these profits is plowed back into the economy in the form of investments, while another part goes to the government in the form of taxes. The social costs of capitalism consist only of the actual *consumption* of the capitalists, their families, heirs, servants, and retainers. While ruling classes in preindustrial, agrarian societies have often consumed a very substantial part, or even a lion's share, of the total social product, the consumption of the capitalist "class" has, in industrial society, always been a relatively small part of the social product,[e] hovering in the vicinity of 10 per cent.

And it could, in fact, not be otherwise *in an industrial society*. It is possible in an agrarian society that the sultan lives a life of sensuous luxury in his palaces, with his harems, his jewels, and his slaves, while the vast majority of his subjects live in mud huts on a near starvation level. In this case, the consumption of the rich is indeed a very substantial part of the total social product, and the plight of the masses could be substantially improved by the distribution of upper-class income.

However, this is so only as long as wealth consists entirely of land, durable consumer goods, and slaves or serfs. In industrial society, wealth consists, for the most part, of industrial and commercial establishments. These establishments do not constitute wealth unless they can be operated in such a way that the output is worth more than the input; they can be so operated only if they can profitably sell a large output of goods; and that is possible only if the broad masses of the people rather than merely the rich are able to buy them. Hence, while in preindustrial society vast wealth can exist

[e] Oliver Wendell Holmes, who had no special "training" in economics but was endowed with a strong sense of reality, once said on this subject: "In all the books that touch on social themes, I noticed the same assumption, expressed or implied, that ownership means consumption of the products, that the ever repeated ownership of 9/10 by 1/10 means that 10% of the people consume 9/10 of the products—the *emptiest humbug that ever served as a red flag* . . . I believe that the drain on the public resources by the consumption of the few is an insignificant item."[10] Yet, this humbug is one of the mightiest forces of history because envy is a most powerful motive force in the uncreative.

on top of mass poverty, in industrial society great wealth can exist only on top of considerable mass purchasing power; for this reason, the appropriation of goods for their own consumption, by the capitalists and their retainers, can, in industrial society, never amount to more than a modest share of the national product. The Marxist picture of the final stage of capitalism, envisioning a few immensely rich capitalists exploiting a vast majority of people who live in abject poverty, *has not only actually* not materialized but *could not possibly have come to pass* because it is self-contradictory; it is a wooden iron. It reflects the inability of Marx to comprehend the crucial difference between agrarian and industrial society, i.e., between primitive and capital-intensive production.

These considerations are rather similar to the Marxist reasoning that capitalist society is self-contradictory and doomed to destroy itself: but what is self-contradictory is Marx's *picture* of capitalist society, and the proper conclusion is not that "capitalist society" must perish from its inner contradictions but that the *picture is incorrect*.

If the social costs of capitalism are but a small fraction of the social product, the economic aspirations of the workers cannot be satisfied by a redistribution of income because even a complete distribution among the workers of the income consumed by the capitalists and their dependents cannot greatly raise the workers' income; at the present time, the social costs of capitalism which, at most, might be available for distribution amount in some countries to less than the *yearly* increment of the social product.

These considerations are still based on the optimistic assumption that the social costs of capitalism could be *completely* saved. However, the capitalists and their dependents are not simply the absentee landlords of a stationary agricultural society; they run the economy—not necessarily by always being its actual managers but in the sense that the decisions about the employment of primary resources, fundamental in every economy, are steered by their proprietary interests, regardless of whether these decisions are made by them personally or by their appointed managers. Their income must therefore be considered as *administrative costs* of a market economy. These costs cannot be completely saved and made available for distribution since somebody will have to do the administering and that will involve social costs.

It may, of course, be possible to do this administration at smaller costs than is done by capitalism; the administrators of the socialist economy of, say, China probably consume a smaller fraction of the national product than the capitalists in the Western countries, but that does not mean that the workers will always gain from such savings. The living standards of the workers depend not only on the distribution of the social product but also, and above all, on its size. A saving in the administrative costs is of advantage to the workers only if it does not bring about a drop in efficiency;[d] and capitalist economy has been, and is, on the whole, an enormously efficient machine for the production of wealth. Even a relatively small drop in efficiency would more than cancel out what might be saved in administrative losses. All in all, it appears that the key to economic abundance for the workers lies primarily in the increase of the national product rather than in its redistribution—a conclusion that has been amply borne out by the history of the most developed countries.

It is probably characteristic of the anticapitalist, or socialist, position that the problem of efficiency has not been seen at all; or, rather, that it has been seen only as a matter of exertion and sacrifice on the part of the workers, and of inspiring leadership and determination on the part of the managers.

---

[d] This has been dramatically demonstrated in recent years by the great difference in income between workers in West Berlin and their opposite numbers in East Berlin, and by the considerable economic losses suffered by the Cuban workers after the Castro Revolution, both due to the wastefulness of the central economic management. Glaring though these facts are, they are unlikely to impress many believers in socialism; for as I have observed more than once, if one considers a theory as self-evident—as the exploitation theory of capitalism undoubtedly is considered by the economically unsophisticated—incongruous experience alone is not likely to shake the convictions.

What has not been seen is that it is, above all, a question of the *optimal allocation of resources*—raw materials, installations, machinery, and labor—at every point of the production process.

Characteristic of this blindness is the belief that all depends on *production*. Yet, there is no simple production except, perhaps, in a very primitive economy which uses only manpower (which under such conditions is in ample supply) and no tools or only very elementary, durable tools. In an economy in which capital goods are extensively used, however, "production" is actually the *transformation* of goods, and welfare depends not on the amount of production as such but on the relation between the values of input and output, measured in terms of consumers' preferences. Production can increase indefinitely without any improvement of living conditions, or indeed even while living conditions are deteriorating.

In order to make sure that output will be worth more than input, in terms of consumers' preferences, it is necessary that every single step in the economic process be measured in terms of consumers' preferences; this measurement is, under conditions of capitalism, a function of the market. In practice, this gauge is often distorted through the intervention of government, which lays down the rules according to which the game is to be played, or the interventions of private power; but except when these interventions have surpassed certain limits, the gauge has worked well enough as a promoter of welfare.

The market economy is, of course, efficient only in terms of consumers' preferences, i.e., in terms of human welfare as seen by the people themselves. It is not suitable, or "efficient," whenever the rulers pursue other goals—e.g., military power—and want to mobilize for these purposes resources which the people would probably not allocate to them through their own private decision; or when the rulers pursue goals which they consider to be in the long-range interest of the people but which the people either do not see in this light, or for which, if they do see them, they would not make the necessary sacrifices on their own initiative.

The role of the market in securing, within the framework of the prevailing rules of the game, the optimal allocation of all resources is the *raison d'être* of a capitalist or market economy; the crucial problem of a "planned," i.e., a command, economy is therefore what other solutions to the problem of economic rationality it can provide. These facts were clearly seen half a century ago by Ludwig von Mises and Max Weber.[11] Socialist planners as well as the vast host of anticapitalist intellectuals have been blissfully unaware of the existence of the problem until this day. Lenin thought on the eve of the Bolshevik Revolution that the job of management could be reduced "to the extraordinarily simple operations of watching, recording, and issuing receipts, within the reach of anybody who can read and write and knows the first four arithmetical rules."[12]

It is worth noting that there are now economists in the Soviet Union and in the Communist countries of Eastern Europe who are aware of the problem. They demand that there be only an overall central plan (*macroplanning*) and that *microplanning* be left to the individual enterprises; the latter, while of course all state-owned, should nevertheless operate independently in a competitive market.[13]

Engrained beliefs have collided with experience; whether facts will induce men to change their beliefs or beliefs will make them disregard or distort facts is still hidden in the future. It would be ironic if the nations which were first to succumb completely to Marxism should turn out to be the first to extricate themselves completely from it.

THE ANTI-SEMITIC CASE

The anti-Semitic case that holds the Jews responsible for all and sundry frustrations inherent in the industrial development is even weaker and more patently paranoid.

Anti-Semitism is an ancient and complex phenomenon and it has meant different things in different places and at different times. There is in it the reaction to an alien group—alien in religion in times when religion was the main constituent of community and alien ethnically at a time of nationalism in which, over most of the globe, ethnic coherence was the main constituent of community; in this aspect, anti-Semitism is comparable to the antagonism of Greeks against Turks in Cyprus, or of Turks against Greeks in Turkey. There is also in it the resentment of a group on the ground of characteristics frequently found among its members or because of the positions frequently held by them; in this aspect it is comparable to anticapitalism or anti-Americanism. Finally, there is in it a more enduring, metaphysical aspect, in the sense that the Jews are viewed as the eternal embodiment of Evil; in this respect anti-Semitism is unique.

The last aspect is the disastrous heritage of the tragic concatenation of Jewish and Christian destiny in the early days of Christianity. It has its basis in the fact that the ministry of Jesus, which was part of the Hebrew Messianic movement, was rejected by a majority of the Jews and accepted by the Gentiles, with a definite anti-Jewish implication. Jesus' own activities seem to have been limited to the Jewish people; "I am not sent but unto the lost sheep of the house of Israel" (Matthew 15:24). Paul carried the message to the Gentiles; it is doubtful, however, whether Paul found much support in the Christian community in Jerusalem at the time. The turning point seems to have come with the Jewish War (66-73). When the zealots had their way and the Jews took up arms against the overwhelming power of Rome, the Christian community seems to have dissociated itself from the Jewish destiny and taken pains not to be identified with Judaism. The Gospel of Mark, presumed to have been written at about that time, contains traces of this process. The centurion who commanded the Roman detachment at the execution of Jesus is supposed to have said: "Truly, this man was the Son of God" (16:39). It is difficult to take this report at face value. Roman

officers were not likely to think in terms of Hebrew Messianism and to look upon a delinquent as the "son of God." Roman soldiering was a cruel thing, and men of compassion
were not likely to rise to the rank of centurion; the execution
of rebels in the provinces was a routine job for them. It is far
more plausible to consider this passage as an addition to the
historical truth that would make the point: the Messiah was
rejected by the Jews but was recognized by the Gentile soldier: hence, this was not a Jewish affair.[14]

This historical development gave Christianity its anti-Semitic stance; the Jews were the murderers of God, both in the
literal sense of having demanded the crucifixion of the incarnate God and in the figurative sense of having closed their
eyes to his divinity.

This ancient tradition gives to anti-Semitism in the countries of Christian culture its metaphysical, indestructible,
background. Anti-Semitism has, so to say, three layers, two
normal and one psychotic. "Normal" anti-Semitism consists
of the negative reactions stimulated by some reality. It is natural for people to resent the outsider in their midst; and it is
natural for people to resent the worldly success of their
brothers (unless they have accepted this inequality as part
of an immutable, cosmic order); all this is normal, though
not necessarily praiseworthy from a moral point of view.
Much of anti-Semitism is comprehensible in these terms. Antagonism against the alien intruder is comparable to other
attitudes of religious or nationalistic exclusiveness, and resentment on the ground of success in terms of modern, alloplastic, civilization is fully analogous to the hostility directed against other success groups such as the rich in general
(capitalists, Americans).

Some of the allegations made against capitalists, Jews, Westerners, and Americans, are almost literally identical. We may
read today that the Panamanians are embittered by the fact
that Americans in the Canal Zone live in conspicuous wealth,
oblivious of the poverty that surrounds them. The same accusations have been made against Jews in Central and East-

ern Europe. In a meeting of a students' relief organization at
the University of Vienna at the end of World War I in which
I protested against an anti-Semitically inspired motion, one
student shouted furiously in my face that "The Jews in Leo-
poldstadt [the Jewish quarter in Vienna] have indulged themselves while our people have been starving." Adalbert Stifter,
the nineteenth-century Austrian writer, described in a novel
the life of a North African Jew who lived with his wife in a
cavern under Roman ruins.[15] Outside, it was all shambles, but
inside, his apartment was furnished luxuriously. He himself
appeared in public clad only in rags so as not to arouse the
envy of the surrounding Arabs. He did not long succeed; one
day he returned home and found his wife slain and his home
looted.

Yet behind this layer in which anti-Semitism is merely one
case of what Nietzsche called "the resentment of those who
have fallen behind,"[16] there is the other, paranoid layer in
which the Jews appear as the eternal source of all Evil, as Sa-
tan Incarnate. In the anti-Semitism of men like Adolf Hitler,
Paul Joseph Goebbels, and the whole academic riffraff and
would-be intellectuals that formed the core of the Nazi
leadership, one can see clearly enough the resentment
of those who in an open contest of the intellect would have
to stand behind; but there is also, particularly in Adolf Hitler,
the psychotic core of a fight against Jewry as the principle of
all Evil.

When von Ribbentrop traveled to Moscow to sign the
Nazi-Soviet pact, Hitler sent his photographer, Paul Hoff-
man, along and ordered him to observe Stalin carefully and
to report to him the details of Stalin's behavior; in particular,
he instructed him to watch whether Stalin's ear lobe stuck to
the underlying skin.[17] There was a superstition that that was
a characteristic of Jews. Thus, Hitler suspected that Stalin
was actually a Jew masquerading as a Georgian who would at
the end give himself away by an inherited physical mark of
Jewishness.

Here, anti-Semitism assumes a psychotic character. This

aspect stems from, or at least is rationalized in terms of, the tradition of the events of the first century of our era which attributed to "the Jews" the role of Evil in the momentous drama of the incarnation and execution of God.

The tradition has often been dormant, but has never been fully detoxified and laid to rest. It provides the background that may give to the ordinary conflicts and frictions between groups a special, metaphysical and paranoid, significance and transform limited antagonisms into unlimited destructiveness.

A merchant, for instance, who operates a small business along traditional lines and who feels squeezed both by department stores and trade unions, may have seen Jewish faces among the executives of large commercial firms as well as among labor agitators. Out of the reservoir of ancient hatred, there emerges in him the suspicion, soon to harden into conviction, that the Jews are playing a double game with divided roles, inciting one part of the population against the other, for their own benefit.

The importance of this factor in the virulence of modern anti-Semitism can hardly be exaggerated. J. L. Talmon writes with reference to the "Messianic" movement of Saint-Simonism and the rising industrialization in early nineteenth century France:

> We have already noted in passing the presence and part played by individual Jews in the [Saint-Simonist] movement. Olinde Rodrigues and his younger brother Eugene, their cousins, the brothers Emile and Isaac Pereira, Gustave d'Eichthal, the poet Léon Halévy of the family of the composer, Moise Renaudet, Félicien David. The fact did not fail to attract the attention of contemporaries. Much of the bitter antisemitism of Fourier and his disciples may be ascribed to the bitter rivalry between the two schools. On the opposite end, a poetic drama by the Polish ultramondane poet Zigmunt Krasinski significantly called "The Godless Comedy" . . . and composed in the 1830's depicts Saint-Simonism

as a Judaic plot to subvert Christian civilization and to plunge the European nations into an abyss of social anarchy and moral debauchery.... The phenomenal success of Rodrigues and the Pereira brothers in business, their decisive role in vital branches of the French national economy, coupled with their socialist and universalist ideas, was calculated to present to the enemies of Jews the pattern of an *antisemitic myth* which was revived with such frightful results in the second quarter of the twentieth century: *capitalism and communism have both been represented as Judaic weapons of war* wielded by a sinister cosmopolitan force, alien and hostile to any national tradition, and acting everywhere as a poisonous agent of disintegration.[18]

Since Jews have ancient rationalistic proclivities, they are particularly fit for all kinds of mental activity that involves emancipation from traditional patterns,[e] and one must expect to meet a disproportionate number of them in new business organizations as well as in political protest movements and in many other developments, too. Contrary to the suspicions of our hard-pressed merchant, however, there is no cooperation between Jews in these various pursuits, and the idea of concerted action, perhaps consciously steered by some "Elders of Zion" or coordinated instinctively, is manifestly psychotic.[f] Above all, these modern developments are so vast that they cannot be attributed with any degree of plausibility to a small group of people, handicapped, to boot, in many

[e] On what these "proclivities" are based is a matter of speculation. It is not impossible that a genetic factor is involved, in the following way: most European Jews are probably descendents of inhabitants of the ancient Mediterranean world who in Hellenistic or Roman times were converted to Judaism. Those who preferred the austere Jewish religion, which offered no appeal to the senses, over the colorful mythology of paganism may well have been men and women of a particular bent of mind, and so may have represented a genetic selection. In this sense, there may be a germ of truth in the myth of the "Jewish race."

[f] The most scurrilous stories have been spread and have found believers. After the First World War, a story was told that the War was decided upon by the Elders of Zion whose representatives—Albert Einstein, Leon Trotsky, and Lord Rothschild—met at night in the Jewish cemetery of Prague some time in June, 1914.

places, by various social restrictions. Moreover, the modern movement has spread over most of the globe and is now going on, in essentially similar forms, in countries in which there are no Jews at all.

THE ANTI-IMPERIALIST CASE

Finally, the poverty of the "underdeveloped" world is not the doing of the highly developed countries. It is not the fault of the United States if the masses in Venezuela or, far more, in Haiti, are poor. In fact, it is misleading to ask who is responsible for the poverty in these lands; the question seems to imply that man was created in a state of affluence, with ample food, decent houses, and air-conditioned offices ready for him. In fact, however, man came into this world naked and helpless, and he has pulled himself up by his own efforts. He has done so *everywhere*; he has gone everywhere a long way from the time of the cave dwellers. In some parts of the world he has gone farther than in others, and he has gone farthest in the northwestern corner of the map. The question to ask is not why Haiti is poor, for this is the older condition, but rather how it has come about that Europe and North America have become affluent.[g] And to this question an answer should not be too difficult.

It is in the countries of the northwestern corner that the demythification of the world has taken place and the new attitudes have been shaped: a new philosophy with its new approach to the world, a self-perpetuating science of nature, its quick technological application, and a perpetual revolution of agriculture, industry, and commerce through these inventions. There has been, in these lands, an extraordinary sequence of men of genius who have made these innovations— thinkers, scientists, inventors, entrepreneurs. Religion had

[g] It is characteristic of the current propaganda that the poor of Latin America are often referred to in the press as the "impoverished masses," thus subtly suggesting that they had once been prosperous and that someone had taken their prosperity away from them.

to withdraw to an innermost redoubt, to what Cardinal König recently called the fundamental religious question, the problems of Purpose and Meaning, and leave the problems of the world of Being to the new approach. Ancient beliefs and social customs were no longer permitted to stand in the way of science and technology. There was nothing like the sanctity of the cow in India to stand in the way of the breeding of cattle for human food or to make it impossible to prevent cattle from roaming freely over the countryside and destroying the crops—a major cause, in the judgment of some experts, of starvation in India, where about half of the world's starving are. There were no ancient rules of ritual purification to interfere with the quite different modern concepts of pasteurization or sterilization, no ritual implications of, say, threshing as a communal activity to interfere with the growing of a new type of grain that would require a different threshing technique,[19] no caste system sufficiently rigid to interfere with the development of large-scale industry.

There were the corresponding social valuations. The characteristic occupations of the new system—the businessman, the scientist, the engineer, the professional man—came to carry more prestige than the leading occupations of a preindustrial age—the landlord, the officer, the cleric, and the civil servant. Work not only lost its previous social stigma and became honorable, but, in the countries that were to become the most advanced ones, work became honorific; the gentleman of leisure became an object of disdain. The children of the upper and middle classes in the United States take it for granted that during their vacations from high school or college they will work as camp counselors or accept whatever employment is available to them.

Finally, within relevant areas of human activities—the economic life and the political life within the national state—a development took place which in terms of psychoanalytic theory might be described as a progress from the pleasure principle to the reality principle;[20] i.e., human behavior, in these areas,[h] ceased to be largely ruled by impulse and became more and more the considered choice between alternate courses of action in the light of their anticipated consequences, with ever more distant events being taken into consideration. The arch from impulse to action lengthened and stop-look-and-listen mechanisms were built in. One might say, in Bernard Shaw's words, that people learned "to choose the line of greatest advantage instead of yielding in the direction of least resistance."[21][1]

A characteristic example of such a development toward the reality principle is the awareness of abstract time—of the kind of time that is shown by clocks—and the willingness to operate within its rhythm; tomorrow at 8:00 A.M. means just that, not some time in the indefinite future. It is another example of such development that countries which stand to gain from foreign investments or foreign credits will refrain from confiscating, wholly or partly, existing investments or renege on their promise to foreign creditors, tempting though the foreign possessions or claims may be in their defenselessness. It is an achievement equal to the one in ancient times when man learned to trade with the merchants who brought their wares to his shores, rather than seizing their property and their persons, too.

Another example is the willingness to accept the fact that in social life one cannot have all one's way all the time, and the consequent willingness to accept compromise, which is the basis for the development of stable government and the rule of law.

The so-called underdeveloped countries differ greatly among themselves in their stage of development, their his-

---

[h] It must be emphasized that such progress applied only to these areas. The intense nationalism which led to the era of the European wars of hegemony and, through them, to the overthrow of the European world system and which today still prevents the unification of Europe (a development that technological conditions seem to require) does not suggest that realities, in this area, have been squarely faced and acted upon.

[1] Caesar's characterization of the Gauls is interesting in this respect. He ascribed to them lightheartedness (*levitas*) and inability of sustained purpose (*infirmitas animae*). Much the same has been said by Westerners about Indonesians, Laotians, Africans, and many others.

torical background, and their sociocultural conditions; but they all lack several of the conditions that have made possible the modern development in Europe and its transoceanic settlements. The introduction in the underdeveloped countries of Western techniques which they so eagerly covet is then, in the words of the physicist Francis E. Dart, who had worked in the Point Four program, "like an attempt to transplant cut flowers."[22]

In addition to this, the policies of these nations are often self-contradictory. They want rapid industrialization, which requires vast investments. At the same time they often want land reform, the splitting up of large agricultural estates into small peasant holdings, a reform which, as long as the peasant has few needs beyond bare subsistence, is likely to lead to a decline in agricultural output. The new owner, who no longer has to pay rent to a landlord, grows only what he needs for his own and his family's consumption. Thus, at the very time when hard currency is most urgently needed for the importation of producers' goods, the only existing source of hard currency dries up.

Furthermore, the people in many countries want both industrialization and a welfare state, and sometimes more of the latter than exists in the most advanced countries. Hence, every investment has its labor costs increased by the often considerable costs of social contributions, and those enterprises that could be operated economically at the prevailing wages but cannot carry the additional load are thus rendered uneconomical. That the rich in, e.g., South America, often show more resemblance to a feudal than to a capitalist class has been widely publicized; the hardly less important fact that workers' and employees' organizations in some countries play a similar role seems less well known.

Finally, while private investment is desired in many developing countries, measures hostile to foreign property, or to private property in general, are often adopted at the same time. In this way, an industrial concern that might be interested in investing in a particular underdeveloped country must realize that if the enterprise should turn out to be successful, local legislation will trim the profits or interfere with their monetary transfer; in the end, the businesses will probably be expropriated, in one form or another. In these circumstances, foreign investments are likely to be made only when they promise exorbitant returns fast so that the whole investment can be written off in a short time. In addition to deterring the foreign investor, policies hostile to private property will often also lead to a flight of domestic capital so that at a time when investment capital is most urgently needed, local surpluses leave the country.

There are many examples of self-contradictory policies of this kind on the part of the underdeveloped countries. These policies increase the difficulty of speedy industrialization which these countries so eagerly desire.

CONCLUSION

It is easier to blame one's frustrations on the capitalists, or the Jews, or the imperialists, or on the whites, than earnestly to investigate a problem and to face the stubborn facts. It is far simpler to see specific groups as the sources of all Evil in the world and to sound the clarion call to attack. It is not too astonishing that the voice of reason is feeble, hardly audible, against the shrill shrieks that call the masses of the world to a lynching which offers them an immediate outlet for their pent-up, or stirred-up, aggressions and promises an easy road to the fulfillment of their aspirations.

Charles L. Sanford remarked about the devil theories as against what he called the tragic sense of life:

> The demonic view of history is ... extremely immature, not to say irrational. ... The more mature tragic sense of life is held by relatively few people. It probably contributes little in the short run to the making of history, because, keyed to the understanding of human limitations rather than human potentiality, it is not aggressive. It transcends a simplistic moralism by seeing elements of good and evil intermixed in human character and events.[23]

7

Future Prospects of the Modern Development

Men perish because they cannot connect the beginning with the end.

—ALCMAEON (6th c. B.C.)[1]

Since the emergence of historical consciousness, men have speculated about the course of their history. The grasp of its laws—if any there are—would permit us to view the past as necessary and in this sense as meaningful, and to foresee, at least in broad outlines, the shape of the future.

THE IMPOSSIBILITY OF A COMPLETE FOREKNOWLEDGE OF THE FUTURE

Certain developments can be predicted as probable as long as one concentrates on a limited system and assumes that there will be no interference from outside the system; *ceteris paribus*—all other things being equal—such and such is likely to happen. All other things being equal, one knows fairly accurately how many of those living today will be dead in a particular year, but major advances in medicine or a major war would play havoc with the prediction.

It can be shown conclusively, it seems to me, that a *general* prediction of the future, not qualified by such a constancy clause, is, and always will be, impossible because it has implications which are patently absurd. Such predictability implies foreknowledge of every future discovery and so, in effect, a total *a priori* knowledge of reality.

It will hardly be questioned that technological developments have had a great impact on life. Without advances in industry and agriculture, it would not have been possible to feed, even if often inadequately, the large populations living today; the population could not have increased to the present level without them. Equally, without these advances of production and the simultaneous advances in medicine, life expectancy could not have risen to the three score and ten it has reached in the West. There is the entirely new problem of how to spend one's leisure time. Automation will further revolutionize living conditions. That the discovery of nuclear explosives has a major impact upon the course of events is equally obvious. The consequences would be beyond imagination if these weapons ever were used in war. Even if, as we all hope, they are never used, however, they will still have greatly influenced the course of history by their very existence; for they will have brought about the substitution of one form of violence for another—i.e., the current pattern of revolution, guerrilla war, and low-grade civil violence in place of the old pattern of periodic wars between territorial states—and so have changed the basis of the power relations between the nations.

The proposition that technological innovations have an important impact upon history is therefore well established. Thus, the possibility of predicting the future implies the possibility of predicting future technology.

Technology is applied science, however, and one cannot predict future inventions unless one can predict future scientific discoveries. To assume that this is possible would imply a kind of *a priori* knowledge of all nature. To foresee the dynamo, men would have had to foresee the discovery of electromagnetic induction, i.e., they would have had to have something like an instinctive knowledge of electromagnetism. To foresee the nuclear explosives, men would have had to have a kind of instinctive knowledge of the fact that nuclear fission, with the release of energy, is possible and that, in certain circumstances, a self-sustaining chain reaction can be produced. A knowledge of all facts of nature would have to be imprinted in the genes—an absurd assumption.[a]

All this comes down to the simple fact that, from time to time, new things appear in history such as, e.g., the discovery of hitherto unknown facts of nature, which cannot be foreseen and which influence the course of events.

FURTHER DIFFICULTIES OF A THEORY OF HISTORY

Even apart from the impossibility of including the genuinely new, there are further difficulties for a general theory of history. In the various theories of history, men have tried to discover a trend, a consistent melody, in what had unfolded of the story of mankind up to their time; they then generalized the trends which they believed to have found into a general theory of history. In this, they assumed, without evidence, that the future would continue along the path of the past. They extrapolated from the part of the curve which they knew to the part unknown; such extrapolations, as physical scientists are well aware, are hazardous undertakings. If we raise the temperature of a liquid, it will at some point become a gas; if we lower the temperature, it will turn into a solid; if we lower the temperature still further, close to the absolute zero, there will be another spectacular change of characteristics. Living beings who know only a small temperature range would arrive at wrong conclusions if they extrapolated their observations in both directions far beyond the range of their actual experience.

The perils of extrapolation are particularly great if we

---

[a] Karl Marx did not foresee the immense technological development that was about to come. He wrote in 1875: "A *general prohibition* of child labor is incompatible with big industry and is therefore a pious wish, devoid of meaning."[2] If Marx were to return to life today, he would be surprised to find 35-hour weeks, spreading automation, and much discussion of what to do with leisure time.

There is no reason to criticize Marx, or anybody else, for not having foreseen what the future would bring, but there is ample reason to criticize those who claim that with the help of "Marxist science," or any other system, they can foresee the future.

know only a relatively short segment of a curve. Our historic knowledge extends, at the most, over about 5,000 years, or something like 200 generations of men. That is a short time in the history of a species. Of the millions of years that human life has spanned, we know little beyond the fact of a few advances in matters of technology.

Moreover, the shape of the curve is not clear within the segment that we actually know. Throughout this time, change in the control of man's environment was very slow in the beginning, gradually gathered momentum, interrupted by plateaus and regressions, became rapid in one part of the world in the last 200 years, and has been accelerating ever since. At the same time, change in other aspects of life did not seem to follow a recognizable pattern at all. A secularization of life had been going on in the later ages of classical antiquity; it was followed by a millenium dominated by supranatural religion, after which the road of secularization was resumed. Under such conditions, we are dealing not only with the precarious nature of all extrapolations but with the even more elementary difficulty that within the known part of the story a pattern can be found only by neglecting, in cavalier fashion, some aspects of reality—things which have brought life and death, elation and despair to millions.

There is the further difficulty that even where existing trends may plausibly be projected into the future, these are often conflicting trends, and we have no way of measuring or estimating their relative strengths—a point about which more will have to be said later.

The only real patterns in history may well be not laws of history but rather patterns of life or psychological laws, somewhat along the line of what Charles Beard said in his mellow old age, as reported by George Counts:

Having been profoundly impressed by the vast range of his [Beard's] knowledge and thought, a range that seemed to embrace the entire human record from ancient times, I asked how long it would take him to tell all he had learned from his lifetime study of history. After contemplating the question for a few moments he replied that he "thought" he could do it in "about a week." We drove on a short distance in silence. Whereupon he said he could probably do it in a day. After another brief pause, he reduced the time to half an hour. Finally, bringing his hand down on his knee, he said: "I can tell you all I have learned in a lifetime of study in just three laws of history. And here they are:

"First, whom the gods would destroy, they first make mad.

"Second, the mills of the gods grind slowly, yet they grind exceedingly small.

"Third, the bee fertilizes the flower that it robs."

About ten days later we took a stroll. . . . Evidently he had been giving further thought to my question. At any rate, he said he would like to add a fourth law to his laws of history.

"When it gets dark enough you can see the stars."[3]

The historical interpretations in Beard's published work are open to serious questions; but I doubt whether the wisdom of these casual statements could be much improved.

THE BASIC TYPES OF THEORIES OF HISTORY

The secular philosophies of history follow, by and large, four basic types; we may call them the "pendulum," the "seesaw," the "wheel," and the "arrow."

According to one type, history moves in a kind of orbit; after a certain time, the *wheel* has turned full circle and something closely akin to a previous situation emerges. An old example is the Greek theory of a circulation of political systems. Aristotle, for instance, distinguished three basic types of constitution: the rule by one man, the rule by a few, and popular self-government. Each of these systems appears in a healthy and a corrupt form, according to whether the rulers are guided by the common good or by their selfish interests. The three good governments are therefore kingdom, aristocracy, and constitutional republic; the three corrupt forms, tyranny, oligarchy, and mass democracy. It is then suggested, with some basis in Greek experience, which is understood in terms of trends inherent in the respective systems, that the constitutions tend to follow each oher in typical sequence, eventually to turn full circle.

Closely resembling this picture is that of the *pendulum;* history appears as an oscillation between two types of culture. An example of this view is a theory of history developed in our time by Pitirim Sorokin: history appears as swinging between "ideate" and "sensate" cultures, between a materialistic, sensualistic, and an idealistic orientation.

Another theory chooses the pattern of rise and fall, the *seesaw.* It was already presented in a quite sophisticated form by the medieval Moslem historian Ibn Khaldun. He saw in history an eternal repetition of this pattern: nomadic tribes endowed with qualities of fortitude and endurance become sedentary and accumulate wealth. The moment at which they have acquired the arts of sedentary life without yet having lost the simple virtues of primitive, nomadic existence is that of the highest flowering of culture; but that moment does not last long. The quality of fortitude is not reproduced in the security of urban civilization. The children of wealth grow soft and fall prey to the attack of more virile nomadic tribes.

According to these theories—the wheel, the pendulum, the seesaw—the past is bound to return; the world is round. Still another theory has become dominant in modern times in the West: the theory of progress discussed earlier in these pages. It views history as a linear process with a built-in direction, basically irreversible, a kind of pilgrimage. The forward march may proceed at greater or lesser speed; there may be periods of fatigue or of consolidation in which there is no further advance; there may be temporary setbacks; but in history's good time, the forward march is always resumed. The course of history is represented in the picture of an *arrow.*

The proponents of all these theories derived their views from looking at the human record; but they looked at different parts of it. The advocates of a linear theory of history looked at the development of tools and skills, and later of science and technology, and at the growing size of political units and the extent and intricacy of human organization in general.

The proponents of the wheel as the basic pattern of history looked at the repeated turmoil and political changes in countries they knew, as in the Greek city states. Those who believed in the pendulum looked at events such as the oscillation between periods of religious or ideological passion and periods of skepticism, the alternation in power of rival political parties like Conservatives and Laborites in England or Republicans and Democrats in the United States, or the alternation of influence between rival policies like internationalism and isolationism or private enterprise and government regulation in the United States.

Those, finally, who thought in terms of a seesaw looked at the rise and fall of empires, particularly the Roman Empire, or, in the contemporary world, at signs, real or imaginary, of the waning of a clear orientation in life and, perhaps, a decline of stamina in modern affluent and emancipated societies.

All these theories have a sound psychological basis. The linear theory, the *arrow*, is based on the fact that knowledge and skills, whenever communicable, are cumulative; the sons can take the achievements of the fathers as their points of departure and so expand the horizon of knowledge and raise the level of skills. The *pendulum* is based on the fact that there are no perfect answers to many problems. Each solution adopted is likely to have disadvantages and side effects that are hidden at first and become more conspicuous later; as time goes on, people forget what difficulties originally led to the adoption of the present policies and, in any case, take their achievements for granted, but become increasingly impatient with the shortcomings. The *seesaw* is based on the facts which are summed up in the common saying that it takes three generations from shirt sleeves to shirt sleeves; i.e., that the qualities required for success are unlikely to be reproduced under the conditions brought about by success. The *wheel*, finally, appears when the pendulum or the seesaw operate not in a bipolar, but in a multipolar—albeit still finite—system.

All these theories, therefore, contain elements of truth. There has been linear, cumulative progress. There has been something like a cyclic return of forms which live for some time and decay; and there has been the swing of the pendulum between partial solutions. There have been cycles of rise and fall. These various movements seem to be superimposed upon each other in history; perhaps that will continue to be true in the future as the story further unfolds.

This consideration may lead to an eclectic theory of history, a theory of multiple trends. However, in which degree do these various trends contribute to what might then be the actual pattern? Does the linear movement, for instance, define the *basic* shape of the curve, with the wheel, the pendulum, the seesaw superimposed upon it as secondary movements like the epicycles in the Ptolemaic planetary system? Or could it be that the pendulum or the seesaw determine the basic Gestalt of the process, with the progressive part that impresses us so strongly being merely *one long swing* of the pendulum which will be followed by another, regressive, swing of comparable length? We have no way of knowing. Yet, an attempt to fathom future development depends on such knowledge.

THE QUANTITATIVE PROBLEM

In addition to the difficulties posed by the appearance of entirely new factors beyond possible foresight, another profound difficulty of prediction rests on our ignorance of the relative strength of the competing tendencies. The nuclei of future developments, at least in the short run, have often existed for quite some time before they gathered strength and emerged victoriously. There was, for instance, a revolutionary potential in Russia around the turn of the century: a ruling class divided in itself and alternating between repression and retreat, a middle class largely alienated from the autocracy, an intelligentsia strongly infiltrated by revolutionary ideas, a small but highly active and disciplined core of full-time revolutionaries, a working class susceptible to revolutionary ideas. These conditions seemed to point toward revolution. Yet, there were also reformers like Witte who tried to lead Russia along the road of rapid industrialization and modernization, or Stolypin who tried to create a class of small rural proprietors as a dam against urban revolution. Was the revolution a foregone conclusion or could wiser leadership in St. Petersburg have prevented it? Moreover, once Czarism was actually overthrown, was it a foregone conclusion that the Bolsheviks would seize power? What would have happened if Lieutenant Colonel Nicolai of the German General Staff had not decided to let Lenin travel from Switzerland to Russia in the famous sealed train? Or if the Western Allies had realized that their insistence on Russian continuation of the war would only pull the rug from under the Kerenski government, and had released Russia from her obligation? Or if after their victory over Germany, the Allies had not forced Germany to withdraw from the vast territories she had occupied in the East and thus to abandon her stranglehold over the young Soviet Republic? These are, of course, unanswerable questions, but the impression does not favor the idea of a relentless, inescapable destiny that man will only help along by what he does to escape it.

We can *see the trends,* but we *cannot measure their strength or estimate their growth potential;* hence, the outcome is unpredictable.[b] Freud has clearly formulated this factor as an obstacle to prediction; he thought of individual patients long observed in psychoanalysis, but his argument applies even more strongly to the even greater complexities of the sociopolitical scene:

---

[b] The extrapolation of current trends into the future is nonetheless indispensable for the decision maker because it shows where present trends, if not checked, are likely to lead.

So long as we trace the development from its final outcome backwards, the chain of events appears continuous, and we feel we have gained an insight which is completely satisfactory or even exhaustive. But if we proceed to reverse the way, if we start from the premises inferred from the analysis and try to follow these up to the final results, then we no longer get the impression of an inevitable sequence of events which could not have been otherwise determined. We notice at once that there might have been another result, and that we might have been just as well able to understand and explain the latter. The synthesis is thus not so satisfactory as the analysis; in other words, from a knowledge of the premises we could not have foretold the nature of the result.

It is very easy to account for this disturbing state of affairs. Even supposing that we have a complete knowledge of the aetiological factors that decide a given result, nevertheless what we know about them is only their quality, and not their relative strength. Some of them are suppressed by others because they are too weak, and they therefore do not affect the final result. But we never know beforehand which of the determining factors will prove the weaker or the stronger. We only say at the end that those which succeeded must have been the stronger. Hence the chain of causation can always be recognized with certainty if we follow the line of analysis, whereas to predict it along the line of synthesis is impossible.[4]

THE FUTURE PROSPECTS OF PROGRESS

From these more general considerations of laws of history, we may now turn to our particular problem and reflect on what, if anything, can be surmised about the future of progress. The analysis of the processes of progress which was attempted earlier permits some generalizations about the nature of the problem.

1. It can be said that there are *no inherent limits* to scientific and technological progress. As far as science is concerned, it appears that there is no such thing as an exhaustive knowledge of a subject which leaves no more questions to

be asked; scientific knowledge is not like the catalogue of a library which may be complete. More than a century ago, the physiologist Emil Du Bois-Reymond compared science to an expanding ball; the volume of the ball indicated the existing body of knowledge, outside of it was the unknown, and the surface of the globe symbolized the frontier of knowledge, the open problems of science. The picture suggested that the more we know, the more open problems there are.

There is no inherent limit to living standards either. Karl Marx still thought that there was a point, to be reached largely by expanding capitalism itself, at which people would have enough for their "needs"; from then on, they would hold the output stable and devote their free time to pursuits like philosophy, literature, the arts. Men, freed from the humiliating need to earn their daily bread by the sweat of their brow, could devote their energies to creative pursuits—and the real history of man would begin. It was a viewpoint fundamentally similar to that of Aristotle, who had said that when practically all the necessities of life were provided, men turned to philosophy as a leisure-time recreation; Marx merely thought of "necessities" in a broader sense than Aristotle.

The Marxists, on the whole, have seen things in the same light. They aim at a point at which all "necessities" are provided for; then, communism, the full consummation of history, becomes possible. They do not contemplate the rise of living standards to be a perpetual process; when Mr. Khrushchev saw the long lines of commuting cars in San Francisco, he is said to have exclaimed: what a waste![5]

A Western, non-Marxist, theoretician of economic growth, Walt Whitman Rostow, takes essentially the same view: "the end of all this is not compound interest forever; it is the adventure of seeing what man can do and will do when the pressure of scarcity is substantially lifted from him."[6]

All this is based on the implicit assumption that "necessity" and "scarcity" refer to an eternal norm and are not merely relative to varying standards.

As has been suggested before, however, there is little to

support this contention. Some men have always considered the most recent expansion in habits of consumption as unnecessary or as frivolous, and what they have condemned has later become part and parcel of the basic necessities of life, to be discarded still later as inadequate. When bread was invented, moralists condemned the people for taking to this new-fashioned, luxurious kind of food. It came to be considered later as the very basic necessity of life; "Give us our daily bread," says the Lord's prayer. In our days, nutrition consisting of, or even largely based on, bread, i.e., carbohydrates, is considered to constitute malnutrition or, some would say, a form of starvation.

The virtually unlimited nature of economic aspirations, i.e., the purely relative character of "scarcity," can best be seen in the example of medicine. Modern medicine can now do more than merely prevent, in a multitude of cases, premature death; this was the great achievement of the nineteenth and the earlier twentieth centuries. It now can slow down the progress of degenerative diseases or compensate for them and thus actually prolong life, and a fruitful life at that. This is what the late Dr. Alan Gregg called "great medicine,"[7] but great medicine is very expensive. It is possible, for instance, to keep a person without a functioning kidney alive for a long time, perhaps indefinitely, by having the function of the kidney taken over by mechanical devices. For this purpose, the patient must each week spend some time in a hospital. The treatment must, of course, be permanently repeated and is highly expensive, costing at the present time between 7,000 and 10,000 dollars annually, about three times the annual per capita income in the wealthiest country on earth, or more than the per capita earnings of an entire lifetime in the poorest countries. The cost, of course, presents a grave problem. Not many people can, at the present time, avail themselves of the treatment; social consciousness does not permit the selection to take place in the fashion of a market economy, i.e., that the rich will live and the others must die. In some places, boards are set up to select the beneficiaries of the lifesaving treatment by means of other criteria, in accordance with the current moral ideas; but with time, pressure will surely mount in favor of public funds guaranteeing such treatment to every citizen who needs it. Perhaps, in this particular case, as in others before it, ways of substantially reducing the cost will be found; but other treatments, equally lifesaving and just as expensive, or even more expensive, may turn up. Perhaps in the not too distant future we shall witness the perfection of mechanical devices that will take over the function of the heart—most likely at enormous cost. When this happens, there will be an increased demand and growing pressure to make these benefits of advancing science available to all. Once that has been done, it will probably be pointed out that the difference between the life of Americans in possession of such devices and that of, say, Panamanians, Burmese, or Congolese who must die when Americans can go on living must needs create bitter resentment among the "underprivileged"—a difference which is bound to constitute a threat to peace; and it will be argued, on moral grounds or on grounds of expediency, that it is the responsibility of the West, and of the United States in particular, to make these inventions available to all people everywhere. Thus, "scarcity," relative to rapidly rising standards, is certain to continue; it will be with us even if the present output were to increase tenfold.

There is not only no natural *terminus ad quem;* the ascent is also accelerating for reasons immanent in the process itself. Scientific and technological development proceed in *geometrical progression*. It has been said that there are more scientists alive today than have ever lived in all previous ages. The speed of communications is accelerating at breathtaking rate. Transoceanic travel, which progressed very slowly during the centuries of sailing ships, made a quantum jump in the nineteenth century with the invention of the steamship; the speed of the latter increased faster than that of ships had in preceding times. Then, only a generation ago, came air transportation as another quantum jump. The trip across the Atlantic

by air has since been cut from about eighteen hours to about
six, and plans are on the drawing board for a spaceship that
will cut the time to a matter of minutes.

The acceleration in weapons technology has assumed a
similar tempo; military planners know that the newest inventions may become obsolete by the time they have reached
the stage of mass production.

2. It is increasingly clear that accelerating progress of this
kind *creates new problems* and that one cannot be sure that
these problems will always be readily soluble. There is, for instance, the question of whether there will always be sufficient
raw materials to supply the growing production apparatus.
We are using up in a few generations the energy accumulated
in the fossilized remains of the life of millions of years. Other
sources of energy, it is confidently expected, will take their
place and supply even vastly increased needs for a long time;
the discovery of atomic energy suggests that this may indeed
be the case. Yet, the question remains whether new sources
will *always* be opened up once old ones are exhausted,
though this process may admittedly go on for a long time; the
reckoning may only be postponed, not prevented, and it may
well be the more terrible the later it comes.

Some people think that by the time men have exhausted the
resources of the earth, they will be able to mine the resources
of the planets and of the entire universe. Just as the surplus
population of Europe streamed into the New World, so they
expect the surplus population of the earth one day to migrate
to other planets; and just as the surplus production of the
New World helped to feed the population of the old one, so
will the production of other cosmic bodies help to sustain
those who will have remained in man's original habitat. Perhaps they will; but the obstacles are still staggering. On other
planets, where natural conditions do not favor life, man
would first have to produce these very conditions (such as
air); the costs of such endeavors are, in the literal rather than
the usual figurative sense, astronomical. Eventually, there are
certain constants of nature which set limits to man's expan-

sion and which, to our knowledge, are unsurmountable;
there is the speed of light as the upper limit of the velocity
of motion, and there is probably an upper limit to the length
of the human life span (although it may well turn out to be
higher than the Biblical measure), and both together will
set final limits to man's expansion in space.

All this, of course, still lies in the distant future. In the
meantime, we are already in the midst of considerable difficulties in many areas in managing rationally what we have
rather than being overwhelmed by it. A biologist has predicted facetiously that men will be crowded off the earth by
the accumulation of publications.[8] The growth of the body
of science has reached such dimensions that it becomes a
serious problem how to communicate it to the next generation. One of the consequences of this situation is the pro-
longation of the time of learning and thus the postponement
of professional maturity; and this trend in turn runs against
the far less fluid limits of life expectancy. In some fields we
have already reached the point where a man cannot be fully
abreast of his subject before he has reached the age of fifty.
Perhaps this will turn out to be one of the more stubborn,
built-in obstacles to rapid progress.

Another consequence is an ever-increasing specialization;
the scene is increasingly occupied and dominated by men who
know more and more about less and less. There are countless
experts each of whom supplies a tiny fragment of a complex
picture, and there are fewer and fewer with the breadth of
vision that is necessary to integrate these little tesserae into
a meaningful whole. The result is haphazard; the chances
are that those partial views will prevail whose proponents
have the loudest voices or can generate most pressure by ap-
pealing to the most powerful prejudices.

The result is especially visible in the political and social
sciences. In these areas there are practically no isolated problems that can be answered by one specialist; each phenomenon
hangs together with a world of biological, psychological, and
social facts. The student of these problems should be familiar

with the whole record of human experience, which involves not only the data collected by sociologists and anthropologists for a particular moment of time but their place in time and their comparison with related experiences of men in other places at the present time as well as at other times; i.e., it requires familiarity with history. It likewise requires familiarity with the systematic disciplines which are themselves the extract of historical experience and provide clues for its interpretation: biological disciplines such as ecology, dealing with the interaction of the organism with its environment; the theory of human motivation, embodied, most comprehensively, in psychoanalysis; a theory of rational action, i.e., of action taken after careful weighing of alternatives in the light of their consequences, itself a marginal case of human behavior, but of great importance for economic theory;[c] and a theory of power, an extract from the theory of human motivation vitally needed for an understanding of events of more than individual significance. Nobody is fully abreast of all this or even of a major part of it. Works written by distinguished specialists in the social and political sciences sometimes present results which, however painstakingly worked out and carefully evaluated, are actually invalidated by simple facts which have been unknown to the author because they fall within the competence of another academic department. There still are some scholars whose range of knowledge is vast, but their influence is small for that very reason; they have no real place in an atomized academia and their works are still too exacting for general consumption.

There is, of course, some awareness of this difficulty; remedy is often sought in so-called team work. A group of specialists "trained" in different disciplines are brought together in an institute where they work on the same "projects," each from his own "point of view"; it is assumed that

[c] A theory of rational action is important for economics not because all people or even most people behave rationally in business matters—they don't—but because those who do, at least in decisions of the greatest consequence, are likely to have a greater share in total decision making while those who do not are likely to lose money and thus have their field of action restricted.

in this way nature will take its course and an integrated whole will eventually emerge. I wonder how often it actually does; moreover, the bias due to the specialist's narrow, tubular vision is usually built into the "project" itself.

Examples such as these illustrate the difficulty which confronts man in adjusting to the increasing complexities of the culture he has been building. More will be said on this in Chapter 16.

3. An *end*, or a slowing down, *of progress is bound to have serious consequences*. A large and increasing part of the population works in the growth sector of the society and derives from it income, status, and security; among them are the workers, engineers, scientists, salesmen, and a host of other specialists employed in the production of capital goods (except for the part that is needed for replacement) and the development and promotion of new products. They would all become expendable. It would be a painful and time-consuming process for them to find a place in a restricted economy. Investments in the abandoned or shrunken sector would be wholly or partly lost; that includes a major part of the reserves of insurance companies and pension funds and of the endowments of educational institutions. The consequences would be grave; the cyclic depressions of the past, particularly the Great Depression of 1929, provide a hint of what one could expect.

It is questionable whether readjustment on such a scale could be safely left to private initiative with only such limited government action as is implied in Keynesian economics, or whether public pressure for action would enforce, in one form or another, a substantial government take-over. The latter seems more likely to me. It is probably in the nature of things that a free, pluralistic society requires an expanding economy, while a stationary, and even more a contracting, economy demands a reglemented society.

In the light of the difficulties which industrial expansion sooner or later is likely to encounter, we must expect a substantial slowdown, or even a reversal, of technological progress to happen some day. It does not seem possible to foresee whether this point will be reached in decades, or generations, or centuries. Nor can we gauge the impact of such an event upon culture in general and, in particular, upon the kind and extent of violence and the kind and extent of authoritarianism it is likely to engender. The latter questions point toward the subject of the second part of this study—power and revolution.

If the West were alone in the world, one prescription would perhaps follow from this diagnosis, viz., cautiously to slow down the rate of technological and economic progress. While this step would not solve the problems, it might keep them in more manageable proportions. But this remedy is rendered impossible by the East-West conflict. The numerically vastly outnumbered West cannot hope to survive unless it can stay substantially ahead in technology and wealth. Moreover, the race is forced upon the West not only by considerations of survival but also by the hardly less imperative needs of collective narcissism, i.e., of national pride. Growth has become a gauge of national greatness, and a "sluggish" economy, with a low "rate of growth," has become a badge of shame. There is, at present, no practical alternative to acceleration.

II

An Essay on Revolution

> ... *two things are the signal marks of Jacobinism—its fierceness and its addiction to abstract systems.*
>
> —MATTHEW ARNOLD (1869)

8

The Power Structure

The destiny of men and peoples is determined by two factors: ideas and physical force.

—Friedrich Schwarzenberg (1847)[1]

Human groups, like individuals, are confronted with situations that call for a decision. In such situations, one of three things may happen: either the decision is made by mutual agreement, arrived at by all members of the group; or the decision is made by some and obeyed by others; or no decision is made.

The last is the case of *anarchy*. Anarchy vastly diminishes the chance of a group to deal effectively with danger; the continued existence of the group and perhaps the physical survival of its members are put in jeopardy.

The first case, in which all decisions are arrived at by general, voluntary *consent*, has worked in small groups only, and even then not very often. Perhaps its most important example, from a practical point of view, is the harmonious marriage, in which the partners love each other so that each conceives of the interests of the other as his own, and both see things the same way, either because they have always been similar in their outlook or because through identification they have grown similar in the course of their common life. But marriage is an especially strong community, cemented by sexual communion, joint parenthood, and common social and economic interests; no other group can vie with it in the degree of closeness, and even among married couples

137

spontaneous agreement on all issues is rare. An attempt to make the government of a large country dependent on unanimous consent of the legislative body, as happened in the Kingdom of Poland, ended in disaster.

The second case, in which decisions are made by some and obeyed by others, is the most important one, at least in a complex society; it implies a *power structure* in the group. It may be a fluctuating power structure that is formed whenever a challenge appears and melts away once the dangerous situation has passed; or it may be a more or less stable power structure, i.e., a system in which it is known in advance who makes what decisions, and in which people turn to the designated authorities when specific situations arise.

Power, then, *is the probability that others will obey* one's orders, the probability of having one's will prevail over the divergent wills of others. The degree to which actual happenings reflect the wills of various parties depends therefore on their power (except for accidents or miscalculations); this statement is indeed tautological, a mere rewording of the definition of power.

This meaning of power is inherent in language itself. The word "power" derives from the Latin *potestas,* which has the same root as the auxiliary verb, *possum,* I can, I am able to. From this root are also derived *potential, potentiality,* and *potency.* Similarly, in ancient Greek, the word for "power" is *"dynamis"* which lives on in English words like "dynamic" and has the same root as *dynamai,* I can, I am able to.

It is widely assumed, particularly in English-speaking countries, that power is both evil and dispensable: evil because the quest for power is due to a lack of love, and dispensable because power would disappear once people had learned to love each other as they should.

But power is merely the probability of having one's will prevail. Wherever issues have to be met about which people differ in their thinking, there has to be a power structure, i.e., the will of some people has to take precedence over that of others, if action is to occur at all. Even if all men were to become entirely free of self-concern and devote themselves exclusively to the welfare of others, and if, moreover, they would feel equal concern for all human beings, regardless of the differences between them—even if all this came to pass, it would not change one iota in the formation of a power structure because people would still disagree on what is best for "mankind," and all conflicts, those of conflicting altruisms no less than those of conflicting egotisms, are in the last resort settled by power. One physician may think that surgery is indicated in a particular case, while another physician, no less devoted to the welfare of his patient, may consider surgery to be harmful. Some planners in "underdeveloped" countries may think that as much as possible of the country's ancient culture should be preserved in the process of modernization, while others, equally concerned for their people, may think that all tradition should be ruthlessly uprooted so that the road to modernization will be unobstructed.

In such conflicts, the will of some persons must prevail over that of others, or contestants will have to reach some kind of compromise which will reflect their respective power. The alternative is confusion, which has no survival value.

Power is necessary not because men are evil or lacking in love, but because they differ in their thinking; the struggle between conflicting altruisms has often been fiercer than that between conflicting egotisms.

THE FORMS OF POWER

Power may be *physical* or *spiritual* power. In the first case, the wielder of power can inflict punishment on others—physical or mental pain or frustration—sufficiently intense that people will prefer obedience to the penalties of resistance. Spiritual power, on the other hand, is the authority one person has over the mind of another.

The differentiation, in reality, between physical and spiritual power has its roots in the separation between the secular and the spiritual arms in Western Christendom, between Empire and Papacy, the king and the Church. Secular power held sway over the *body* of men, spiritual power held their *conscience* in its keeping. "Render unto Caesar what is Caesar's and unto God what is God's," said Jesus; and these words seem to have inaugurated the division of power in the world of Western Christendom.

Sometimes secular and spiritual authorities have worked together, hand in glove, as was the case, e.g., in Spain during the Counter-Reformation; sometimes they fought each other, as in the struggle between Empire and Papacy, a struggle which was particularly fierce in the two centuries from Gregor VII to Boniface VIII.

Whenever secular and spiritual authority are concentrated in the same hand or cooperate with each other, the resulting power is overwhelming and leaves practically no opening for resistance; whenever they are in conflict with each other, there is some leeway left for individual freedom, which may get a measure of protection from one power being pitted against the other. It is sometimes easier to have two masters rather than one, viz., when the two are at cross-purposes with each other, one power can be played against the other.

The division between secular and spiritual authority, however, was not fully accepted in *Eastern* Christendom. The proud statement with which the Byzantine Emperor Leo the Isaurian is said to have defined his position to the Roman pontiff ("I am emperor and priest") may or may not be apocryphal, but it is a fair enough approximation of the actual relationship.

Moscow, the heir of Byzantium and hence the third Rome, entered into this heritage. There is no tradition of separation of secular and spiritual power in Russia. The Czar was the autocratic head of the State and head of the Orthodox Church at the same time. The Communist party, in our day, continues this combination in modern form; it holds complete physical power and is at the same time the guardian of thought, the only legitimate interpreter of the Marxist-Leninist tradition.

When Michael Bakunin, sentenced to death both in Austria and in Saxony for his activities in the revolutionary year 1848, and extradited to Russia which had older claim for his person, was imprisoned in the Peter-Paul fortress and awaited trial, there appeared one day in his cell one Count Orloff, adjutant to Czar Nicolas I. He put paper and pencil on the table and brought Bakunin the "order" of the Czar, as his spiritual overlord, to write his confession. And so Bakunin did. The document, with marginal notes from the hand of the Czar, was found in the Archives by the Soviet government and published by it in the early years of the Soviet regime. It is a strange hybrid between a confession and an appeal, the result of a compromise between obedience to the Czar's order and an attempt at maintaining Bakunin's inner independence and his revolutionary pride.[2]

In effect, Bakunin appealed to the Czar—to Nicolas I, of all people—to put himself at the head of the revolutionary movement in Europe. The document may be looked upon as a kind of precursor of the "confessions" of defendants in the purge trials in Stalinist Russia (or in Mao's China)—except for the vast difference of intolerance; for while Bakunin got away with his pseudo confessions full of mental reservations, no defendant in the Communist purges, to my knowledge, could get off that easily.

In Western Christendom, however, Church and State were separate. Some time around the Renaissance the spiritual power of the Church began to decline as fewer and fewer people looked upon her as the keeper of their consciences; more and more, the autonomy of every man in matters of religious belief, and eventually in matters of thought in general, was upheld. This concept of the human mind unfettered by any dogma was fundamental in the new scientific movement. The Royal Society, chartered in 1660, had inscribed on its arms the first three words of the principle, *nullius in verba iurare magistri*, never to swear on the words of any master. Man, then, was subject to physical authority but master of his own mind, approximately along the lines of the words of Shakespeare's Henry V: "Every subject's duty is his King's, but every subject's soul is his own."[3]

We see the emergence of a new attitude which respected a man's opinion as his private domain; even arbitrary, despotic, power asked only for behavioral compliance and did not try to enter into the sanctum of the subject's mind. This tradition prevailed until revolutionary totalitarianism revived the unlimited claims of authority of earlier ages and required men not only to obey its orders but also to think the official thoughts. How it proceeded to bring this about will be discussed in Chapter 9.

Power can also be classified according to the *motives of obedience*; this classification will lead to approximately the same division. One may obey another man out of *fear* of the punishment he may inflict for disobedience; or because one *loves* him and therefore does not want to displease him; or because one is *confident* that he is well-intentioned and equipped with superior knowledge or wisdom; or because one feels that one owes *allegiance* to him or to the order or idea which he incarnates or represents.[a]

Fear makes the prisoner obey the rules of the jail; children who are well behaved in the classroom with a teacher whom they like do it out of *love*; *confidence* in his doctor's good intentions and professional competence makes a patient follow the doctor's orders; and the alumnus who answers an appeal of his school for contributions may do so because he feels an *obligation* to the institution.

Where obedience is rendered out of fear, we may speak of *physical* power; where it is due to love, confidence, or loyalty, there is authority over the *minds* of men.

In reality, power is often made up of ingredients of both kinds. A man may file his income tax return both because he considers it his duty as a citizen and because he is afraid of the consequences if he fails to do so; in a fund-raising cam-

---

[a] These three motives of voluntary obedience correspond to the three systems of the mind in psychoanalytic theory; they come from the id, the ego, and the superego.

paign he may make his contribution both because he considers it his obligation and because he is afraid of the criticism of people whose goodwill he wants to maintain. In a case like the latter, in which it is not clearly defined what is proper for him to do, a combination of both motives may induce him to make a greater contribution than he would have made had he acted only out of enlightened self-interest or only out of a sense of obligation.

THE BASIS OF GOVERNMENT

The power of a government in a functioning state which endures longer than a brief moment rests on two fundamental laws:

1. The power of government is always mixed. A single man, or a small group of men, cannot maintain power for any length of time by inspiring fear alone. There must be some people who obey the ruler, or rulers, out of love, confidence, or loyalty. On the other hand, no state has so far been able to exist on voluntary consent alone and thus been able to dispense entirely with physical coercion as *ultima ratio*.

2. The smaller the basis of love, confidence, and loyalty, the more physical force is necessary to maintain a regime; the broader the basis in the love, confidence, or loyalty of the people, the less violence is needed for its maintenance.

Ad. 1. A tyrant—a Caligula, a Peter the Great, a Stalin—may inspire great fear: his mere appearance may strike terror in the hearts of his subjects. But his rule cannot endure on fear alone; there must be some men—at the very least, an armed palace guard—who are genuinely devoted to him. If this were not the case, if all his ministers obeyed only in fear and trembling, the regime could not last long; for the tyrant is still a mortal man. He cannot be omnipresent, and there must be moments in which he is defenseless; at the very least, he has to sleep.

There would come a time when his terrified subjects would suddenly understand each other without any words being spoken and each would realize that the others feel what he does, viz., hate submerged by fear; at that moment all fear would be gone, they would feel their united strength and proceed together to kill the tyrant. Once the first step in this direction was made, there would be no turning back and safety could lie only in carrying the deed to its successful conclusion.

The situation is not too different if the tyrant has only a few loyal friends, perhaps his family and a few favorites. In order for a system to be stable, there must be a *sizable core* of men loyal to the ruler or to the system for which he stands—the *Verwaltungsstab* (administrative staff) in Max Weber's terminology. This core of loyal followers, however, need not be a majority of the people. A relatively small minority can hold power, as was the case, e.g., in some slave societies and in the Roman Empire, particularly in the latter days of the Republic, before the enfranchisement of large numbers of provincials; the slave owners as well as the Roman citizens constituted a small minority in the state.

While government cannot be based on coercion alone, it cannot do entirely without it either. Even in systems which rest on widespread consent, there is an irreducible remnant of persons who do not cooperate, be it for selfish, pathological, or ideological reasons. It is a dream both old and new that force should be not only at a minimum but entirely dispensable. Ovid places the fulfillment of this dream in the remote past, the beginning of Time—"the golden age in which men did the right thing and were loyal to each other out of their own free will, without judge or law," an age that did not know "punishment or fear."[4] Christian eschatology put the "Peaceable Kingdom," in which the sheep will lie quietly next to the lion, at the end of Time. Modern prophets like Marx and Lenin expected the "withering away of the State" in the near future, after the liquidation of capitalism. A perfectly just order, so these and other thinkers believed, would be voluntarily accepted by all, and there would be no need for coercion.

The latter belief is ultimately based on the assumption that all men are satisfied with justice— an assumption that is open to doubt.[5] Even if it were true with regard to man's conscious intent, there remains the fact that man's judgment is influenced by his emotions, i.e., that bias leads him to be more impressed by the merits of his case than by those of others. Above all, there is the difficulty, previously discussed in a different context, that not all people have the same idea of justice and that one man's justice is another man's oppression. Force may well be needed to make one interpretation of justice prevail over another which is held with equal sincerity, and the struggle between rival moral creeds has often been more ferocious than that of rival greeds.

Ad. 2. In ancient Rome there was a law according to which the whole slave household, men, women, and children, were to be put to death whenever a slave owner was murdered by someone inside the household. This extreme threat made it the vital interest of every slave to watch unceasingly over the safety of his master.

Tacitus tells us that after Pedanius Secundus, a city prefect, was murdered by one of his slaves, public opinion, apparently for the first time, showed pity for the innocent: there were 400 souls in the household of the slain man. Many people spoke of mercy; even in the Senate there was some sentiment in favor of clemency, but one Caius Cassius pleaded for the ruthless application of the old blood law: "There are many preliminaries to guilt," he argued; "if these are divulged by slaves, we may live singly among numbers, safe among a trembling crowd." His view prevailed and all 400 slaves were put to death.[6]

Where obedience is based broadly on loyalty, coercive measures can be few in number and moderate in execution. This has been largely the case in countries such as Great Britain or, until very recently, the United States, because the existence of the body politic and its constitutional form have been taken for granted, or approved of, by a vast majority of people.

As was already suggested, it would be an oversimplification to think of the subjects as being either wholly loyal to the government or wholly subdued by fear. While there are some who are unqualifiedly loyal and some who submit while they hate, most people probably obey out of a mixture of fear and loyalty. One may represent a political system by the picture of concentric rings. In the center are the rulers. Around them is an innermost ring of those who follow exclusively from loyalty; around the inner core is a broad belt of those who cooperate out of a mixture of loyalty and fear; and finally there is an outer fringe of those who are constrained by fear alone. It is part of the Western ideal of society that the area of consent should be as large and the area of coercion as small as possible.

Fear and loyalty are not independent of each other. Fear, as will be discussed in Chapter 9, may generate a loyalty of sorts; the existence of a loyal body of followers, on the other hand, means that men are gripped by fear at the first heretical thought and at dissent merely imagined.

THE MINIMUM RATIO OF CONSENT TO COERCION AS A FUNCTION OF THE TECHNOLOGY OF VIOLENCE

The amount of consent that a government must have in order to be able to govern, as against the degree to which it must rely on force, depends on the nature of the coercion, i.e., on the existing technology of violence, on the one hand, and the moral climate which determines what kind of force can be applied, on the other. The latter point is self-evident; a man who, for inner reasons, cannot use force can only try to persuade. The first point, however, seems in need of amplification.

A few can effectively control if the situation is such that a small *Verwaltungsstab* can keep a monopoly of the tools of coercion, i.e., if these tools are either so expensive that they are not accessible to many, or if a large organization is needed to operate them, or if they cannot easily be hidden from the eyes of the authorities. If, on the other hand, arms are cheap, can be easily operated, and can be smuggled across borders, buried in back yards or hidden behind wallboards, governments cannot easily control a population by force and they will last only so long as they are based on a large measure of consent.

In the feudal era, armored knights on horseback were greatly superior to infantry. The cost of horses and equipment was very high for the meager resources of the age; and feudal lords, well entrenched in castles virtually impregnable to the offensive arms of the time, could keep a large countryside in submission. Only in places detrimental to the development of cavalry, e.g., in the mountainous regions of Switzerland, could a peasant infantry hold its own against the knights on horseback, and the peasant succeed in defending his independence.

The same military conditions which gave the lords their advantage over the peasantry offered no advantage to the kings; there were no weapons which they alone could own or operate and with which they could subdue the willful barons. This situation changed with the advent of the cannon. Here was a weapon too complex and too expensive for every baron to own; it naturally became the weapon of larger sovereign units such as princes or leagues of cities. The cannon could reduce the baronial strongholds and thus transform independent magnates into courtiers; it ushered in the age of monarchical absolutism—the Tudor monarchy, the age of Louis XIV. A small core of loyal followers could then be the pivot of a long arm of coercion.

This situation changed again when the rifle appeared on the scene. The rifle is a weapon which every man can own and operate and which he can easily hide from the searching eyes of the authorities (as was demonstrated by the failure of Bazaine's attempt to disarm the Mexican peasants). In emergencies "minute men" could now improvise a defense at the spur of the moment. The new spirit found expression in Dean Inge's words that a man can build himself a throne of bayonets, but he cannot sit on it.[7] This situation favored the rise of democracy.

In our time, there are tools of coercion that cannot be hidden behind bedboards and that need a large organization to operate them, e.g., tanks; and determined minorities can keep large populations in submission if they are not encumbered by inhibitions in the use of force.

At the same time, however, a new method has been invented to overthrow a modern state, viz., internal war such as guerrilla war. A well-organized minority of malcontents, ruthless toward others and impervious to danger, can disrupt the functioning of government through civilian terrorism, frustrate all efforts at pacifying the country, and in the end marshal to its support the common man's desire for peace. Thus far nobody has developed an effective technique of controlling this kind of internal war once it has started; but the highly developed modern technology of communication enables a totalitarian government to abort, as it were, any internal war before it has seen the light of day, by effectively atomizing society and so preventing any opposition from ever becoming organized;[b] and a political organization is a prerequisite of internal war. Once again, modern technology favors totalitarianism.

FREE, AUTHORITARIAN, AND TOTALITARIAN SYSTEMS

All systems of government can be classified in two groups according to whether or not they permit opposition to the government. In some countries, people are permitted to "assemble peacefully and to petition the government for a redress of their grievances"; criticism of the government, expressed by the spoken or printed word, is permitted, and opposition can organize itself with a view to winning friends

---

[b] There was a newspaper report about two policemen in East Berlin (Vopo) who escaped together by jumping side by side from a building into Western territory. Up to the last moment they watched each other with distrust, suspicious lest the other might be an *agent provocateur*, trying to get him to jump first and then shoot him.

and influencing people. These are what are commonly called *free* countries. In other systems, opposition is illegal and subject to punishment (which may vary greatly in severity). Many people may feel that freedom of opposition is not a sufficient reason to call a country free, and that much higher requirements should be met before a society can so qualify. Accordingly, they do not consider the United States and other Western countries as genuinely free; or, perhaps, it is the other way around, i.e., those who wish to denounce Western freedom as a sham define freedom in such a way that this conclusion must follow.

Some people, for instance, argue that Americans are not really free because they are forced to surrender a substantial part of their incomes to the government, which uses them for purposes of which they do not approve (which may be social security in the case of rightwingers or nuclear arms in the case of leftwingers). Freedom, in this case, is understood as a condition in which men are *not subject to laws of which they disapprove*. Or it is maintained that Americans are not free because they may have to accommodate their employers; a junior executive, for instance, may have no practical alternative but to comply with company requests such as private entertaining along prescribed lines, or submitting to regular physical checkups by the company physician. Or it is pointed out that a man is not really free to express his opinion if by so doing he risks adverse criticism, perhaps unpopularity. Freedom, in these instances, is conceived as *absence of social pressures*. Or it is held that a man is not really free to go to a restaurant of his choice if he does not have the means to meet the bill. Freedom, then, is understood as the *power to have one's wishes fulfilled*.

It is, of course, true that once such criteria are adopted, the United States and other Western countries do not qualify as free. But this truth is not of great interest because there exists no society in which nobody is subjected to laws which he dislikes, nobody is subject to social pressures, and everybody has the power to have all his wishes fulfilled.

Yet, whatever the restrictions under which human beings in society operate, there is a great difference between countries in which opposition to the government is permitted and countries in which it is not; Westerners who have lived, for however short a time, under an authoritarian or a totalitarian regime have no doubt about it. Out of the freedom of opposition comes the upward pressure which is the core of the difference between a free society and a tyranny, as it was once formulated by Thomas Jefferson: in a tyranny the people are afraid of the government, while in a free country the government is afraid of the pople.

Systems in which opposition is not permitted may be subdivided according to whether citizens are required to display active, perhaps enthusiastic, support of their rulers or whether mere silence on political issues is acceptable to the regime. In the latter instance, the politically inarticulate citizen can go about his business unmolested; this is the case in the *authoritarian* state. In the first case, the silent citizen is suspect and may be subject to reprisals; a citizen is safe only if the government is satisfied as to his positive loyalty. This is the case in the *totalitarian* state.

The difference between authoritarian and totalitarian systems is not widely appreciated.[8] The Western public is inclined to lump them both together as "undemocratic." Actually, the difference is enormous with regard to the impact of either system on the daily life of the people, as is shown by the only objective test there is, viz., the migratory pressure. There are practically no refugees from authoritarian countries except for active politicians, naturally a very small group; there is mass flight from totalitarian countries.

We thus have three kinds of systems:

a. Political systems in which the expression of opposition to the government is permitted within wide limits (*free* countries).

b. Systems in which opposition is not permitted, but citizens who obey the laws may remain inarticulate without the government trying to penetrate into the secret of their hearts (*authoritarian* countries).

c. Systems in which silent obedience of the laws is not sufficient to satisfy the government, and in which citizens are required to love their government; in order to be safe, the people must be able to convince the government of the genuineness of their affection (*totalitarian* countries).

The difference between the latter two classes is largely a difference regarding the presumption of loyalty and the burden of proof. In the authoritarian systems, the citizen is presumed to be loyal to the government until proven disloyal by his behavior; the burden of proof rests with the state. In the totalitarian systems, the citizen is presumed to be disloyal until he can prove his loyalty; the burden of proof rests with the citizen.

In recent times we have witnessed two types of totalitarianism, viz., totalitarianism of the Left and totalitarianism of the Right. Their difference lies in their ultimate vision: in the case of Left totalitarianism, it is an egalitarian society; in the case of Right totalitarianism, it is an elitist, hierarchical society. This difference is extreme, but it is so only on the abstract, ideological level; in their actual impact upon the individual, the difference between the two types may be slight and may even be nonexistent. The lot of deportees to Soviet labor camps was—with the exception of the Jews—hardly better than that of inmates of Nazi concentration camps, and the fact that Soviet policies were inspired by the ultimate vision of brotherhood gave no more comfort to its victims than the fact that Christianity was a religion of mercy gave to the victims of the Inquisition.

If we rank the totalitarianisms of twentieth-century Europe according to their inhumanity, the Hitler regime holds unchallengeably the first place; no other regime has transported children wholesale across a continent for the purpose of extermination. But the Soviet regime, a Left totalitarianism, must be given a second place, not altogether outclassed, for the first thirty years of its existence; while it has by and large eschewed the sadistic obscenities of the Nazi regime, the number of its victims may be actually greater than the number of Nazi victims.[e]

The Right totalitarianism of Fascist Italy, Germany's ally in the war, follows at a great distance; its victims can be counted in the thousands, not in the millions.

The difference is further blurred inasmuch as elitist elements become more pronounced or more outspoken within Left totalitarian movements and regimes.

In addition to the relatively clear cases discussed, there are also unclear, or mixed, cases on record such as Peronism in Argentina.

[e] It is unfair, however, to compare thirty years of Communist rule with twelve years of Nazi rule. There is no way of knowing what records the Nazis would have established, had their empire lasted another eighteen years.

9

The Influence of Physical Force upon the Mind or How Might Makes Right

The concept of force must be made central in any attempt to think clearly about human relations....

—Simone Weil[1]

We must now inquire whether physical coercion and psychic authority are independent of each other or whether one can reach into the domain of the other; whether physical force can influence what people think; or whether psychic appeal can stay the hand of force.

THE EDUCATION OF THE YOUNG

Those who wield physical power, first of all, are virtually unlimited in their ability to influence the minds of people if they use this power to get control of the education of the young; if complete control is achieved and exercised, the minds of the wards can be inculcated with practically any desired norms because it is in childhood that standards of conduct and loyalties are acquired, through internalization of adult commands and prohibitions. The best troops of the Turks were the Janizaries, kidnaped Christian children who were reared by their captors and imbued by them with a fanatical loyalty to the Padishah. They proved fully reliable soldiers during two centuries of wars with the Christians.

The situation is more complex, however, when those who hold power assume only partial, not full, control of the education of the young. In partitioned Poland, e.g., educators in the schools preached patriotism for the new fatherland—Russia, Prussia, or Austria—but the children were allowed to grow up in their families where they were imbued with a spirit of Polish rather than Russian, Prussian, or Austrian patriotism; in these circumstances, the influence of the school proved insignificant as compared with that of the home.

The situation is less clear today in countries like Eastern Germany and Hungary. On the one hand, children are brought up in families where the parents, for the most part, have allegiances at variance with those demanded by the new Communist rulers; on the other hand, the efforts at indoctrinating the young, while not extending into the home itself, are far more extensive than they were in Czarist Poland. The state is active in the education of the young far above and beyond patriotic indoctrination during school hours. Moreover, an atmosphere of intimidation engulfs the parents and if it does not make them into propagandists of the regime, it at least deters many of them from actively indoctrinating their children with ideas opposed to those of the regime. Such restraints are further strengthened by the encouragement given to the children to emancipate themselves from control by "reactionary" parents and, sometimes, to keep an eye on their parents' loyalty. Finally, while loyalty to the Czar of Russia was clearly incompatible with Polish patriotism, loyalty to Communism as a universal philosophy is not necessarily incompatible with Polish patriotism; even support for specifically Russian interests can, to some extent, be justified in universalist terms ("the fatherland of socialism"). For all these reasons, the present ruling power has a better chance of establishing itself in the hearts of the young in countries such as Poland, Eastern Germany, or Hungary than had Russian patriotism with Polish youth in Czarist times, even though the children continue to receive their basic moral education in the home. What the results will be it is too early to judge. Old loyalties have probably not been entirely rooted out, at least for the time being; for how long this will be so is an open question.

It is noteworthy that the two actual rebellions against Soviet-supported Communist regimes in Eastern Europe took place in Eastern Germany and in Hungary, i.e., in two countries which had fought in the war on the other side of the fence, and to which Soviet armies had come as conquering enemies; while something close to a rebellion took place in Poland, which had been only partially an enemy during the war—Germany was Poland's main enemy, Russia her secondary enemy—and to which the Soviet army had come in a role of both liberator and oppressor. It thus appears that old loyalties were operating against Communist indoctrination in these countries—more so in Eastern Germany and Hungary than in Poland. There was no sign of rebellion in Czechoslovakia, where people had sided unambiguously with the Soviet Union during the war and where the Soviet armies had been greeted as liberators plain and simple.

My remarks so far have been concerned with the education of the young. But what about the adults? Can those who wield physical power change the already established moral standards of adults and alter their fundamental loyalties?

THE LEVERAGE OF LOYALTY

One way in which Might can generate its own Right is based on the fact that many people are inclined to think that their rulers know best, and that it is the duty of the citizen to obey them. This is essentially the attitude of children to their parents before the beginning of adolescent rebellion. It is an unsophisticated attitude, assumed without reflection: "Nothing is more customary in man than to recognize superior wisdom in the person of his oppressor," as de Tocqueville remarked.[2]

Sometimes, however, this attitude is assumed as the result

of reflection as, e.g., in the Christian doctrine that governments are instituted by God and men owe them obedience.

However, obedience on these grounds, whether naïve or reflective, is not without limits; governments must not overtax the loyalty of their subjects. In the case of naïve obedience, this means that while governments can to some extent remodel the consciences of the people, they cannot radically uproot the moral principles that have been inculcated in childhood. It is somewhat like the situation in hypnosis: the hypnotist becomes a kind of parasitic superego for the hypnotized person and so can influence him considerably. But if he makes demands that all too sharply contradict the rules of conduct which the hypnotized person has made his own—e.g., orders a lady to undress in the presence of men— he will probably not be obeyed and his subject will wake up from the hypnosis.[3]

Similar limits can also be found in the reflective, sophisticated version of the attitude that invests the government with moral authority. The same Christian doctrine that made it the citizen's duty to obey duly instituted government also made resistance to tyrannical government, i.e., to government that makes demands in contradiction to the law of God, permissible and at times obligatory.

The psychic operations at stake can easily be expressed in psychoanalytic terms. The superego—the internal law—is, on the whole, the result of an internalization of parental commands and prohibitions. Sometimes the internalization is complete; the moral law becomes a categorical imperative, independent of the attitude of outside authorities or of the opinion of one's peers; that is the position which Luther expressed in the famous words: "Here I stand—I cannot do otherwise. God help me." On the other hand, there are many people in whom the superego does not become completely separated from outside authorities but continues to communicate with them. It remains plastic enough to receive new imprints from new objects; internalization still can, to some degree, be undone if a new parental figure appears—perhaps an inspiring leader—in the outside world. The superego is then re-liquified, as it were, the inner law reverts to dependence on an outside authority, and a fresh internalization of the new object will take place.

Not all people, of course, have the same attitude of either naïve or reflective submission to their government; nor do people have the same attitude all the time, in all situations. In modern Germany, e.g., the authority of government *qua* government has been very great; in modern France, very low.

COERCIVE PERSUASION

While the leverage of loyalty as discussed above represents a gentle way of influencing the minds of people, there is also a more coercive, hard approach. Edgar H. Schein has called it coercive persuasion;[4] it is commonly known as brainwashing. On the surface, it may seem impossible to coerce the mind: one can coerce the behavior of people, what they do and what they say; under torture, they can be made to confess to sins they have never committed and to implicate others. But that does not reach their minds. The woman who confessed under the agony of torture that she had been a witch, had cohabited with the devil, and had brought sickness to her neighbors' children and to their cattle, knew that what she said was untrue. One's mind is not in the public domain, like one's speech and actions; it is one's very own possession; and whatever one may be forced to say or do, by penalty of intolerable suffering, one can still think one's own thoughts and keep one's mental reservations.

This conclusion seems to follow *logically* from the fact of the privacy of thought; and it is true, to a degree. But *psychologically* it may be difficult, very difficult, for men to maintain this mental reservation; and it is in this sense that we can also speak of the mind being coerced.

The mind cannot be coerced, of course, if the new leaders approach their subjects in a genteel fashion and tell them in effect: "We do not ask you what you think of us; that is your business and, in any case, we respect your feelings. We request only that you obey the laws and refrain from public criticism of the government." This is essentially the approach of the authoritarian, as distinguished from the totalitarian, system; it respects the autonomy of the individual conscience, and under such conditions this autonomy flourishes.

Things are different, however, if the new rulers approach the people with the attitude that everybody who is not for them is against them, that being against them is being evil, and that it is up to every citizen himself to prove his loyalty and to convince the government of the sincerity of his allegiance.

If this is the approach of the regime to its subjects, and if it is amply buttressed by the threat of force, conversions come about in this way: coercion makes the subject do or say things for which he will feel either ashamed (because they are deeply humiliating) or guilty (because they are immoral). In this way, an inner conflict is produced in the subject, a conflict between the forces of self-preservation which counsel compliance with the rulers' requests, and the feelings of shame or guilt. Inner peace is lost. It can be regained, however, if the subject can convince himself that the rulers' request was actually right; for if that were the case, there would be no reason for shame or guilt.[5]

The essence of this view of the nature of "brainwashing" was probably first expressed by a social scientist, Albert D. Biderman, in an Air Force report in 1954 reproduced by the Senate Permanent Investigations Subcommittee:

> Communist terror confronts the individual with a choice between external punishment if he does and thinks what he regards as right, and internal punishment [guilt] if he begins to do or think as the Communists demand. One way out, of course, is for him to change his conscious idea of what is right and wrong to accord with that of the Communists. The heavy emphasis in Communist coercive interrogation upon "moral" arguments attempts to provide the victim with a new "moral" justification for his behavior.[6]

The process of "coercive persuasion" is going on wherever rulers hold out their ideas to the vanquished with the request, backed up by the threat of physical force, to accept them and to make them their own—whether or not special programs for re-education or reindoctrination have been devised. The thought reform of German civil servants under the Nazi regime, without any special institutions for reindoctrination such as were later instituted by the Chinese Communists, has been described in simple terms by the noted German economist, Wilhelm Röpke, who fled Germany in the first days of the Nazi regime and who, after a brief period in Turkey, lived for the rest of his life in Switzerland:

> They told themselves and others that if they remained at their post they could "prevent worse things," that they must not let themselves be "frozen out," that "hanging on" demanded greater sacrifices than resigning, that "one must not leave the Fatherland in the lurch at this difficult time," and made all sorts of similar excuses. . . . But anyone who had once given his little finger very soon felt himself compelled to be silent where his conscience would have told him to speak, to do nothing where as an honest person he should have acted, to descend to lying and hypocrisy or to do something that made him an accomplice. Then there remained only three alternatives: it was still possible to make the decision to break with the regime; or every fresh day would inevitably bring fresh cause of self-contempt; or the effort must be made to persuade oneself that in one's judgment of National Socialism one must, after all, have been a little mistaken. For the first alternative many people had no longer the courage, and the second would have been against human nature. Thus there remained only the third course; men began to talk of "the good sides of the regime that do after all exist," of the possibility of gradual normalization, or of the supposed necessity of helping the "decent" Nazis against the worse ones.[7]

One can often see this psychological process going on before one's eyes. Ervin Sinko, the Hungarian Communist who as a youth of twenty was Commandant of Kecskemet during the brief Communist regime of Bela Kun in 1919 and who after many trials and tribulations has finally found home, work, and recognition in Yugoslavia, tells the story of his stay in Moscow, 1935-1937, where he tried to get a novel on the Hungarian revolution published. For part of his stay, he shared an apartment with the writer Isaac Babel. One day, so Sinko recounts, he came home and saw in Babel's room the famous film director Eisenstein in a somewhat disheveled condition. Sinko wanted tactfully to retreat, but Babel encouraged him to come in, as though he welcomed an opportunity to terminate the situation. Eisenstein actually left shortly thereafter and Babel told his roommate what had happened.

Eisenstein had just finished, after two and one half years of work, his great film about the collectivization of Soviet agriculture. The film had been privately shown to the Party leaders, who had turned it down. The film pictured the pre-revolutionary conditions in Russia in the darkest colors, as had been customary, but the Party line with regard to Russia's past was just about to change. The Party anticipated war and wanted to harness the great moral reservoir of patriotism to its cause rather than alienate it any further. The leaders decided not only that the film was not to be shown but also that all copies should be destroyed.

Eisenstein, desperate at the threatened destruction of a sizable part of his life's creative work, had come to plead with Babel to let him hide one copy and thus save it for the future. He had thereby put Babel in a most embarrassing position; Babel felt that he should help, but he could not: "If somebody stands before us," said Babel to Sinko, "whom one should help but whom it is not possible to help . . . a man whom I cannot help, whom I simply cannot help, whom I can no more help than I can help myself. . . ." Babel's frustration gave way to resentment of Eisenstein's request: "Why does he torment me, why does he humiliate me by making me the impotent witness of the injustice which he has suffered?" But only a few moments later there is a new twist in Babel's feelings; he said, according to Sinko: "Eisenstein is a genius, but particularly with men of genius the danger of grave errors is very great. I have often mused about Eisenstein taking the wrong direction and neglecting important points of view which might have been considered, which indeed should have been considered."[8]

Only a few moments earlier Eisenstein had been the victim of injustice; but it now appeared that he had brought his misfortune upon himself, by his own errors or sins.

It all begins with a conflict in Babel's mind between a sense of obligation and the demands of self-preservation. Once the latter have prevailed, there comes shame and soon resentment at the supplicant for having put him into this position. One further step, and Eisenstein is guilty of negligence, hence the author of his own misfortune, and Babel is relieved of some of his shame. The aggression that first worked against Babel himself as a kind of self-hatred is then again turned toward the outside world, not against the Communist leaders who had done to Eisenstein what no "bourgeois democracy" would have contemplated doing to an artist, but whom it was dangerous to hate; rather it is directed against Eisenstein. The personal predicament is eased, one can find inner peace again.

This appears to be, in a nutshell, the psychological mechanism that makes for the remolding of thought through terror. There are no mysteries of hypnotism, no tricks of Pavlovian conditioning, no weird consequences of isolation from outside stimuli, no physical and mental exhaustion through the unceasing struggle of cell mates to make the prisoner reform; all these and many other means of physical or mental torture may be applied, but they are not indispensable requirements in coercive persuasion. What is indispensable is the *uncompromising demand for genuine allegiance and the stark realities of power.*[a]

[a] Today many persons insist on experimental evidence as the prerequisite of their accepting any interpretation of events as valid; without it, they will at best consider it a hypothesis.

There is no chance that a proposition such as the one presented above could ever be tested by experiment because it is practically impossible and would

It thus appears that when men, under conditions of terror, are confronted with the request not only for obedience to the regime but also for a convincing display of affection for it, *the inner acceptance of its norm becomes a matter of adjustment.*

There is, however, one further condition which has to be fulfilled if the conversion is to occur, viz., the circumstances must be such that the conversion is *credible.* At the time of Cortez' first expedition the Aztecs sacrificed some Spanish captives at the altar of their god Huitzilopochtli. If they had not done so but had instead set themselves the task of converting them through "coercive persuasion," i.e., through the combination of propaganda and threat, to their Mexican religion, they might have succeeded in having Spaniards go through the motions of the Aztec worship, but they would hardly have succeeded in making any Spaniard believe, for instance, that for the sun to rise every day and give men light and warmth, Huitzilopochtli had to be fed human blood.

The Spaniards felt vastly superior to the Aztecs and in some crucial ways they were; above all, they were a great distance removed from cannibalism, and the abandonment of cannibalism is so important a step in the development of a civilization that the civilized man, who is revolted at the thought of consuming human flesh, *cannot but look down* at those who have not made this step. Moreover, the Christian beliefs, though by no means free from magic, did not contain

---

be morally impermissible to reproduce in the laboratory the terror of the individual who is naked in the face of ruthless power. For the sake of an experiment people have been put under all sorts of stresses, but these stress situations were different in kind, not merely in degree, from the terror that grips an individual who finds himself in the merciless hands of fanatical men, utterly self-righteous and therefore impervious to pity; an individual who is subject to a steady diet of humiliating and demoralizing treatment and uncertain of what the next moment will bring, who may never see his family and his home again, and who feels utterly forsaken by his own people who seem either to have forgotten him or to lack the power to help him. Above all, the stresses of an experimental situation are of an artificial kind and can always be terminated if the subject so desires.

magical concepts as crude as those that related blood sacrifices to the light of the sun. If a Spaniard had joined in the
behavior of Aztec worshipers, it would have been clear to
others and, above all, to himself that he did so to save his
skin, and nobody, including himself, could have believed
that he did so from genuine conversion.

In order to believe in the moral claims of the victor, one
must either believe that he is, in some ways at least, a better
man, a man who for some reason has the right to command,
or there must be something in his idea that appeals to one's
own conscience. It must be added, on the other hand, that
belief in the victor's right to command comes fairly easily on
account of the fact of victory itself. "Nothing is more customary in man than to recognize superior wisdom in the person
of his oppressor," in de Tocqueville's previously quoted
words. If one is to resist this reaction, there has to be a strong
conviction of the victor's inferiority, which must be manifested again and again in daily contact.

Thus, the ruler's demand that he not only be obeyed but
also loved or at least accepted as legitimate is successful only
if he appears to be superior, naturally endowed with the
ability to command, or represents an idea which one recog-
nizes as valid. The *former* condition was sometimes realized,
for instance, in the case of the ancient Romans and, in our
days, in the case of the Nazis in their dealings with *conquered*
peoples; the *latter* was most widely realized in the case of
the Nazis in their dealings with the *German* people themselves (and in the case of any nationalist movement in its dealings with its own people).

The ancient Romans approached other people with the
naïve claim that the world was rightfully theirs, that therefore everybody owed them allegiance, and that those who
opposed Roman rule were by definition traitors. Although
by their efficiency and monstrous cruelty they succeeded in
making the world tremble before them—never mind if they
hate us as long as they fear us, as Accius put it—the Romans

for a long time did not succeed in getting their subjects to accept their rule as the right order of things. Similarly, Hitler did not get very far in winning non-German people over to his message of the German master race.

CONCLUSION

It thus appears that there are essentially three ways in which Might determines what will be considered Right. Might becomes Right
—through education of children in which the requirements of the educator become embodied in the child's superego;
—in more unsophisticated people, through the transfer of a child-parent attitude to their relation to the rulers, and thus the inclination to consider actual authority as rightful authority;
—through coercive persuasion (commonly called "brainwashing"), i.e., the construction of situations in which a person is by terror forced to act against his own conscience and his pride so that the ensuing feelings of guilt and shame will be a constant irritant, and the desire for inner peace will persistently work in favor of a revision of the superego.

10

Polemic Supplement: Underestimation of the Role of Violence

For, he reasons pointedly,
That which must not, cannot, be.

—CHRISTIAN MORGENSTERN[1]

There has been in the Western countries, and particularly in the United States, a widespread tendency to disregard the role of violence in the affairs of man and to make plans on the national or on the international scene without considering the possibility of violence and the natural apprehension of its prospective victims. This attitude apparently takes three forms:

1. *Naïve* disregard, i.e., the failure to recognize the role of violence in stable, quiet times, in which there is little or no manifest violence and in which the hidden influence of potential violence can be surmised only through reasoning; and reasoning is never as convincing as direct observation.

2. The belief that violence is of little or no relevance in human affairs, for one of the following reasons:

(a) because violence is *immoral* and will therefore not be practiced; or

(b) because it is inherently ineffective, at least in the long run, and its application therefore *inexpedient*; or

(c) because violence, though effective throughout most of human history until quite recently, has now become ineffective and self-defeating through the invention of weapons of indiscriminate mass destruction, i.e., because violence has become *obsolete*.

3. It is claimed in some quarters that violence, though effective as such, *can always be overcome by spiritual* or mental *power*.

NAÏVE DISREGARD

If one walks through a peaceful countryside in which civil order has not been challenged for a long time, he may take this condition for granted, either as innate in human nature or as following easily from tradition and enlightened self-interest, and may overlook, or underestimate, the share which the deterrent power of the state as a potential wielder of overwhelming physical power had, and continues to have, in the establishment and maintenance of the peace. It is easy to attribute the peace to general consent alone and to overlook the hidden potential of violence which looms in the background as *ultima ratio* of the regime. The same applies to an international order.

Throughout the century between the Congress of Vienna and the First World War, Europe enjoyed a time of relative peace. Wars were few in number, of short duration, and limited in aim and geographical scope. They were fought for delimited adjustments of the map rather than for the obliteration or total subjugation of other countries; and they were fought largely within rules of combat comparable to those of a gentlemen's duel.

The diminution and partial domestication of violence between nations were often seen as manifestations of a more enlightened age, as a step in the moral progress of mankind. They can also been seen, however, as the consequence of a "balance of power," the analogy, on the international scene, of the system of checks and balances set up by the Founding Fathers of the American Republic. The European balance of power was not self-regulating but needed continuous adjustment by an outside balancer, a role that was played for some time by Great Britain which had no interest in the various issues of Continental politics though it was greatly interested in the maintenance of the equilibrium. It was the *Pax Britannica,* kept, in the last analysis, by the British fleet; but since the fleet did not fire its broadsides—its prestige was great enough so that nations did not desire to test its military power—its vital role in the European system was not obvious. As happens so often, the very completeness of the success obscured the fact that success it was.

When in the 1930's the power of Hitler Germany began to challenge the post-Versailles European order and the British people uneasily felt the forebodings of a "gathering storm" in which they might be called upon to fight the War of 1914-18 all over again, Englishmen looked for possibilities of escape from such a calamity, and some of them began to play with the idea of withdrawal into neutrality. Why could not Britain be like Sweden, it was asked, cultivating her own garden, and let the storms of history pass by? Sweden had prospered in this way, why could not Britain?

To others, however, it seemed clear that the peaceful condition of Sweden was due not simply to the Swedes' decision to mind their own business but to the *Pax Britannica* which alone made this neutrality possible, i.e., in the last resort, to the power of the British fleet. Sweden was shielded by a system which Britain was forced to defend in her own interest and to which Sweden therefore did not need to contribute.

It has sometimes been suggested that the domestic independence which Finland has been allowed by the Soviet Union is a proof of the Soviet's fundamentally defensive goals; for would a Russia bent on world domination have failed to subjugate Finland? Others are inclined to think that Finland's precarious freedom is but the *quid pro quo* for

Sweden's neutrality. If the Soviet Union were to incorporate Finland or to make a satellite out of her, Sweden would probably seek a Western alliance; to forestall this possibility is for the Soviet Union well worth her tolerance of domestic Finnish independence. Conversely, according to this interpretation, if Sweden were to enter a Western alliance, Finland would find herself subject to greatly increased Soviet pressure.

The fact that there was no popular uprising in Cuba at the time of the Bay of Pigs invasion is frequently cited as evidence of popular support of the Castro regime. So it *may* have been; but it may also have been that many people, though disaffected with the regime, feared to show their hand before they knew how things were going. The regime would have had little mercy for those who had revealed themselves as its enemies.

Similarly, the inability of the armed forces of a government to suppress a guerrilla revolt of a few thousand people is often quoted as evidence of popular support for the guerrillas. It does, of course, prove that the population has been giving aid to the guerrillas—at the very least did not inform the authorities about them. Such collaboration *may* be due to popular sympathy with the guerrillas; but it may also be due to fear of the swift and ruthless retaliation that will strike those whom the guerrillas consider traitors. Death and mutilation are persuasive arguments.

Guerrillas are a kind of subterranean government; and, like any government, it rests on a combination of loyalty and fear, needing more of the latter the less it has of the former. A guerrilla force of a few thousand men may move easily among a sympathetic civilian population, like a "fish in the water," in Mao's famous phrase. But *if* it has the unwavering loyalty of its own men, it may well rule the countryside by *terror alone.*

We may remember that the pre-Fascist governments of Italy failed for generations in their efforts to suppress the

Sicilian Mafia because the population did not cooperate with the authorities; the hold of the Mafia over the people rested on their fear of reprisals. Only the Fascist government succeeded largely, though not completely, in suppressing the Mafia because, being a very strong government, it either gave the people confidence that it could protect them against the revenge of the Mafia or it intimidated them more than the Mafia had done. After the fall of Fascism, the Mafia was revived and it is now said to be as powerful as ever: witnesses of the numerous murders have seen nothing and remember nothing.

In the history of American cities, we find repeatedly that quite small extortionist groups have terrorized a trade for a long time, without being hunted down by the police with all its resources.

Failure to understand an implicit threat of force is a failure to identify oneself with those under duress; and the latter may be due to lack of experience, i.e., to *genuine naïveté,* or to an unwillingness to put oneself in the place of some people, i.e., *to bias.* In the latter case one sees clearly enough the threat of violence implicit in a situation and denounces it sharply whenever one is in sympathy with the victims, but one fails to see it when the victims are on the other side. Many of those who do not see the duress under which the civilian population lives in a ruthless guerrilla war are probably biased rather than really naïve. There are none as blind as those who would not see.

Those who fail to understand the all-pervasive influence of latent force, or "Force in Being," behind a peaceful surface frequently look upon negotiations as an alternative to force. Negotiations, however, are also a form of force rather than an alternative to it; to be sure, they are not coercion carried out but coercion threatened. In one case, there is actual shooting; in the other, the contestants show their guns and battlements to each other, as it were, and settle along the terms that are likely to emerge from an actual contest of

strength. When union and management negotiate a contract,[a] the possibility of a strike (or, in times of economic con-
traction, of a shut down) is never far from the minds of
the negotiators. They arrive at a settlement if they
can find terms which each side prefers to the recourse to
force; the terms reflect the relative strength of the contenders.
It is usually possible to find such terms if both sides have the
same estimate of their relative strengths and thus of the probable outcome of a strike; but *if their estimates do not coincide*, if one side hopes to gain more from a break than the
other fears to lose,[b] there is no settlement.

This was the case in the outbreak of major wars. "Negotiation" could not prevent a war when both sides disagreed in
their strategic estimates and one side believed that it could
insist with impunity on what the other believed itself capable of withholding with impunity. In 1914, Austria-Hungary believed that she could make war on Serbia with impunity because she was backed up by Germany, which was
considered invincible. Russia believed that, with French help,
she had a good chance of staying the hand of the Central
Powers. Hitler believed in 1938 that he could decisively defeat his European enemies one by one and that American
help would never come; England believed that, in the long
run, she would once again prevail.

These conditions coincide with observations made on subhuman behavior. S. L. Washburn and I. De Vore reported
that fighting among baboons breaks out *when the order of*

---

[a] The example is actually not quite apt because the conflict between management and union is far less fundamental and therefore easier to mediate and
to settle than the more serious political and ideological issues of the day.
Management and labor, under present conditions, do not intend to extermi-
nate each other. Labor unions do not wish to drive business into bankruptcy,
and business does not wish workers to starve or to emigrate in desperation.
Thus, there is a basic recognition of each other's right to exist, and thus a
common ground on which to negotiate. This is not the case in the present
great international issues, in which irreconcilable moral concepts clash.

[b] This does not necessarily mean better terms. Sometimes one side prefers to
fight, not because it has much hope for better terms, but for such reasons as
saving face or making one's own camp more amenable to compromise.

dominance is doubtful; where the social order is clear, everybody abides by it without fighting.[2]

Those who believe that negotiations are an alternative to force, i.e., that one side can be naked in terms of force and still protect its vital interest effectively by "negotiation," assume that all participants are motivated by a philosophy of live-and-let-live and nobody will press his advantage against a defenseless adversary. This is a utopian assumption. But their error goes even beyond this illusion. Even if all people purged themselves of individual and collective self-concern and were as much interested in the welfare of others as they are in their own, disagreement would still be possible; both sides, equally "idealistic," might nevertheless disagree on what is best for the good of all concerned. Conflicts over moral issues are not any less serious than conflicts over frank personal advantages; moral conflicts usually are even less tractable than the latter because both sides can go to any length with a perfectly good conscience. Negotiations would be a genuine alternative to, rather than merely a form of, settlement by force if both sides were not only equally unselfish but also had identical views of how best to serve their self-negating goals.

A more sophisticated version of the disregard of violence is the doctrine according to which defenselessness as such will disarm a potential aggressor. Thus, Bertrand Russell, pleading in the Hitler era for British disarmament, pointed at little Denmark as a living example of the safety which impotence can bestow: "When disarmament is suggested, it is natural to imagine foreign conquests would inevitably follow.... This is a mistake as the case of Denmark shows.... [The Danes] are defended by their very defenselessness."[3]

To other people, including the present writer, the defense of Denmark did not lie in her nakedness but in what still remained of the *Pax Britannica,* i.e., the danger that an attack upon Denmark, or her subjugation by armed threats, would involve the aggressor in war with Great Britain. It is in line with this interpretation that four years after Russell's words had been written, Germany, already at war with Great Britain, did invade Denmark when this seemed strategically advantageous to her leaders; the threat of a war with England could not deter her at a time when such a war was already a reality. Defenselessness, in any case, did not protect Denmark in that hour.

IMPOSSIBLE BECAUSE IMMORAL

Force is often considered evil, regardless of circumstances. It is thus taken for granted that what should not be will not be. In fact, some people consider the mere belief in the possibility of evil a sign of a cynical or morbid or evil mind. On the other hand, a person who believes others to be guided only by noble motives is called an idealist, in an odd confusion between the *devotion* to a moral ideal and the *delusion* that this ideal has been universally realized. Such expectations overlook not only the existence of patent Evil but also the fact of sharply divergent views on what constitutes the Good. What some call idealism must appear to others as rank irresponsibility.

FORCE AS INEXPEDIENT

In the period between the two World Wars, for instance, it was often claimed, particularly in the United States, and by no means only by outright pacifists, that "war settles nothing"; from this the conclusion was drawn that there was no point in arming oneself or in taking a stand, buttressed by force, on international issues.

The view that "war settles nothing" probably owed some of its popularity to the general disillusionment about the results of the American intervention in the First World War. The war had been fought "to make the world safe for democracy," to end forever "the game of power politics," and to put an end to all wars. When it became clear that these objectives had not been realized, and that the problems posed by the rival nationalisms of Europe continued to plague it and the world, it was obvious that the intervention had not attained all its goals.

Yet, this was an emotional reaction rather than a conclusion reached by calm reflection. If the victory of 1918 had not brought the desired results, it did not necessarily follow that force could settle nothing. Perhaps, the goals had been set too high, in the realm of Utopia; perhaps, also, the American people had expected that all the wished-for changes would come about as the result of one great but brief exertion, whereas more might have been achieved had they been willing to make a sustained, protracted effort.

A glance at the history of America might actually have suggested that force had indeed settled a number of things for a long time and that these are still with us. Force decided that the country became a European settlement and did not remain the hunting ground and the grazing land of Indian tribes; that its culture became fundamentally English rather than French or Spanish; that it became independent of Great Britain and opened its gates, for some generations, to unlimited European immigration; that it remained one nation, with slavery outlawed, rather than being divided into two nations; and a few more things besides.

Like many erroneous ideas, the idea that force cannot settle conflicts has a nucleus of truth. If by settlement we mean a condition that does not for its maintenance require the continued support of force—at least, of Force in Being—but that has an "intrinsic survival value" (Alfred North Whitehead), then peace achieved by agreement among equals[c] is perhaps more likely to produce such a state of affairs than peace imposed by the victors upon the vanquished. However, such an agreement voluntarily entered into is not

[c] The settlement of 1815 was, to some extent, an example of this type of agreement.

always possible; the conflicting parties cannot always find a common denominator sufficiently broad to overcome their particularistic interests and passions.

Moreover, although the mild application of force as practiced, e.g., in the peace of Versailles, was ineffective, there is reason to assume that under certain circumstances a more determined application of force could bring about a state of affairs which might, after some time, have intrinsic survival value. If the victor destroys all possible nuclei of resistance around which opposition might crystallize and if he takes the children and the young, isolates them from discordant influences, and indoctrinates them to "the gills," his order of things may well, after a generation or two, survive by its own devices and require no further outside intervention to uphold it.

Perhaps, the kernel of truth in the assertion that force does not settle issues might be formulated in the following way: *force which is inadequate for the task at hand* or force which provokes the opponent without annihilating him, in Adolf Hitler's phrase, *is inexpedient.*[4]

The idea that force is ineffective is so obviously contradicted by everyday experience that it has often been modified to the more modest claim that its triumphs are ephemeral. In this form, the argument is unassailable, if only in the sense that *all* things human are finite and transient. There is no reason to assume that the handiwork of force is necessarily more ephemeral than other products, at least within the short time span that we, at this stage of the human story, can oversee.

In many cases those who have taken up the sword have perished by the sword, like Napoleon or Hitler; but others have died in their beds at the height of their power, like Genghis Khan or Stalin; and still others have built edifices that lasted for centuries, like Caesar, Augustus, or Tamerlane. In which category a case belongs seems to depend more on the conqueror's resources, prudence, and luck than on his moral restraint.

Moreover, knowledge of the transience of the fruits of force is poor consolation to the victims of violence. It is like the solace of the ancient Stoics and Epicureans, the *Consolations of Philosophy* which the doomed Boëthius wrote in prison. It may be the counsel of wisdom but of a wisdom too high and too detached for most mortal men, particularly in a time of otherwise extreme alloplastic orientation.

After the younger Scipio had given orders that Carthage be razed to the ground and its people be sold into slavery, he watched the flames consuming the once proud and prosperous city and was overtaken by emotion at the thought that there might once be a day of doom for Rome, too; he is said to have shed tears and declaimed the Homeric lines about the future fall of Troy:

> Once will come the day when the sacred Ilios will perish
> And Priam and the people of the king with the ashen spear....

But his sentiments changed nothing in the plight of the Carthaginians.

FORCE AS OBSOLETE

Finally, there is the most recent version of the argument according to which force has become obsolete through the advent of the nuclear age—as obsolete, it is said, as the tools and weapons of the horse-and-buggy age.

There is a great deal of truth in this argument. The resort to nuclear war as an instrument of national policy is clearly irrational, as the costs, in terms of death and destruction, outweigh all possible gains by many orders of magnitudes. And it is equally irrational for any nation or group of nations to corner a great nuclear power and drive her into a situation in which resort to nuclear arms may be the only desperate alternative to national humiliation and recognition of defeat.

But this does not mean that all force has obsolesced. There

is still a vast range of force that neither is nuclear nor involves much danger of escalating into nuclear war, and there is little reason to believe that these forms of violence have become obsolete. They include domestic revolution, civil war, and guerrilla war—perhaps morally encouraged and sometimes also materially supplied from beyond the border—and conventional wars between nations which have no nuclear arms; they also include competition for strategically important bases in countries in close proximity to the adversary.

It is not force as such that has become obsolete but rather *certain extreme forms* of force in which the risks and costs are no longer commensurate with the potential gains. This is not a totally novel situation, although the destructiveness of nuclear arms has increased the irrationality of unlimited violence and dramatized it as never before. There have always been limits to the *rational* application of force, as there are rational limits to any pursuit, because rationality consists in the weighing of means against ends. Measures that were apt to provoke an antagonist without being able to incapacitate him have always been irrational. It was only the doctrine of total war, discarded after the disasters of the Wars of Religion and revived in more modern times, not by military professionals but by politicians, which blinded people to the limits of a rational application of force.

THE ALLEGED SUPERIORITY OF SPIRITUAL WEAPONS

There are those who point out that the capacity to inflict great harm upon an aggressor cannot be relied on to dissuade all kinds of aggressors, and some people have suggested that other policies might be more effective. In the last analysis, they appear to have faith in the capacity of spiritual power to hold its own, and in the end to prevail, against the power of the sword.

The nature of the power of ideas and its relation to physical power will be discussed in a different context (Chapter

11); for the moment, it may be sufficient to say that the extravagant claims in favor of the former are not borne out by the historical record.

There is, of course, a wide area of life in which strong persons feel love and affection for weaker ones as, for instance, parents do for their children. They are then open to appeal from the latter. And this is true also in a number of other conditions, for example, when there are bonds of common interest between the stronger and the weaker ones which outweigh the differences, or when the strong adhere to a liberal philosophy. But whenever the strong have no love for those in their power and embark upon enterprises at variance with the interests of the latter, the achievement record of appeal and persuasion is exceedingly poor.

Many examples come easily to mind: the fate of the Carthaginians at the hands of the Romans; of Roman Britain at the hands of the Saxon invaders; of the Cathari, inoffensive heretics, at the hands of the Roman Church; of slaves throughout the ages; or, in our times, the fate of the bourgeoisie, the Kulaks and the non-Communist leftists at the hands of the Bolshevists and eventually that of real or suspected dissidents within the Party at the hands of Stalin; the extreme fate of the Armenians at the hands of the Turks and of the Jews at the hands of Hitler. The words *vae victis* are writ large over the firmament of history.

In these and in countless other cases the words apply which Thucydides attributes to the Athenians in the Melian dialogue: "You know as well as we do that right, as the world goes, is only in question between equals in power, while the strong do what they can and the weak suffer what they must."[5]

In our time, faith in the superiority of spiritual over physical power is usually expressed in trust in the efficacy of *Satyagraha,* the methods of nonviolent resistance. Thus, a well-known psychiatrist, Dr. Jerome Frank, suggested that the United States should lay down its arms, and pondered the question "whether a disarmed America could maintain and defend its way of life." He focused on what in his opinion is the sharpest form that the enemy threat could take, viz., the "nightmare of hordes of Chinese, for example, swarming over our defenseless borders and proceeding to enslave us." He suggests, first of all, that "our defense against such a calamity would start before they left China, in the form of a massive propaganda barrage describing our preparations to resist them and the advantages for them of remaining home." If, however, this "propaganda barrage" should not be successful and the Chinese should land, nevertheless, Professor Frank would have recourse to nonviolent resistance:

> Modern weapons and methods of transportation and mass communication have undoubtedly greatly increased the ability of small groups to subdue and control hostile populations, but they do not protect the occupiers against psychological pressures. Occupying forces have certain psychological vulnerabilities that, recent experiences suggest, can be effectively exploited by a subject people. The chief weapon would probably be non-violent resistance . . . non-violent movements led by Gandhi in India and Martin Luther King in the United States suggest that they may have achieved a breakthrough in the conduct of human affairs that holds great hope for the future."[6]

The success of Gandhi's nonviolent independence movement has apparently inspired many advocates of nonviolence. Gandhi's successes were won against Great Britain, a nation in which the greater part of articulate opinion had ceased to believe in her right to rule over foreign peoples and therefore no longer countenanced the use of such force as would have been necessary to subdue a large population; a nation in which even the imperialist minority was not sufficiently self-righteous to go to great lengths in the defense of Empire; a nation, moreover, that was no longer strong enough to disregard the intensely anticolonial trend of world opinion. The success of nonviolent resistance against Englishmen in the mid-twentieth century permits no conclusion about its feasibility against rulers deeply convinced of their right to rule and therefore unencumbered by inhibitions, and in possession of the physical means of coercion—against, say, the China of Mao or, indeed, even against the England of Robert Clive and Warren Hastings.

Whether the movement commonly associated with the name of the Reverend Martin Luther King is a perfect example of nonviolence is an open question. If people appear in numbers in offices or stores, settle down and refuse to leave, it is not merely a case of spiritual appeal. Rather, it should be described as a case of low-grade violence, with the attempt to shift responsibility for escalation to the other side.

In any case, however, the experience of this movement does not warrant the conclusions which Professor Frank draws from it. For one thing, it is not thinkable that a disaffected minority could in a Communist dictatorship—e.g., in Cuba or in the German Democratic Republic—hold protest marches and meetings, and sit-ins in public or private places, all openly organized by a general planning staff with nothing more to fear than, at most, a few hours in prison. Furthermore, the Negro movement in question has not greatly diverted the Southern authorities from their traditional course; what successes it has achieved have been due to the intervention, on its behalf, of the federal administration and the federal judiciary; and the federal government is largely representative of articulate Northern opinion, which sympathizes with Negro demands (at least as long as they do not directly infringe upon one's personal interests), is in some degree dependent on the Negro vote, and is very responsive to Asian and African opinion. What the successes of Negro demonstrations and marches suggest is not that nonviolent resistance is an effective weapon against tyranny but rather that in a nation traditionally favoring the (real or alleged) "underdog," the dramatization, by an underprivileged group, of its grievances, as it is possible in a free country, is a way of winning the support of public opinion and with it of governmental power; and that the white man has to walk warily in the face of the world revolution of the colored peoples.

However, it is impossible to see what bearing this experience could have on the effect of nonviolent resistance in a tightly organized terror system in which all organizations that might have become nuclei of resistance have been systematically destroyed and the population effectively atomized.

GENERAL CONSIDERATIONS REGARDING NONVIOLENT RESISTANCE

In the history of warfare new weapons or tactics, offensive are defensive, have traditionally had the advantage until a new weapon or a new tactic was found that would effectively counter them. The machine gun made cavalry obsolete and extorted a frightful toll of blood from infantry; the tank, combining fire power with mobility, rendered the trenches with their machine gun nests obsolete.

In a somewhat similar way, there are also new inventions in the creeping civil war, the fight between governments and rebellious citizens. Martyrdom is an ancient invention in the fight against tyranny. In the Roman circus, where men and women suffered an agonizing death for the amusement of the crowds, some endured their fate with such fortitude and equanimity that they won, for moments at least, the sympathies of the crowd and in some cases even won new adherents to their creed. As a weapon, it was of low efficiency, for small gain was bought at a terrific cost in agony. Nevertheless, the fact that some men and women could, for whatever reason, better than others endure anguish and pain, allowed them to die with the hope that their suffering would bring about good. It was with this kind of conviction that countless resisters went to their deaths right down to our time.

But one thing is necessary for martyrdom to have an effect upon the minds of men: the martyr who becomes a "witness" for his cause must have an audience before which to make his existential deposition. It is in this respect that modern totalitarianism has found an answer to martyrdom and made it a blunted weapon. The would-be martyr, in modern totalitarian states, does not get his "day in court"; he is either broken in torture until he is willing to disgrace himself in public or he dies in loneliness, and nobody knows of his cause and of the way he bore testimony for the truth of his belief.

A Gandhi, e.g., would have been utterly ineffective under the Hitler regime. He would probably have died unnoticed in a concentration camp, and all the public would have heard, in the enforced unanimity of a controlled press, would have been a trumped-up story about crimes that he had allegedly committed. The Nazis were fond of pinning two things on their helpless adversaries: homosexuality and embezzlement, both equally unsuited for a hero legend.

A special and rather mild case of martyrdom is the hunger strike. It has been a most effective weapon of the opposition against conservative or democratic states, but nobody has ever heard of a hunger strike being successfully used by the prisoners of a Communist or Fascist state.

At the time of the Irish revolution following the First World War, Terence MacSwiney, Mayor of Cork, went on a hunger strike. At that time the British still believed that it would mean abdication for a government to release a prisoner because of his resistance, without legal grounds; and they let MacSwiney die. Yet, again in accordance with the standards of a state ruled by law, they put no particular pressure on the prisoner, nor did they prevent news from the prison to be disseminated all over the country, nor did they stop people from expressing their sympathies. Daily bulletins from the bedside of the man who was slowly losing strength fed the hatred of the Irish people; his funeral procession was a demonstration of the mourning and the determination of the nation. The British learned their lesson; in the subsequent Indian struggles, they released Gandhi quickly when he began to fast. The government capitulated before the prisoner who had resorted to the hunger strike.

Nothing was heard of similar successes under the Nazi regime. No doubt there have been men of similar will power, but the Nazis would at best have let such strikers die in anonymity—and they may also have humiliated and tortured them.

It is more interesting to inquire what answer the Communists have found to the threat of hunger strike; for the Communists, while hardly inhibited in the use of force for the attainment of their ends, have nevertheless shunned the obviously sexual embellishments of brutality in which the Nazis delighted and, except for the height of Stalinism, have taken something like an artisan's pride in using the minimum amount of violence that would deliver the goods.

So it was like learning about a simple solution for a puzzling problem when I heard about the experience of some persons who had been imprisoned in the German Democratic Republic and who later, after their release, escaped to Switzerland. These men reported that they had gone on hunger strike; the answer of the authorities, according to their story, was as simple as it must have been effective; they merely turned off the water.[7] It is possible for men of will power to abstain from food; but it is beyond human capacity to stay without water for any length of time. As the body gets dehydrated, people go mad, possessed with an uncontrolled urge for liquids. Men tortured by thirst have eagerly gulped down salt water though they knew that after a little while they would suffer even more grievously; so imperative was the need for immediate relief, whatever the cost in later agony.

In circles in which it is firmly believed that the laboratory holds the answer to all human desires, it has occasionally been suggested that "research" should be done on nonviolent resistance in order to advance the cause of peace. There is a simple experiment that could easily be tried and that does not require large grants and expensive equipment: just to see how long a man can hold out, and keep up morale, without water.

CONCLUSION

The Victorian age went to great lengths not to recognize the sexuality of man. Women went for a swim dressed from neck to foot. Pregnancy and delivery were talked about in a whisper as though something shameful had to be covered by discreet silence. One did not speak of the "legs" of a piano—the word had become indecent by association.

That has changed with a vengeance. Women's bathing suits have gone to the opposite extreme and are reaching the vanishing point. Intimacies of erotic relations and obstetrical details are discussed in public. But the very attitude of nonrecognition or belittling that once prevailed with regard to sexuality is now at work to deny or to minimize the role of violence, practiced or potential, in human affairs.

Man in earlier ages was quite aware of the power of force once the protective layers of law had been stripped away. The tenth-century Byzantine historian Leon Diakonos tells the story of the murder of the emperor Nicephorus Phocas.[8] The leader of the conspiracy, one John Tzimiskes, was the Empress' paramour. She let him secretly into the palace and he helped his fellow conspirators to get in at night through the windows. They found the Emperor, mistreated him for some time, and finally killed him. While all this happened, word of suspicious goings-on had reached the palace guard; they assembled before the palace and tried to break the doors. When John Tzimiskes heard about it, he ordered one of his followers to cut the dead Emperor's head off and show it to the soldiers outside through a small opening in the palace door. Those who do not think much of the efficacy of violence in human affairs might now expect that the soldiers, already aroused at their Emperor's peril, became further infuriated at the evidence of this outrage and stormed the palace to avenge their master. But this is not what happened; the soldiers were terrified, fell on their knees and proclaimed John Tzimiskes emperor.

The various theories regarding political behavior which leave out or minimize the role of violence may nevertheless be accurate for "ordinary," "civilized" conditions in which there is no manifest violence and in which the issue of self-preservation does not present itself. These are conditions in which the law, though originally imposed by force, has come to be universally recognized.

Those who have never themselves met the fearful might of force, wielded by men either without moral restraint or, worse, of utter self-righteousness and hence not only free from inhibitions but spurred on by their ideologies, cannot imagine it. They have grown up in countries like the United States in which a humane law has long been established, in which unlimited power, or even a high concentration of power, has not existed for centuries, and in which all institutions have been designed to prevent such a concentration of power from ever materializing; and they take it for granted that tactics of opposition which have proved expedient under conditions of *fragmented* power are equally applicable under the conditions of *total* power.

11

The Influence of Ideas
upon Force

*... it may well happen that times change and that men
who are usually fair in remote things but changeable
in those that concern them directly, adopt another
opinion. ...*

—ABELINUS (1630)[1]

When barbarians could invade the Roman Empire with impunity and people lived in constant dread of wholesale murder and pillage, bishops often acted as the protectors of the
people. When Attila the Hun invaded Italy and approached a
trembling Rome, legend has it that the Bishop of Rome, Leo
III, went into his camp, unarmed, and persuaded him to turn
back.

Whatever the reality behind this tradition may be, the fact
remains that Christianity rose from a small congregation of
humble folk in a despised colonial country, against the oppression of one of the mightiest empires the world has ever
seen, into the Church Triumphant—the most inspiring tale
of the victory of mind over matter in all European history.

Inspiring as this story is, the historical record does not fully
bear it out. Faith and suffering—martyrdom—alone did not
suffice to conquer; more than two hundred years after the
Christians perished in the gardens of Nero, Christianity was

still an illegal creed, tolerated only by default, and spasmodically persecuted. It eventually triumphed nc through the irresistible power of the spirit over brute force but *through a deal with Caesar*—with Constantine the Great, one of the least attractive of the Roman Augusti, a group of men not distinguished for their virtue. Bernard Berenson called the Church of Rome a blend of Hebrew messianism, Greek metaphysics, and Roman imperialism; it was the deal referred to that brought the third ingredient in, and the Roman Church has never fully recovered from the moral consequences.

But be that as it may, there can be little doubt about the fact that ideas influence people; that, as Max Lerner put it, "ideas are weapons."[2] "Mad men in authority, who hear voices in the air," said Keynes in an often quoted passage, "are distilling their frenzy from some academic scribbler of a few years back."[3]

The Marxists, to be sure, have minimized the influence of ideas by insisting that ideas are merely a secondary product of economics and that, as Marx put it, socioeconomic reality determines socioeconomic consciousness.[4] But their actions have belied their professed beliefs; they have untiringly propagandized their ideas throughout the world and so demonstrated by their actions that they expect ideas to influence events; where state power is in their hands, they prevent the dissemination of ideas opposite to their own, and so again show their implicit belief in the power of ideas.

THE LEVERAGE OF IDEAS

If we compare the influence that men of the sword can have upon the thinking of the people with the possibility that the promoters of ideas may sway the minds of those who are in power, one important difference suggests itself immediately. Those who wield physical power can take children at their most receptive age and mold their minds; the promoters of new ideas have of themselves no access to children and can indoctrinate them only if those in charge of the children permit it. Thus, the man of ideas, as a rule, can reach people only at a later age, in *adolescence or adulthood.* At this later age, the mind is no longer a complete blank: a fundamental framework, a basic superego structure, has already come into being; it is still flexible in some degree, particularly during adolescence and early adulthood, but not of unlimited plasticity, and this flexibility diminishes with advancing age.

New ideas may be advanced by *new men,* leaders who so impress themselves upon the minds of people that they take the place of an earlier authority, already internalized but not yet so strongly entrenched that it could not be ousted again by the appearance, in the outside world, of a new leader of great appeal. The likelihood of such an event diminishes with advancing age; with most people, it remains permanently possible, to some degree, in hypnosis and in mass situations (which are a kind of collective hypnotism).

Apart from the impact of personalities, however, new ideas also find entrance through the *rills and fissures of inadequately patched-up inner contradictions and inconsistencies,* either among the moral tenets themselves or between moral tenets and other needs and aspirations of the person. In this way, they may find an Archimedean point within the existing personality structure to get the leverage for a breakup of the existing moral tenets and beliefs. The entry wedge of egalitarianism, for instance, was the secularized version of Christian charity; that of nationalism was the obligation to one's kith and kin.

But man's tolerance for contradictions is great and challenges to inconsistencies have therefore, with most people, little immediate effect; the influence is slow and great changes do not take place in a short time. It usually takes several generations until a radical change is brought about.

Furthermore, ideas do not seem to triumph as long as the ruling strata are solidly arrayed against them; *infiltration of the establishment* is a prerequisite of the victory of new ideas.

Christianity had its followers among high Roman society from a very early time; above all, and decisively, there was Constantine the Great. Luther had the protection of powerful princes, which Hus lacked. The American Revolution had support even within the royal house. Aristocrats were among the sponsors of revolutionary ideas in eighteenth-century France. The socialist movements of the last few generations have largely been manned, and practically exclusively been led, by men of upper- and middle-class background.

UPHILL AND DOWNHILL FIGHTING

We see, on the one hand, that the Communist state in Russia could model the thinking of the Russian people in something like forty years to such a degree that external coercion could be drastically reduced. During this time, opinion leaders of opposition views—Monarchists, Cadets, Social Revolutionaries, Mensheviks, and other dissident Leftists—had either been eliminated through liquidation, exile, and demise from natural causes or been paralyzed by intimidation, and the Russian youth had been brought up on the ideas of Leninism. As a result there is now, according to informed opinion, a generation of young men and women who take the *essence* of Communism for granted. If they are critical of conditions in the Soviet Union, as they apparently quite often are, their criticism is *immanent* criticism, i.e., they criticize Communist reality in the name of Communist principles. *Transcendent* criticism, i.e., criticism that challenges the basic assumptions of Communism, seems to be largely limited to surviving members of a prerevolutionary generation—a Pasternak, for instance.

A similar situation prevailed in Nazi Germany in the slightly more than twelve years of its rule. Adolf Hitler succeeded to a great degree in unteaching the German people the principles of Christian and humanitarian morality. If his reign had lasted twelve more years, it would probably not have been necessary for the Nazis to build their charnel houses away from areas where most of the people lived, and they could have performed their work of destruction in the full view of a meanwhile sufficiently brutalized people, as happened in the circuses of the Romans or the mass sacrifices of the Aztecs.

Ideas which are not supported by coercion, on the other hand, grow much more slowly. While physical force can work great changes in the thinking of men in a single generation if it is used with no restraints other than those counseled by prudence, the impact of ideas unsupported by the instruments of force seems slow, somewhat like an uphill struggle, and it takes several generations until any great change can come about.

In the last stage of the victorious career of an idea, its representatives usually get hold of the reins of government *without* the idea having won in the hearts of *more than an active and articulate minority* of men. Control is gained either through a deal with those who wield physical power (as Hitler rose in 1933 through a deal with the clique around President Hindenburg) or by effectively gaining the support of those in a strategic position (as Lenin's revolution succeeded through the support of the Moscow and Petrograd garrisons on whom Lenin's propaganda had deliberately concentrated). From then on, the further advance of the idea is a matter of fighting downhill, with physical force on its side.

AN EXAMPLE OF THE CAREER OF AN IDEA: THE STORY OF GERMAN NATIONALISM

The rise of German nationalism is a case in point. It began to make its appearance around the turn of the eighteenth century. By then, the ideology of nationalism that had been born and nursed in Western Europe arrived in Germany, the next station on its triumphant trip around the globe. The humiliations which the Germans suffered at the hands of Napoleon probably accelerated its growth. German national consciousness began to crystallize and German pride to assert itself;

there were Fichte, Kleist, Schelling or, on the more popular level, Jahn. It received its baptism of fire in the War of Liberation against Napoleon. Goethe, farsighted as he so often was, warned against the future rise of a German Napoleon and cursed him and his followers in advance.

The new movement was still largely liberal in feeling, and remained so a generation later when, in the revolutionary year of 1848, German delegates assembled in St. Paul's Cathedral in Frankfort to restore a united German Reich. The germs of nationalistic ferocity were visible to only a few. The Austrian poet Franz Grillparzer, to be sure, said his famous words about development going from humanitarianism through nationalism toward bestialism. And when Grillparzer was bitterly criticized for having taken the Habsburg side in the revolution, he said in his apology, among other things, that there was so much pretense and conceit among the German educated classes that there was no chance of anything reasonable and moderate coming out of it.

But Grillparzer was a lonely Cassandra, and for most people German nationalism seemed wedded forever to liberalism, like two sides of the same coin. As late as 1911, Vienna's leading liberal daily, which was read largely by the Jewish middle class, celebrated the electoral victory of German nationalists—most of them, by then, quite rabid—over clerical conservatives as a victory for "liberalism."

A generation after Grillparzer's warning, German nationalism gained further ground at the expense of traditional, humanitarian morality. Bismarck had brought about, with "blood and iron," the unity of Germany which the liberals of Frankfort had vainly sought to accomplish by consent. From then on, German nationalism was less encumbered by inhibitions from traditional moral sources. It remained heterodox only in Austria; in Germany, with the foundation of the Reich, it became the official creed.

The further career of German nationalism went from the arrogance of the Treitschke generation through the even more aggressive nationalism of the Wilhelmine era, which was bred by the combination of the frustration of new world-wide ambitions with a feeling of superior strength, to the final consummation of Grillparzer's prophecy, an outcome of the frustrations and humiliations of 1918 with the temptations of great latent power. But this part of the story lies outside of my proper subject.

THE APPEAL OF IDEAS

There remains the question: what is the nature of the appeal of ideas? What makes people believe in one proposition at one time and in the opposite proposition at another? What, for instance, made people whose forebears had shown the normal human appetites for sensual pleasures embrace an ascetic religion which considered this world only as a preparation for an eternal life of the soul and which shunned sensual pleasures as blocking man's way into this blessed Beyond? What made men of the sixteenth century, whose forebears had lived for centuries in the medieval order which, while allocating to men vastly different stations in life, had yet balanced, in principle at any rate and often also in practice, the rights and responsibilities of all classes—what made these men suddenly embrace a doctrine of monarchical absolutism, not matched by any obligations? Why do men at one time consider conformity in religion, not only in basic tenets but down to the most intricate theological points, so overriding a necessity that its enforcement is worth any price in blood and goods, while at another time they consider a ceremonial noncompulsory appellation of a Supreme Being without denominational specifications in a schoolroom an intolerable invasion of the freedom of their consciences? Why do people at one time consider private property so sacred and inviolate that it cannot even be temporarily restricted in a supreme emergency such as the Irish Famine, and at another time look upon it as an unmitigated Evil and the prime source of all Evil?

Why do people at one time consider the essence of morality to lie in the restriction of sexual activity—complete except for marital duties in a woman, less complete but subject to discretion in a man—at the same time being indifferent toward the abuses of men by men inherent in social stratification; while at another time they find nothing objectionable in a virtually uninhibited expression of sexuality, at the same time condemning the slightest manifestation of status seeking? Why at one time are external wars, i.e., wars between sovereign states, accepted as a necessary, legitimate, and perhaps even ultimately beneficial event and internal wars—civil wars —looked upon as a crime, to be atoned on the gallows, while at another time external war is considered a monstrous crime whose initiators should be executed, and internal wars are condoned or even praised as worthy endeavors?

Why did British Moralists at one time urge their government to take over African tribal lands and to bring to the natives the blessings of civilization, while the same kind of people at another time consider colonialism not just a misguided policy but the crime of crimes? Why do people of Caucasian or Mongol stock at one time consider African Negroes as a permanently inferior race that can never equal or approach the achievement of the peoples who have so far been the bearers of civilization, despite the fact that history provides examples of backward peoples without historical consciousness who have later moved into the forefront of civilization; while at another time insisting that the differential in achievements *in matters of alloplastic activities* is entirely due to white oppression, despite the fact that the level of achievement of Africans who have never been in contact with the white man and so have never suffered oppression or discrimination is lower, not higher, than the level of those who have had this contact and with it the experience of discrimination?

There are perhaps no fully satisfactory answers to questions of this kind, any more than we can really explain, on a much lower level of historical significance, why a fad like the hulahoop suddenly appears, spreads all over the globe, and fades into oblivion after a few months' time.

"The wind bloweth where it listeth, and thou hearest the

sound thereof, but cannot tell whence it cometh and whither it goeth."

Least of all can it be explained in the way of many modern sociological studies, by correlating things with other contemporary phenomena and claiming that coincidence means causation. It may, however, be made understandable historically. History, aided by the insights of psychological studies of individuals in depth, can offer plausible hypotheses concerning how things have grown out of pre-existing situations, conditioned by the challenges with which men were confronted at the time and the nature of their previous experience, both collective and individual, and so make the developments *comprehensible*. In this way, historians may succeed in demonstrating that what happened was a *possible* outcome, under the conditions then prevailing, but not even the most thorough and most subtle historical analysis can demonstrate that what happened had to happen this way, as the *sole* possible outcome of the circumstances. We are again touching the problem of prediction, which was discussed earlier.

12

Utopianism

You are mistaken, Licinius, if you believe that sensuality and failure to do one's duty are characteristic of our age; they are the vices of man, not of the times.

—SENECA[1]

Some of the revolutionary religious movements of the past have been inspired by messianic expectations; some of the secular political movements of modern times seem to be inspired by what may be called a secularized version of messianism, viz., utopian ideas. This subject was latent in the discussion of the modern scapegoat movements; it requires direct attention.

We may call utopian the striving for unrealizable goals. It may be convenient to distinguish between the two types of utopian aspirations:

1. Cases in which people aim simultaneously at two goals, one of which excludes the other.

2. Cases in which the means are grossly inadequate for the achievements of the desired ends.

There is a group of utopian aspirations which falls sometimes in the first category and sometimes in the second, viz., aspirations regarding human behavior which imply so high a degree of moral excellence that most people can live up to it, if at all, only for brief moments of supreme effort or great enthusiasm—a "rendezvous with destiny"[a]—or that their attain-

---

[a] Followed not infrequently by periods of exhaustion.

ment would exact too high a price in terms of other values such as, e.g., mental health or happiness. This type will be discussed separately.

MUTUALLY CONFLICTING GOALS

As has been pointed out earlier, liberty and equality, closely associated in Left thought, become mutually contradictory as soon as liberty refers not only to the relation to an outside oppressor but also to the relations within the peer group.

As has also been previously discussed, a great many people want affluence, ever more affluence, i.e., mass production, but without organization and the organization man. They aim at the complete liquidation of poverty; they ask that a floor be guaranteed below which nobody will be permitted to sink, and that this minimum level be periodically adjusted upward. They demand vast and increasing outlays for education, for scientific research, for various groups considered "underprivileged," such as an internal Marshall Plan in the order of magnitude of a hundred billion dollars to raise the socioeconomic level of the Negro population or vast programs to further Asian, African, and Latin economic development. All this is possible only through streamlined mass production and automation. At the same time, however, these people are horrified at the view of a mass society in which everybody is a faceless cog in an immense machine. They want to combine the output of the supermachine age with the cozy human relations of the horse-and-buggy age.

Higher education, it is demanded, should be not for the few, but for all; yet the very students for whom universal higher education is a morally self-evident postulate resent bitterly the factorylike anonymity and bureaucracy of the "multiversity."[2] They demand that their professors be available to them for discussion and consultation. They want millions to be educated by good teachers, in an individual tutor system or in small seminars, and all this without administration.

For the last two hundred years, liberal and radical intellectuals have asked for an effective democracy in which people are free to work out their own destiny and in which incomes are high and widely distributed, with income differentials small and declining. But at the same time, most of them cling to aristocratic values. They are horrified at the vulgarity of taste in, say, mass-produced furniture or automobiles or in the entertainment offered by the "mass media." But the latter is unavoidable, at least for a generation or two, when purchasing power has suddenly come to uneducated and traditionless masses. The noted sociologist Seymour Martin Lipset remarked with regard to this and similar situations:

> We cannot have the advantage of an aristocratic *and* a democratic society; we cannot have segregated elite schools in a society which stresses equality; we cannot have a cultural elite which produces without regard to mass taste in a society which emphasizes the value of popular judgment. By the same token, we cannot have a low divorce rate and end differentiation in sex roles, and we cannot expect to have secure adolescents in a culture which offers no definite path from adolescence to adulthood.[3]

It is a frequent experience that labor congresses and similar bodies request, in times of economic retrogression, the immediate liquidation of unemployment and the introduction of a minimum wage law, or the raising of the wage floor where such laws already exist. Yet, the enaction of a minimum wage law, or the raising of existing wage minima, will drive marginal producers out of business and thereby create unemployment. It is possible (though not assured) that in the long run such unemployment will be absorbed by the more efficient producers, but in the immediate future such legislation is apt to increase unemployment.

President Wilson proclaimed in 1918 the right of self-determination of all peoples, large or small. The idea appealed widely, the spark kindled a fire that spread rapidly over the entire globe. The assumption was, of course, that the self-determination of all peoples is mutually compatible.

Taken literally, it may well be the case that the freedom of each individual to decide which sovereign unit he wishes to join, or in conjunction with others like-minded to establish, is compatible with the equal freedom of all others. But the self-determination of some will seriously impede, or cancel out, the military security or economic viability of others, and without the latter "self-determination" is an empty gift. The exercise of self-determination of the Sudeten Germans, for instance, made the Czechoslovak rump state nonviable.

The principle was first announced in connection with the aspirations of the alienated nationalities in the Austro-Hungarian Empire, particularly the Austro-Slavs. Their secession was to make the Austro-Hungarian state nonviable; it was felt at the time that the self-determination of the Austro-Slavs must have precedence over the viability of the Austro-Hungarian state.

But the exercise of this right immediately opened the question of similar rights of the minorities in the new independent states, e.g., the German minority in Czechoslovakia. Granting them the right of self-determination, too, would cancel out the viability of the Czechoslovak state, and it was decided at the time that the latter had precedence over the right of self-determination of the Sudetens.

That was, of course, in accordance with the age-old privilege of the victor to arrange things in accordance with his interests. Had it been openly presented in this way, it might have been accepted and the victors might even have been praised for the moderation with which they had used their victory. But sailing under the flag of a moral principle which was claimed to be of universal validity, the settlement was unacceptable and led to the intensification of a self-righteous, disillusioned, and vindictive German nationalism which brought on the Second World War, with all its disastrous consequences.

The utopian illusion behind a principle of universal self-determination, subject to no qualification, was the assumption that the self-realization of one is always compatible with the self-realization of all others. But this is not the case, as countless examples could illustrate; the unqualified self-determination of Jews, for instance, is not compatible with an equally unqualified self-determination of Arabs.

As a rule, men are not greatly disturbed by contradictions in their thinking as long as it conforms with their wishes. De Tocqueville called it "one of the most ordinary weaknesses of the human intellect to seek to reconcile contrary principles and to purchase peace at the expense of logic."[4]

How far the tolerance of contradictions can go may be demonstrated with a rather abstruse example. When I came to the United States from Central Europe in the late '30's, I was astonished to see how many people, reaching from the extreme Left well into the business community, believed that the spectacular confessions of defendants at the Moscow purge trials were genuine. Such belief was rare in Central Europe; one was too close to Russia geographically and too many people knew individuals both in Russia and outside whose alleged counterrevolutionary and treasonable activities had been "revealed" in the Moscow confessions to give the latter any credence. But even without any firsthand knowledge and on the basis of the official Moscow reports alone it should have been entirely clear that the confessions could not all have been trustworthy. After the great purges of the old Bolsheviks, the so-called Yeshovshchina, there followed a period in which officers of the secret police—the Chekists—were put on trial; they confessed to having extorted confessions by torture and were executed for it. If their confessions were accepted as trustworthy, some of the previous confessions could not have been true; and if the confessions of the Yezhovshchina were all genuine confessions of repentant sinners, those of the Chekists could not have been. Yet, when I called attention to these incongruities in conversations in this country, the result was not that people reconsidered their view of the matter but rather that they resented my argument. It had been a trespass upon a preserve of collective daydreaming.

Numerous people believe at the same time in the evolution of the human species, in the sense of Darwinian theory, and in the basic inborn equality of all men, without significant difference in their genetic endowment. Yet, Darwinian evolution consists in the selection, by nature, between different genetic endowments; without genetic difference there can be no Darwinian evolution.

The thought processes are quite clear: genetic equality is only *just;* it would be a grave injustice if different individuals entered this world with greatly differing endowment. Evolution is *noble;* it leads man to ever loftier heights. The Darwinian theory is *scientific* because it deduces evolution from intrinsic necessities of nature. How could good things such as justice, nobility, science, not be in harmony with each other?

The favorite motif of utopian thought is the disappearance of conflict, and of the suffering caused by it, from the human scene. Complete harmony is envisaged between man and man, between man and society, between desire and duty. There is an implicit assumption of a prestabilized harmony in human affairs, thus far disturbed only by evil and, happily, transient institutions—for instance, private property. Once these conditions have been removed by human action or have disappeared in accordance with the "laws of history," conflicts which have been an integral part of all known history and a motif of so much of the world's literature are bound to disappear and the interests of every man will be in harmony with the interests of every other man and with the interests of future generations as represented by society.

A conservative thinker, Michael Oakeshott, described the working of this kind of mind in politics:

> ... they tell us that they have seen in a dream the glorious collisionless manner of living proper to all mankind, and this dream they understand as their warrant for seeking to remove the diversities and occasions for conflict which distinguish our current manner of living. Of course, their dreams are not all exactly alike, but they have this in common: each is a vision of a condition of human circumstance from which the occasion for conflict has been removed, a vision of human activity co-ordinated and set going in a single direction and of every resource being used to the full. And such people

appropriately understand the office of government to be the imposition upon its subjects of the condition of human circumstances of their dreams. To govern is to turn a private dream into a public and compulsory manner of living.[5]

If this kind of thought is carried to its logical conclusion, humorless and merciless, it inevitably leads to terrorism: for once the planners encounter the resistance of what they wish to mold, they have recourse to violence; no ordinary moral consideration can stay their hand when the eternal happiness of mankind is at stake. Again, in Oakeshott's words: "The combination of dreaming and ruling generates tyranny."[6]

INADEQUACY OF MEANS

The principle of contradiction is almost universally recognized, though in practice honored more often in the breach than in the observance. When we proceed to the second type of utopianism, however, we are on more controversial ground: for there are no clear criteria of what is and what is not achievable with the resources at hand. One man's utopianism is another man's bold vision and imagination; one man's sense of reality is another man's dried-out heart. Most of the cases that will be discussed in the following pages as examples of utopianism may appear to others as entirely realizable projects; and if attempts at realizing them have failed, the failure will be attributed to accidental circumstances such as mistakes of execution rather than to intrinsic impossibilities. To call a person's aspirations utopian will appear to him as an ideological device used by defenders of the *status quo* or, at best, as a "lack of imagination." Since there is neither objective evidence nor practical consensus as to what is possible and what is not, caution is indicated in arguments of this kind and any judgmental stance should be avoided.

What is or is not factually possible should be considered separately for the inanimate world and for living organisms, and among the latter for the subhuman and the human part. We have become very hesitant today to condemn ideas re-

garding the inanimate world or plant and lower animal life
as forever impossible; so many things have become reality in
recent times which only a short while ago would have been
fairy tales. If then someone suggests that another planet will
some day be farmed and mined for human benefit, or that
migration to other planets will take place to find room for expanding populations, few will dare to go on record with the
prediction that such things are forever impossible. Yet, purely physical limits of humanity—of the amount of production,
for instance, that can be wrung from resources within reach—
may well exist although so many estimates of these limits, like
those of Malthus, have so far proved wrong. The limits that
seemed so clear at an earlier age,

> Where Hercules of old set up the marks,
> As signs that man should never venture farther,[7]

have faded away, the sky is no longer the limit either, and we
do not know whether and where such barriers, temporary or
permanent, will yet be found.

In the control of lower organisms such as plant pests and
parasitic invaders of the human and animal body, man has
achieved the most staggering successes in the last hundred
years, beyond all expectations of an earlier age. Yet, there
seem to be certain limits; the very greatness of the success has
carried us to the point where they become visible. Nocuous
organisms can be destroyed by suitable preparations, but new,
resistant forms often turn up. The disturbance of the balance
of nature which is caused by the intervention of man makes
itself felt in various unwelcome ways. It has become increasingly apparent that in the war with parasites one can hardly
expect any final victory. New tasks will present themselves in
consequence of our solution of the old ones.

The same, approximately, applies to medicine in general.
Its magnificent successes are clearly shown in the lengthening
of the human life span. But it also becomes clearer that new
illnesses appear as old ones are liquidated and that the idea
of extinguishing all illness is probably an illusion.

When it comes to human behavior, the possibilities of influence are slimmer still. Changes in human behavior since the days of early man are not as well documented as the changes from Stone Age tools to computers. Great expectations regarding human potentialities are not supported by gigantic accomplishments of the past, and skepticism cannot be discredited by recalling the long record of myopia of outstanding men in the face of new inventions—e.g., Thiers, who saw the demonstration of a small railroad in a Paris exhibition and was sure that this would never be more than a novelty article.

A few examples may illustrate what I would consider utopian goals of the second type.

When the United States entered the First World War, the American people saw themselves fighting not merely in defense of national interest. The war was not to be fought for trivial ends such as temporary security; it was to be a war to end all war. A just peace settlement would remove all causes of discontent; the nations, liberated from belligerent monarchs, would henceforth live in peace with each other, to work for their economic betterment in an atmosphere of mutual goodwill.

When President Wilson returned from Paris with the treaty he had negotiated with the European allies, there was an outcry of indignation. This was not the absolutely just settlement that alone would justify the spilled blood and guarantee eternal peace; it was a product of "power politics," it embodied the parochial interests of the great European Allies and was unfair to both the minor Allies and the former enemy. So it was, in fact, to some degree; it was not the judicial verdict of an impartial court. Though imposed by the victors upon the vanquished, and applying a double standard of morality, the settlement did not completely disregard the interests of the latter; it merely gave preferred consideration to those of the victors. As compared with what had happened immediately before, in Brest Litovsk, and with what happened later, in 1938, 1940, and 1945, and what is happening today, it almost appears as a great document of justice.

But for many men in America it was the great betrayal. They would not settle for less than total justice and perpetual peace. Given the enormous power of the United States at the time, the United States might have had a chance of securing peace in our time if this had been its goal. Turning away contemptuously from such mean aspirations, their eyes firmly fixed on the ideal, the American people permitted the opportunity to slip through their hands. Disillusioned by the refusal of their wartime associates to forego the pursuit of their immediate interests and guarantees of their security and to throw their all in the basket of a promise of universal brotherhood, the American people adopted a cynical attitude, swore never again to be swayed by idealistic appeals, and "returned to normalcy," convinced that the tender shoots of idealism had been killed by the early frost of European "power politics."

However, the goal had been set too ambitiously: *perpetual* peace is hardly a reasonable object of statecraft. As Winston Churchill once said, "it is not given to human beings ... to foresee or to predict to any large extent the unfolding course of events";[8] man cannot reasonably plan very far into the future. The greatest statesmen have been those who have built for generations; eternity is not within our reach.

When in the mid-30's the United States Senate held hearings on the mandatory neutrality law then in consideration, Henry L. Stimson, who had been Secretary of State in the Hoover Administration, testified before the Committee. A lawyer by profession, he reminded the Committee of the many testators who want to foresee all possible future contingencies and make appropriate arrangements for each of them; "the Lord Almighty," he said, "has the embarrassing habit of bringing confusion to such efforts."[9][b]

We often hear the proposal that all nations should sur-

---

[b] This little episode may show how closely the various motifs of the modern age are interrelated. Those who feel humble in the face of a personal God or of a Cosmos far beyond their comprehension will scarcely set their goals so high, but utopian goals are chosen by those who believe that there are no limits to the realization of human ambitions.

render their sovereignty in favor of the "United Nations" and
so promote "peace under law"; the United States is urged to
take the initiative in this matter and set the example which
others, it is hopefully assumed, will follow. Carried away by
their enthusiasm, the proponents do not bother to question
the nature of the law into which we should deliver our destiny; whether it would be a law based on the *golden rule,* or a
law that puts a particular ideology ahead of the golden rule,
and if so, *which ideology;* whether it would be a law that *defends the status quo* in a particular aspect of life or one that
legalizes revolutionary demands, or a law that compromises
and mediates between these possibilities, and in what areas it
would do the one, in what the other. Would such a law condemn India for seizing Goa, or Indonesia for threatening to
seize Western New Guinea; or would it condemn Portugal
and Holland for not having surrendered them in the first
place? Without clarification of such points, the demand for
"strengthening the U.N." and for "peace under law" is mean-
ingless; and without some reason to believe that it would be
the kind of law under which we would find life livable, it is
misleading.

What the proponents of these ideas have in mind is, of
course, a world federation comparable in legal structure and
actual behavior to the federation of the American colonies into the United States of America; but this goal presupposes a
change of behavior in hundreds of millions of people—a feat
which is entirely beyond the means of the United States to
effect.[e]

    [e] The apparently ineradicable American belief that community can be es-
tablished by conscious, rational action derives its strength and tenacity from
the experiences of early American history, just as in personal lives ineradicable
convictions are based on, and maintained by, the impact of early childhood
experiences. The United States is indeed the conscious, reasoned creation of
men. It is the *only* example of a community that had not grown historically
but was artificially created by the will of a small number of men, with the
consent of their contemporaries.
In evaluating this unique event, however, two circumstances which are not
easily repeated must be considered. First, the men who created this community
were not very far apart in background; they were all European colonists; they

Another proposal commonly heard is that the constitution of the United Nations be altered to make it a more effective organization; perhaps, that the big power veto be abolished, or that a system of weighted voting be introduced in the Assembly. No attention is paid to the obvious fact that the first proposal has no chance of being considered by the Soviet Union as long as she is in a minority in the Council and the second proposal has no chance of being considered by the Asian and African states which would thereby be partly disfranchised.

Utopian was Mussolini's aspiration to establish Italy as a world power, to restore, as it were, the Roman Empire, because Italy was too narrow a power base for so ambitious an endeavor. The moderate size of her population; the absence of any military spirit among them; the paucity of essential raw materials; and, above all, her vulnerable geographical position—all conspired to make a bid for the highest stakes inauspicious. Mussolini could only have recourse to gambling, first by trying to be the pivotal force between the larger powers of Germany and Western Europe, and, when Italy proved too weak for this role, by allying himself with Hitler, a step which ended in his becoming Hitler's satellite. Another great Italian, Machiavelli, had warned statesmen against entering into an offensive alliance with a stronger partner because, by so doing, they would lose, whatever the outcome of the joint aggression: if it failed they would face the consequences of

---

had all been subjects of the British Crown; they spoke the same language and lived under the same law; and they had all just gone through the common experience of the struggle against England. There were no vast differences like those which separate the various branches of mankind today.

Second, the conscious creation of the American commonwealth occurred at a particular moment of history—perhaps the only moment in which such an act was possible at all, viz., at the height of the Enlightenment, in what Thomas Paine called the "Age of Reason." That moment lasted for only a generation. By 1800, it was probably already too late; the worship of Reason was already giving way to the worship of other, more traditional goddesses—the romantic reaction to the Enlightenment had set in. But even in this most propitious moment, the artificial creation of a community took place only in North America, where historical allegiances were weakest.

defeat, and if it succeeded they would be left alone with a superior power. At one point or another, the delicate balancing act which such games require is likely to go awry, and Mussolini's fate corroborated the warning of the sixteenth-century political theorist.

In a similar war, General de Gaulle's present bid for great power status for France is undertaken with inadequate national resources and seems largely based, on the one hand, on alliances with other European nations which are thought willing or obliged to play France's game, and, on the other, on the expectation that the United States will be forced to protect Europe, including France, no matter what additional burdens her allies may put on her shoulders. Such unsound expansionism is likely to collapse some day like the heavy difference buying on the New York Stock Exchange before the Great Depression.

While some modern movements appear wholly or predominantly utopian and have therefore been likened by historians to religious eschatological movements of the past and classified as "political messianism" (J. L. Talmon) or "millenarianism" (Norman Cohn),[10] the ideas of modern political parties have often been a mixture of realistic and utopian ingredients. In the United States, for instance, one political party has been more realistic with regard to what is achievable in foreign affairs but has been aspiring in domestic matters to a utopian vision of an "America Unlimited"[11] in which all people will be happy through abundance and justice for all, oblivious to the fact that the goal of abundance recedes with every step made in its direction, that material goods do not make people happy for any length of time, and that one man's justice is another man's outrage; another political party has been fairly well aware of the limits and costs of domestic programs, but in international affairs it has been holding up the utopian vision of a world in which American ideals or American interests prevail all over the globe, without risks or costs, oblivious to the fact that American power is limited by the power of others and that engaging in enterprises be-

yond one's means is courting disaster. Each side sees clearly
and denounces the utopianism of the other; each is myopic
with regard to the utopian elements in its own ideas and eager
to cash in on their appeal to wishful thinking.

Utopian proposals are usually advanced without any serious
effort to think matters through in concrete terms. If a critic
tries to go into the question of implementation, enthusiasts
often reply impatiently that these are "details" which can be
"worked out later." Yet, attractive-looking ideas are "plenti-
ful like blackberries" and it is the details which determine
whether or not an idea will work.

> Ideas can dwell in close proximity
> But hard in space collide the things.
> —Schiller

Proposals like those enumerated have in common a certain
dissociation from reality. Their advocates, apparently, think
in terms of abstract ideas rather than in terms of acting human beings. In their more extreme forms, such utopian proposals become the "addiction to an abstract system" which
Matthew Arnold said was characteristic of the Jacobin.

MORAL UTOPIANISM

Just how much and how far can man's behavior be changed to
make him comply with moral standards, in particular with
the modern standards of social responsibility, concern for others and for the community as a whole, over and above concern
for self and those next to him? The Soviet theoretician
Stepanyán said in 1960:

> The Communist man is no egotist, no individualist; he will
> be characterized by a conscious collective spirit and by con-
> cern for the common weal. The firm basis of this morality is
> his loyalty to the collective, his readiness and *his ability* con-
> scientiously to defend the interests of society.[12]

Loyalty to the collective is here not only a moral demand,
similar to, in times past, the obedience to God or the duty of

a citizen or a soldier, to which people tried to live up, approximating, at best, the ideal without ever quite reaching it. In the case of the Communist man, there seems to be a presumption of his ability to act always in accordance with communal rather than personal interests; Ovid's melancholy complaint —"I see the better course and I approve of it but I follow the worse one"[13]—would then belong, like so many other human failings, to a past that has been conquered for good.

Some questions, however, suggest themselves: Is this devotion to collective interests complete? Does it prevail all the time? Does Communist man never seek any advantage for himself or for his son or daughter? Is his devotion as stern as that of a Brutus, a Cato of Roman legend? Will self-seeking altogether disappear from the earth?

Behind all this lies the basic question whether an ethic that demands the complete abandonment of self, its total merger in the community, is *realistic*, i.e., whether it can be fulfilled by a large number of men without producing other consequences even less desirable.

This kind of ethics may be looked upon as a secularized offspring of the preachings in the Sermon on the Mount. Ethical demands of total self-abrogation belong to the messianic tradition of Judaism. Close to the time when these messianic ideas found their most powerful expression through Jesus of Nazareth, another Jewish teacher, Hillel, who followed the humanistic rather than the messianic tradition of Judaism, formulated principles of another, more modest ethic which allowed self-concern a legitimate place in life. His was the famous saying: "If I am not for myself, who will be for me? Yet if I am for myself only, what am I?"[14]

According to this formula, man is not only permitted to stand for his own interest; he must do so, for otherwise he would not survive. Hillel, apparently, takes the right of self-preservation for granted. Furthermore, he did not believe that men can safely leave their own interests in the care of others. However, a man who *only* pursues his own interests, without regard for others, without dedication to a larger whole, is considered a shabby creature. Each man standing for himself, but from this basis transcending himself to the interest in, and care for, things larger than himself—that is Hillel's moral ideal. It is the *highest ethical ideal short of the total abandonment of self in the messianic message,* if "height" of morality is measured in terms of distance from, or transcendence of, pure self-concern.

It is extremely doubtful whether the prescription of complete self-abrogation can ever be the practice of a large viable and surviving community. There is no reason to believe that monastic orders have ever completely eradicated self-concern, and, in any case, they have never embraced more than a small minority of the people. The Church soon tacitly accepted the fact that the moral prescriptions in question are somewhat like the stars by which the mariner steers his course but for which he does not reach out. She has accepted the sinful nature of man and has moderated utopian moral demands by sacramental ministrations. Some modern theologians have suggested that these prescriptions were not actually meant as laws for a continuing community but were given in the expectation of the immediacy of the end of Time and the coming of the Kingdom of God, as a code of behavior for the faithful during the years of waiting (*Interimsethik*). It is only in more recent times that many men consider a secularized version of messianic morality as something to be realized, here and now, in its entirety.

A view of morality identical with that of Hillel has in our days been defended by Reinhold Niebuhr:

> A valid moral outlook must be based upon an honest regard for the facts in the human situation, and must not construct norms which are impossible to achieve in view of the persistence and the power of man's self-concern, and more particularly of his collective self-concern. It is obviously wrong for either the individual or the group to pursue its interests consistently without regard for the interests of other individuals or groups who are bound to it in the bundle of life. It is also wrong to claim a larger measure of disinterestedness

than is possible for either individuals or groups. But it is possible for both individuals and groups to relate concern for the other with interest and concern for the self. . . .

It is interesting that a valid psychiatry had come to the same conclusions that a valid political science has arrived in regard to communities. This conclusion is that it is not possible permanently to suppress, by either internal or external pressure, the concern of the self for itself. The most loving parent combines with sacrifice for the children a healthy pride in perpetuating himself or herself in the other generation. Even the most loving parent may insinuate the love of power with the love of the child. A valid moral outlook for both individuals and for groups, therefore, sets no limits to the creative possibility of concern for others, and makes no claims that such creativity ever annuls the power of self-concern or removes the peril of pretension if the force of residual egotism is not acknowledged.[15]

What alone can have been meant by a "valid psychiatry" will now be discussed.

THE PAVLOVIAN AND THE FREUDIAN VIEW OF THE SOCIALIZATION OF MAN

Can man be remade into a completely social creature, free from (individualistic) sins? Communists seem to believe in the possibility of so remolding man that social behavior will come as naturally to him as a reflex. That raises the question of the *malleability of man*. In the Communist view, man's plasticity is, for all practical purposes, unlimited.

In close proximity of time, two different approaches to the understanding of behavior have been developed, viz., the theories of Pavlov and Freud. Fundamental to Pavlov's view is a mechanical reflex model, modified and enlarged so as to encompass socially conditioned, artificial reflexes. Fundamental to Freud's view is a model which pictures psychic life as an interplay of forces, some inborn, some acquired under the impact of the encounter with the outside world, and which sees behavior as the outcome of conflict and interaction between these tendencies. Freudian theory has no quarrel with the validity of the Pavlovian model under certain conditions which do not involve biological drives (or in which a satisfactory approximation can be achieved without taking this factor into account), and it could admit the Pavlovian model as a *marginal case* of its own model. But it takes a different view where a modification of biological drives is at stake, as would certainly be the case in the socialization of man. In that case, the two models lead to different views about the processes through which a human being becomes a fit member of a human society.

It so happens that the Communist view of the plasticity of man finds its best underpinning in Pavlov's work on conditioned reflexes, which has become an integral part of Soviet philosophy. Pavlov himself was strongly opposed to Communism as a sociopolitical creed and he made no effort to hide his feelings, but he remained unmolested under the Soviet regime. The Communists apparently thought that the good he did them with his biological teachings far outweighed any harm he could possibly do them with his political views.

Let us briefly consider the difference between the two models. A man may have grown up in a country in which traffic moved on the left side of the street and has so acquired the conditioned reflexes that go with these conditions; when starting to cross the street, he looks automatically to the right. Some day, he takes up residence in a country where traffic moves on the right side. He has difficulty in readjusting to the new situation and, particularly in emergencies, he tends for some time to look in the wrong direction. Yet, after a certain time he will probably develop a new set of reflexes appropriate to survival in right-lane traffic; and once this has happened, he moves as easily and effortlessly in his new surroundings as he did in the old ones. Should he change domicile again and move to a country with left-side traffic, he will have to relearn again.

If, on the other hand, a man tries to fight off and to blunt his sexual urges, the picture is quite different. We have

heard of the temptations of the ascetics of old (or, occasionally, of today) and of the lovely shapes which the devil assumed for their perdition. These men were praying for
strength to resist and conquer the temptations. We also know
of the tortures of sexual frustration suffered by prisoners and
others in comparable conditions. Sometimes, such people engage in new activities that appear like outlets of the frustrated desires. Priests have always known that an excessive,
sensually flavored, devotion to the Virgin may be a consequence of the temptations of the flesh. Homosexuality and
other perversions are not infrequent among sailors or prisoners.

The picture in such cases is different from that of reconditioning reflexes to another traffic system and the acquisition
of a new set of reactions with which, once they have been established, man moves as effortlessly as he did in the old one;
it rather appears as a constant struggle against a force, somewhat like sitting on the lid of a vessel in which water is boil-
ing. If inadequately checked, these forces may break through
at any time, and if barred in one direction, they may find an
outlet in another.

The question presents itself whether the socialization of
man is of the first type, viz., a reconditioning of reflexes, or
of the second type, viz., a control or a rechanneling of inborn
instinctual drives. The former would be in the sense of
Pavlovian, the latter in the sense of Freudian psychology.

Both models suggest an explanation of how selfishness and
hostility are overcome. In the first, Pavlovian, case, complete
conditioning and reconditioning of man is possible, and old
habits can disappear without leaving any traces. In the
Freudian picture, on the other hand, the new equilibrium
is not static, and constant effort is needed to maintain it;
under unfavorable conditions such as fatigue, illness, or
great danger, the whole edifice of acquired behavior can collapse and the original antisocial substructure can be regres-
sively reactivated.

If we believe that socialization proceeds along the lines of the Pavlovian model, we can see no limit to the possible re-modeling of man; but if we believe that it proceeds accord-ing to the model of Freud, the original instinctual drives of man cannot be altogether changed and there are limits to the realization of a very exacting reality. If too much is de-manded, if man's personal desires, sensual or otherwise, are not allowed some degree of gratification, they will return and make themselves felt in various, often highly undesirable, ways.

The Freudian view thus implies limits to the ambitions of the new *demiourgos,* the conscious architect of the human mind, while the Pavlovian approach seems to bid him fair speed for his ventures. It is better suited to those who feel themselves called upon to create an altogether new universe.

THE PERFECTLY MORAL SOCIETY

In the Middle Ages, many individuals strove for moral per-fection in an unceasing and lonely uphill struggle against temptation. They chastised themselves in despair over their relapses into sin. The less they sinned—many of them were hermits or monks with little opportunity of sinning except in their thoughts and dreams—the more guilty they felt and the more they chastised themselves.

In our time the scene, in the Western countries and par-ticularly in the United States, has shifted. Higher morality is no longer expected from the lonely struggle of the individ-ual, nor is it set as a goal for the education of the young. With regard to individual appetites and in the education of chil-dren, the atmosphere is rather one of tolerance and forbear-ance if not outright indulgence. Instead, absolute undeviat-ing devotion to the Good is expected of the State in its deal-ings with groups in the lower echelons of the social hierarchy and with foreign countries. Many people seem to believe that this has been guaranteed in the Constitution of the United States.

The United States, it is requested, must totally forgo all

concern for its own interests, including its own security, must refrain from interfering with, or indeed actively support, the exercise of unlimited self-determination by all countries and by all minorities within its borders, with total disregard of the consequences which such actions are bound to have upon its own freedom of movement, its way of life, and its very existence. Attempts at relating "concern for the other with interest and concern for the self," i.e., attempts at reconciling self-concern with moral principle, which Niebuhr described as the essence of a valid morality, are scorned as hypocritical; no attitude on the part of the United States that is not totally and unqualifiedly self-negating is morally acceptable.

This is a complete reversal of the situation that prevailed previously. For centuries, moralists have complained that nations do not recognize any law as superior to them and that they do with impunity what would expose an individual to severe censure; and these moralists have dreamed of the day when the moral law that applies to individuals will be considered as equally binding on nations. We see today, particularly in this country, that moralists demand of their country a type of conduct that they would not dream of expecting of any person in his individual life.

PSYCHOLOGICAL CONSIDERATIONS

The various kinds of aspiration and forms of thinking which we have lumped together on the basis of one common characteristic—the unrealizable goal—are not identical in other respects, such as their psychological roots or their role in life. In some instances we see isolated bits of thought in a person who otherwise has a realistic outlook, a kind of wildlife preserve in a highly built-up country; in this sense, probably everybody has some utopian corner in his mind. In other instances, utopian aspirations permeate or dominate the personality and the entire conduct of life. In some instances, utopian thought is subject, albeit slowly, to the corrective influence of experience; in other instances, it is refractory to it.

In its more benign manifestations, utopian thought is wishful thinking, due either to a lack of experience or sophistication or to the prevalence of the pleasure principle over the reality principle. In its more malignant forms, it reflects a radically different and, to my mind, defective perception of reality. The degree to which utopian thinking permeates life and the degree to which it is accessible or inaccessible to the corrective influence of experience mark the difference.

Sometimes one senses something like a search for paradise, with individual childhood experience probably providing the basis for the firm belief in the existence of a promised land.

Utopianism is frequently associated with perfectionsim— the intolerance toward flaws. Perfectionism has more than one psychological root. One rather frequent condition has been aptly described by Jean Rostand: "The search for the absolute may be nothing but a want of love."[16] Men who cannot love human beings as they are, with all their imperfections, but who desperately want to love—"they are in love with loving," as St. Augustine said—fantasy objects of perfection to which, in fantasy, they can extend their love.

ASSETS AND LIABILITIES OF UTOPIANISM

Utopian expectations, like all very high goals, have fired the enthusiasm of man and multiplied his strength in overcoming obstacles. The utmost human exertions and sacrifices have been due to this inspiration.

But there are liabilities, too. Any rational attempt at improving human conditions depends on a realistic assessment of circumstances. Francis Bacon's word still holds true: Nature, to be commanded, must first be obeyed. Illusions about facts and wishful thinking—of which utopianism is an extreme case—preclude the rational approach.

Furthermore, utopian expectations, like all very high expectations, are based on man's willingness to pay any price for the achievement of his goals; questions of costs are altogether neglected. In particular, utopianism may unleash ruthlessness and cruelty. Who but the coward and the neurotic would hesitate at individual sacrifices or the impediments of conventional morality when so much is at stake? Moreover, high goals not only can weaken moral inhibitions; they may also serve as an ideology by means of which ruthlessness and cruelty can masquerade as idealism.

Finally, there are the consequences of disappointed utopian hopes. Some people react to such disappointments by realizing that their expectations have been inordinately high, and adjusting their expectations accordingly. Others hold on to their philosophy and lay the rebuff of fate at the doorsteps of others. In this way utopianism may lead to scapegoatism.

This is what Grillparzer had in mind when he said that "the very unrealizability of the philosophical and literary theories has opened the door to all depravity."[17] And Goethe, presumably, meant something similar when he wrote:

> One should crucify every dreamer in his
>   thirtieth year;
> Once he knows the ways of the world, the
>   dupe turns into a knave.[18]

13

Three Current Views of Revolution

It isn't ignorance that causes the greatest harm; it's knowin' so darned many things that aren't so.

—Josh Billings

THE DEVIL THEORY OF REVOLUTION

Among the theories of revolution which are currently in vogue there is, first, a particularly simple theory which attributes the outbreak of revolutions to the activities of persons who have made it their business to arouse the people against the government. Agitators, usually from "foreign parts," have descended upon an otherwise peaceful countryside, have promoted discontent and stimulated the people into seditious and eventually revolutionary actions. The theory is quite old; King Frederic William IV of Prussia, for instance, believed that the 1848 revolution in Berlin had been engineered by foreigners (which to him meant Southern Germans, Poles, and Jews). This theory is widely believed today by whites in the South of the United States and in South Africa. It is also the official Soviet version of the Hungarian revolution of 1956.

It is easy to see that, whatever the content of truth in this theory may be, it cannot be the whole story. In order to accept it as a comprehensive theory, one would have to assume that any group, or at any rate the particular group in question, can be stimulated to revolutionary activity by any kind of agitation at any time. If this were the case, it should also be possible for the defenders of the *status quo* to dispatch their own agitators to a population infiltrated by foreign agitators and arouse them to rebel against the latter. Something of this kind did in fact actually happen, e.g., during the rise of National Socialism in Germany, when Nazi agitators succeeded in inflaming a small part of the working class—in particular, of the unemployed—against the labor leaders. But at other times, attempts of this kind have proved failures; in the present climate of Negro opinion, e.g., the chances of such counteragitators appear to be slight.

If this is so, it follows that not only the fact of agitation but also the *responsiveness* of the population to it must be considered; i.e., it must be taken into account that the soil may be more or less fertile for influences of a particular kind and that the ideas which agitators disseminate may have a greater or lesser appeal to people in a given situation. The outcome appears to be the result of both agitation and receptiveness of the soil, rather than of agitation alone. The immodest claims which have been made for the agitation theory as an allegedly complete explanation of a revolutionary movement have probably prevented many people from considering such elements of truth as the theory may nonetheless contain.

INJUSTICE, OPPRESSION, AND POVERTY

The most widely accepted theory sees the cause of revolution in social injustice, oppression, poverty. Examples that fit this picture come easily to mind: the revolt of the Roman plebs; the class war in the late Roman Republic; slave revolts in Antiquity or modern times; the peasant revolts in feudal Europe. An old German song has put it in these terse words:

A God who made iron grow
Wanted no slaves.

This theory is widely taken for granted. Current United States policies toward the "underdeveloped" world in general and toward Latin America in particular are based on the assumption that the likelihood of violent revolution declines with rising standards of living. While in official policy these considerations are qualified by others which reflect an awareness of complexity, the American and particularly the British press publish a constant stream of articles in which the United States government is urged to understand that the worldwide unrest is due to oppression and poverty, to discontinue all nonsense about political and military measures designed to stop the spread of Communism, and to get down to what is obviously its clear moral obligation and only chance of survival, viz., to remove injustice and oppression everywhere in the world, to bring affluence to the people of all lands, and to do so immediately because next year may be too late.

Like the previously discussed agitation theory, the oppression theory does not offer a complete explanation of revolution. Some facts do not seem to fit in easily with it:

1. For centuries men have quietly borne misery and oppression as great as, and sometimes greater than, those believed to have led to revolution.

2. Revolutions have broken out, as a rule, not in countries with the greatest poverty and most brutal oppression at that time, but in countries with relatively higher standards of living, considerable social mobility, and a measure of political freedom; and they have been carried out not by the poorest and most oppressed but by groups belonging to relatively higher strata of the social order.

3. Revolutions seem to occur most frequently just after conditions have markedly improved and while they are continuing to improve.

Ad 1. Poverty, oppression or, in more scientific terms, a low position in the hierarchies of power, income, status, and safety cannot in themselves be sufficient cause for revolt since such conditions have existed everywhere for long periods of time without generating revolution or revolutionary unrest.

There is the question: what constitutes unbearable oppression or poverty? What is poverty to an Italian peasant may be opulence to an Indian peasant; poverty and oppression, in any case, can be defined only in relative terms. Even within the same culture and in plain view of each other there may be great discrimination between groups which is not felt as unbearable. The untouchables of India have lived lives of extreme degradation, despised by all other castes, crowding themselves against a wall lest their shadow pollute a high-caste passerby, their wives walking for miles to carry on their heads the water for their household because they could not take it from a nearby high-caste well, their children tied inescapably to the same lot. Yet, there was no rising of the untouchables. Hindu women lived lives of total submission to their husbands and had to die on the husband's funeral pyre if he preceded them in death; extreme though this is in the eyes of Europeans—or, for that matter, contemporary Indians—we know nothing of a rising of Hindu women against their male oppressors.

Conditions comparable to the Indian caste system existed in medieval Europe. There were occupations which were not part of the guild system; due to ancient taboos, the practitioners of these trades stood outside of decent society and carried an invisible badge of shame. These included not only hangmen, gravediggers, and latrine cleaners, but also others like millers, weavers, potters, shepherds, barbers, chimney sweeps, and errant musicians.[1] Yet these outcasts did not rise against society.

The reason seems to lie in the fact that such conditions, and others equally revolting to contemporary feeling, were considered part of a sacred or otherwise immutable order and so accepted.

It cannot be true that a humble station in society is in itself sufficient cause for revolt; for in that case, as Bertrand de Jouvenel has pointed out, no society could last:

... no society could endure if, as it is sometimes implicitly assumed, its members became hostile to it by reason of and in proportion to their lowly status within it. Should you so plan a society as to establish and maintain equality in every respect you can think of, *there would naturally be a restoration of scarce, desirable positions, by nature attainable only to a minority*. You can allot equal time to each member of an Assembly: but you cannot ensure that each will command equal attention. *You can chase unequal ... distributions out of one field after another: they will reappear in new fields*. Nor are men so base as to be disaffected from any ordering in which they are low-placed: they are indeed lavish in the precedence they afford to those who excel in performance they value. What exasperates them is a system of qualifying values which seems to them scandalous .... [2] [a]

In earlier ages there was often a legend of a supreme outrage of tyranny that made the long-suffering people rise, a drop that made the barrel overflow, as the rape of a virgin (Lucretia by Tarquin), the blinding of a man for a trivial offense, or the wanton brutality of a satrap (Gessler forcing Wilhelm Tell to shoot the apple from his child's head). Such acts may be looked upon as psychological equivalents of castration or enforced self-castration. There is no evidence that there always was such a climactic event to trigger the revolt.

Ad 2. Revolutions did not break out in the lands of the greatest privation and they were not made by the poorest and most oppressed classes. In 1789 the revolution broke out in France and not in Spain or Russia where oppression was far more extreme than in France. H. R. Trevor-Roper said in his essay on "The Spanish Enlightenment": "It is not the backward countries which need revolutions. Being backward, Spain had not yet developed those internal strains which made France, with all its enlightenment, a social volcano."[3]

The same seems to be true of colonial revolutions in our

[a] Perhaps one can add to the last sentence that under conditions of great social mobility men have little difficulty believing that the system of qualifying values, or its application in their case, is scandalous.

day: they have come first in the countries which had a liberal colonial administration. In Latin America, revolution came to Cuba, one of the most "advanced" countries both in terms of industrialization and social legislation. Pre-Castro Cuba ranked third in per capita income ($454.00) in Latin America, topped only bc Argentina and Venezuela. The corresponding figures were $118.00 in Peru, $109.00 in Bolivia, $93.00 in Ecuador, $62.00 in Haiti.[4] Urbanization had progressed to the point where more than half of the island's population lived in the capital city of Havana alone. Economic progress had reached the stage where foreign (i.e., American) owned investments were already being progressively repatriated. Cuba was not an underdeveloped country like India or Nigeria or Haiti but well advanced along the road to industrialization. Why, in terms of the theory, did revolution come to Cuba rather than to Haiti or Ecuador?

The revolutionaries themselves did not come from the oppressed or poor strata. When President Eisenhower visited Chile in 1960, the Association of University students presented a memorandum to him in which it was stated:

> If the present injustices are all that Christianity and democracy have to offer to our Continent, nobody should be astonished if the best sons of the nation, in their striving for the foundation of morality and civilization—food, shelter and education—will turn to Communism.[5]

Be it noted that the memorandum did not state that, unless given justice, the *desperate masses* will take their destiny in their hands and put their faith in Communism; what it said was that "the *best sons of the nation*," i.e., presumably, they themselves, sons of upper- and middle-class homes, would do so. They would do it, it is true, in the name of justice for the masses, or under that flag, but that is something altogether different from the theory that poverty itself breeds revolution. The Chilean students had, in fact, unwittingly given support to another theory of revolution that was held by European conservatives under the impact of the experience of the French Revolution.

"The governments," wrote Clement von Metternich to Czar Alexander I in 1820, "having lost their balance, are frightened, intimidated, and thrown into confusion by the cries of the *intermediate class of society* which, placed between the kings and their subjects, *breaks the scepter of the monarchs and usurps the cry of the people.*"

Experience also lends support to a modernized version of this view which is expressed, for instance, by Hugh Seton-Watson: "The frustration of the intellectuals is a more immediate cause of Communist and other anti-Western movements than is the poverty of the masses."[6]

A prominent contemporary historian, reporting on a trip to Venezuela, said that the country was seething with revolt. He saw the reason for it in the contrast between great wealth and stark proverty; he compared it to the tension between two high electrical charges that will result in a lightning discharge. But after having stated what appeared to him the basis of the revolutionary situation in the country, he noted with astonishment that the acts of violence had come not from slum dwellers but from middle-class intellectuals. He drew no conclusion from such incongruity between theory and fact.

It is, indeed, hard to discard a theory that seems self-evident merely on the ground of unaccommodating facts. One is more inclined to hold on to the theory and to assume that the incongruity is due to some incidental, basically irrelevant, disturbances, such as the static in poor radio reception.

The assumption that revolutions are always "right," virtually by definition, i.e., that they occur only under conditions of avoidable injustice and refusal, by the rulers, of proper redress, is deeply rooted in the prevailing ethos, the "unwritten philosophy" of the time. It is a bias which comes through in the presumably dispassionate, descriptive language of scientists and scholars. Thus, the political scientist Chalmers Johnson states in a recent, systematic, if brief, treatise on revolution: "Multiple dysfunction plus elite intransigeance plus X equals revolution."[7]

If "dysfunction" means merely that the *status quo* is not to the liking of the revolutionaries, and "elite intransigeance" means merely that the government does not capitulate before their demands, the statement is a truism. But apparently the author means more than just that; the statement suggests that the grievances of the revolutionaries are *justified* in terms of moral principles which have to be accepted as sound, and that it is within the power of the rulers to redress these grievances at no greater cost than they can legitimately be expected to bear, but that they wilfully fail to do so. This amounts to taking it for granted that revolutionaries have never made demands which interfered with what others considered just or fair and have never resorted to force except for unexceptionable causes and sound reasons. That may all be true in individual cases, but to make it a *universal* assumption is absurd. This becomes apparent once we shift from the national to the international scene. Who would claim that no international war has ever been started except for the redress of wholly legitimate grievances? Who would accept Professor Johnson's formula for revolution (= internal war) when it is translated into conditions of international war, in which case it would read like this: "Multiple dysfunction in the international order plus intransigeance of the *status quo* nations plus X means war." It would also be equivalent to the assumption, in a theory of individual homicide, that all victims of homicide deserved their fate.

Ad. 3. The South of Italy, the *Mezzogiorno,* was the underdeveloped part of the peninsula. This land of high ancient and medieval civilization was ruined in modern times by soil erosion. It preserved the mores of an age of chivalry which are not conducive to modern industrial and commercial development and it suffered further for generations the loss of its more active, enterprising people through emigration. Thus, while industrialization was rapidly developing in Northern and Central Italy, the *Mezzogiorno* remained a distressed area. Through all this time, the region elected conservatives to Parliament while the industrial North was a hotbed of radicalism.

In recent years, conditions in the *Mezzogiorno* have been changing. A large reforestation program, begun early in the century, is beginning to bear fruit; industry has been steered into the region. It is *now* that Communism finds followers there.

Italy as a whole has made great strides in its economic development in recent years; one speaks of an economic miracle. She is about to enter the ranks of the highly developed nations, and the "age of mass consumption," the "affluent society," is about to be born. Yet it is at this point that the Communist Party registers gains at the polls.

THE REVOLUTION OF RISING EXPECTATIONS

Such examples suggest that revolutionary sentiment may appear not when the people are most downtrodden but rather when their fortunes are rising—and rising fast, for that matter. They also suggest that resentment, and with it revolutionary sentiment, is a function of the social distance between rich and poor, though not in the sense implied by the popular theory: the greater the distance, the greater the resentment; but in precisely the opposite sense: the smaller the distance, the greater the resentment. The latter possibility was seen in earlier times by only a few farsighted observers like Alexis de Tocqueville and Jacob Burckhardt, but they have become more and more conspicuous in our days. Negro resentment in the United States, for instance, rose to a revolutionary level only recently, after there had been steady improvement, far beyond what competent observers like Mr. Gunnar Myrdal had expected only twenty years earlier.

For phenomena such as these, Adlai Stevenson coined the witty expression "revolution of rising expectations." Revolutionary sentiment, then, is due to a change in aspirations; though conditions are improving, revolutionary sentiment rises because they do not improve fast enough—aspiration outruns fulfillment.

The basis for this apparent paradox seems to lie in the conditions of adjustment. After the battle of Chaeronea in which he defeated the forces of the Greek city states, King Philip of Macedonia wanted to make a symbolic bow before the intellectual and artistic glory of Athens and so, presumably, prove himself to be a man of culture rather than a Northern barbarian; he set all Athenians among his prisoners free without ransom. Under the conditions prevailing at that time, this was an act of great generosity; the fate of a prisoner of war was a harsh one, and the best he could hope for was to be ransomed eventually, after long tribulations. Prisoners probably accepted their fate by bowing to the inevitable as people accept other disasters about which they can do nothing. The Athenian prisoners, having been set free, showed no joy or gratitude: they came to the King, requested that they be given back their clothes and their blankets, and complained about their treatment at the hand of Macedonian soldiers. Philip was greatly annoyed: "Do you think," he replied, "that you have been defeated in a game of checkers?"

Alexis de Tocqueville called attention to the fact that in an age that cherished equality, small inequalities were more bitterly resented than big ones, and that inequality approaching the vanishing point (without having reached it) generated more resentment than vast inequalities had ever done:

> The hatred that men bear to privilege increases in proportion as privileges become fewer and less considerable, so that democratic passions would seem to burn most fiercely just when they have least fuel. . . . When all conditions are unequal, no inequality is so great as to offend the eye, whereas the slightest dissimilarity is odious in the midst of general uniformity; the more complete this uniformity is, the more insupportable the sight of such a difference becomes. Hence it is natural that the love of equality should constantly increase together with equality itself, and that it *should grow by what it feeds on.*[8]

In another context, he said:

> ... it is not always when things are going from bad to worse
> that revolutions break out. On the contrary, it oftener hap-
> pens that when a people which has put up with an oppres-
> sive rule over a long period without protest suddenly finds
> the government relaxing its pressure, it takes up arms against
> it. Thus the social order overthrown by a revolution is almost
> always better than the one immediately preceding it, and
> experience teaches us that, generally speaking, the most per-
> ilous moment for a bad government is one when it seeks to
> mend its ways. Only consummate statecraft can enable a
> King to save his throne when after a long spell of oppressive
> rule he sets to improving the lot of his subjects. Patiently en-
> dured *so long as it seemed beyond redress,* a grievance comes
> to appear intolerable once the possibility of removing it
> crosses men's minds. For the mere fact that certain abuses
> have been remedied draws attention to the others and they
> now appear more galling; people may *suffer less, but their
> sensibility is exacerbated.*[9] [b]

The French Revolution, Alexis de Tocqueville suggests,
was not a matter of despair but of hope:

> In 1780 there could no longer be any talk of France's being
> on the downgrade; on the contrary, it seemed that no limit
> could be set to her advance. And it was now that theories of
> the perfectibility of man and continuous progress came into
> fashion. Twenty years earlier there had been no hope for the
> future; in 1780 no anxiety was felt about it. Dazzled by the
> prospect of a felicity undreamed of hitherto and now within
> their grasp, people were blind to the very real improvement
> that had taken place and eager to precipitate events.[10]

In his comparative study of the English, American, French,

[b] De Tocqueville's last point was dramatically illustrated in Eastern Europe
after the death of Stalin when the Soviet leaders relaxed their iron rule. Those
countries in which old national loyalties were arrayed against the new indoctrination seethed with discontent; revolution broke out in Eastern Germany
and in Hungary and threatened to break out in Poland. Even in Russia proper,
criticism and subversive attitudes spread among university students, always
the first harbingers of revolutionary sentiment. The leaders tightened the
reins again although not to the previous level.

and Russian Revolutions, Crane Brinton emphasized the same point: "These revolutionaries are not children of despair. These revolutions are born out of hope and their philosophies are formally optimistic."[11] Or, as Nietzsche put it: "It is not hunger that makes revolutions but the fact that the people's appetite was growing *en mangeant*—in the process of eating."[12]

This aspect of the phenomenon is apparently based on the conditions of adjustment. One accepts virtually anything that is unavoidable and adjusts to it as best one can; but if the condition is not clear or not definite, adjustment does not take place. The climate is something we can do nothing about (so far), and while people occasionally complain about the weather, they accept it and nobody is unhappy on account of it; but if it were possible to regulate the weather at will, there would be a great deal of unhappiness, resentment, and bitterness if not our preferences but those of others prevailed. *The inevitable is accepted but not the inadequate.*

Men accept even death when it is unavoidable. A person who has been told by his physician that he is beyond the reach of medical art and that his days are numbered usually accepts the fact, not happily, to be sure, but with composure; but if another physician holds out some hope, high tension will return and the patient will hover between hope and despair.

Hence, if conditions are in flux, one does not accept them and adjustment does not take place. An age of progress is bound to be an age of anxiety and resentment.

Finally, we must consider that new aspirations will appear when old ones are satisfied. The most fundamental aspiration of all is that for life itself, the demand of *self-preservation;* when life is in jeopardy, everything else, for most people, is of little relevance. Once life and the basic necessities of life have been secured, there come the narcissistic desires for *status* (i.e., for individual or collective self-aggrandizement) and the desires for a *good life* (i.e., for various libidinal gratifications). The prisoners whom Philip of Macedonia had set free, finding life and freedom secure, asked immediately for some of the niceties of life. And if the desires for status and for a good life have been satisfied too, there follows the craving for the satisfaction of *creative achievement*. Most women, at least of the childbearing and child-rearing age, satisfy this desire through motherhood; but only a minority of men—those endowed with creative abilities—can satisfy it. The others become restless, bored, striving for all kind of things like the proverbial "solid gold Cadillac" which, once achieved, turn out not to satisfy them for more than a brief moment.

In all this, there is much material for dissatisfaction; and in an age in which people are in the habit of blaming their frustrations on "society," the "system," or the international order, the sluices of aggression are opened.

The theory of the revolution of rising expectations appears to be an important, perhaps crucial, contribution to the understanding of revolution, *particularly in an age of progress*. Like the previously discussed views, however, it cannot be a complete theory of revolution. There are instances in which the specific conditions have existed without producing a revolutionary situation. So it has been, on the whole, in the United States in the last hundred years. Living conditions have been steadily improving and some of the features characteristic of the revolution of rising expectations have indeed made themselves felt, but, except for the Negro community, they have not crystallized into a revolutionary situation. The reason, probably, lies in what has often been called the conservatism of the American people, i.e., the fact that, in spite of the incessant, shrill denunciations of American realities on the part of those who believe that the promise of a land without sin has been dastardly betrayed, the majority of white Americans have *so far* either considered the sociopolitical structure of the country to be fundamentally sound or at least taken it for granted. Frustrations, then, have led to hostility toward persons and groups, toward specific laws, institutions and policies, but not toward the sociopolitical system as a whole.

Moreover, we may accept the concept of rising expectations as fundamentally correct, at least in an age dedicated to progress, and yet wonder whether that necessarily implies a rise of *revolutionary* potential. It is possible that rising expectations lead only to more moderate action, short of a challenge to the core of the sociopolitical structure. The history of the working class movement is a case in point.

There is little doubt that the stance of the working class in the earlier nineteenth century was potentially, and at moments actually, revolutionary. Marx did not see ghosts when he looked upon the industrial workers as a revolutionary class and staked on them his hopes for a different kind of society; he merely erred by sweepingly generalizing from the conditions of his own time. There seem to have been serious revolutionary possibilities in England in 1831/32.[13] Alexis de Tocqueville described the situation in Paris in the spring of 1848 in these words:

> I found in the capital a hundred thousand armed workmen formed into regiments, out of work, dying of hunger, but with their minds crammed with vain theories and visionary hopes. I saw society cut into two; those who possessed nothing, united in a common greed; those who possessed something, united in a common terror. There were no bonds, no sympathy between the two great sections; everywhere the idea of an inevitable and immediate struggle seemed at hand.[14]

This is obviously a far cry from the situation today. True, workers constantly make new demands to improve their circumstances: demands for higher wages, shorter working hours, greater job security, pension rights. But throughout the developed West the revolutionary fire has gone out of the working class movement—so much so that those who aim at revolution have given up on the working class and concentrate all their efforts on "colonial" peoples, Asians, Africans, and Latins, including American Negroes.

It is also noteworthy that this is not only so today when the living standards of the workers have reached those of the lower middle class; it was already visible on the horizon toward the end of the nineteenth century when economic improvements in the worker's life were still rather modest. The rise of revisionists like Edward Bernstein who renounced the idea of revolution in favor of reform was a symptom of the changing situation; and so was, in fact, the rise of Leninism. For Lenin realized in these years that the workers would not rise in revolution by themselves and that therefore, if revolution was wanted—and Lenin certainly wanted revolution more than anything else—it could not be left in the hands of the working class but had to be made the business of an elite party, i.e., of a professional army of civil war. It was this train of thought that led Lenin to the founding of the Bolshevist Party.

We thus see that advances in working conditions and living standards have blunted the edge of the revolutionary sword in the case of the *workers*; but the successes of *nationalist* movements have nearly everywhere led to new, more radical, demands. Why does the fulfillment of aspirations appear as ineffective or even appetizing in others? An understanding of this difference is apparently a prerequisite for the evaluation of the revolutionary potential of a situation.

14

A General Framework for a
Future Comprehensive
Theory of Revolution

OUTLINE

Revolutionary action[1] is a case of human action; and action is never completely explained by impulse or motive alone. A man may feel an impulse to say something unpleasant to his boss and quit his job; this does not mean that he will actually do it. Impulses may be immediately translated into motor activity in early childhood and also later, under conditions of regression which may be due, for instance, to toxic influence (as alcohol) or to brain injuries; but in normal adults impulses must first pass through the critical faculties (the "ego" of psychoanalytic theory) and either overwhelm them (as in emotional outbursts) or be approved by them (as in rational action) before they can find expression in action.

The distinction is between *mere discharge of accumulated tension,* on the one hand, and the *considered choice between alternatives* in the light of their anticipated consequences, on the other. But the distinction is not always quite so sharp; the two kinds of behavior are actually the extreme ends of a continuum, with many intermediate positions. For instance, the critical faculties may, like the weak father of a family, accept and rationalize only what they are powerless to prevent.

An impulse may be rejected for a variety of reasons; among them are fear of consequences (as, in the case of the disaffected employee, joblessness or a reputation for uncivil manners, a sense of propriety or a distate for vulgarity). In dealing with actions, we must note both the existence of a motive and the absence, or inadequate strength, of inhibitions.

In considering the causes of revolution, men of progressive leanings and men of conservative leanings tend to concentrate on only one or the other of these conditions. As is usually the case, both see one half of the truth clearly enough but are myopic with regard to the other half. Progressives emphasize the existence of the revolutionary impulse, which they assume is caused by well-founded and remediable grievances; but they neglect the lack of inhibitions or take it for granted. Conservatives emphasize the absence of inhibitions, which they tend to attribute to general demoralization or to a failure of nerve on the part of the authorities; they take dissatisfaction with government for granted. Since each faces a different part of a composite picture, it is not surprising that they arrive at practically opposite conclusions and remedies: progressives emphasize the need for more concessions; conservatives, the need for more repression.

With regard to both impulse and critical scrutiny, several factors should be considered.

1. The revolutionary impulse may well be said to stem from *frustration*. In a sense, this can be said of all human action which aims at changing the *status quo*. Plato said in his mythical language that *Eros* (Desire) is the child of *Poros* (Wealth) and *Penia* (Poverty); it moves from the latter toward the former.[2] Desire, in this sense, grows out of frustration. But this general characterization requires some qualifications:

Frustration conducive to action cannot be defined in external terms alone. It is not true that people are tempted to rebel if they are starving and not so tempted if their diet is

ample, or that they are tempted to rebel if they live in tene-
ment houses but are not so tempted if they live in modern
apartments or suburban homes. Frustration is experienced
*relative to a standard that varies with time, place, and cir-
cumstance.* The frustrated ambition of an aristocrat or an
intellectual may have a higher revolutionary potential than
the hunger of a peasant.

Moreover, reaction to frustration depends not only on the
distance between desire and fulfillment but also on the degree of *frustration tolerance.* The latter varies greatly both
in general and with regard to particular types of frustration.

Frustration can, but need not, be seen as a consequence of
unalterable conditions either of nature (e.g., the eruption of
a volcano or death in old age) or of the social world (e.g., the
privations of a war deemed to be necessary). If considered
inevitable, they are accepted and lead to autoplastic adjustment; but no such adjustment takes place *if other, better, conditions seem possible.* Frustrations have therefore a revolutionary potential only if their causes, real or alleged, seem
subject to change.

In the latter case, some kind of alloplastic action will follow; but such action will be directed toward destroying or
reshaping the political or social order only if people blame
their frustrations wholly or predominantly on it—only then
does *frustration turn into grievance.*

American immigrants, arriving in successive waves and
coming from various stocks, have begun their American life
in uninviting slums. They had ample opportunity to compare their lives with those of more fortunate groups only a
few blocks away and they did not believe that their condition
was fixed by cosmic necessity. Nevertheless, most of them
sought remedy by grasping opportunities of personal advancement and only a few took to political, collective protest.

But when people take the road of political rather than private action, there are various courses open to them. An American Negro at the turn of the century, for instance, who was

dedicated to the advancement of his race, could go the Booker Washington way of slow educational advance or the Du Bois way of political organization; he could start at the bottom or at the top. Latin Americans, frustrated by poverty in their lands today, may go the way of Munoz Marin in Puerto Rico or of Betancourt in Venezuela or of Castro in Cuba. The road they take may depend on factors such as the record of success or failure of these alternate methods (measured in terms of their aspirations), their patience, the balance of self-assertive and accommodative tendencies, of a liking for peace or a taste for violence, of constructive or strategic talents.

2. Rebellious sentiment alone is a necessary but not a sufficient condition of revolutionary action. As long as a government is a going concern, revolutionary action may still be constrained by *fear or residual loyalties*. Lenin, with all his uncompromising revolutionary zeal, did not consider an armed rising possible once the Czarist regime had recovered from the crises following the Russo-Japanese war; as late as January, 1917, he did not anticipate that revolution would come within his lifetime.[3] When the German opposition plotted the overthrow of the Hitler regime (1944), the conspirators had difficulty finding a man who was willing to kill Hitler. There were many who considered the assassination imperative, but, though of proven physical courage, they could not bring themselves to accept this assignment.[4] Action, though desired, was restrained, in the first case, by fear of the power of a functioning government; in the second case, by residual loyalties in the mind of the oppositionist.

If revolution is to take place, fear and loyalties must have largely disappeared, i.e., the system and its ethos must be in an advanced stage of disintegration.

These points will be discussed in greater detail in the following pages.

THE FRUSTRATIONS

Sometimes uprisings seem to have arisen from the bottom of

the social order—slaves, helots, serfs; some of these men were denied the possibility of satisfying the most elementary needs of life, or even life itself. The most extreme case on record is the revolt of the last remnant of the Warsaw ghetto. These men and women had not only no hope for a betterment of their wretched condition but no hope of survival for themselves and their children under any circumstances and in any kind of condition. They took to arms because only in this way could they exercise the last choice that was left to them: to die fighting rather than be led to their execution, and thus to take some of their torturers with them to the grave.

Other revolutions, however, have been made by people who were far above the bottom of society and whose grievances had nothing to do with a denial of the basic requirements of life or of human dignity. The American Revolution falls into this category. The Southern planters and the New England merchants and professionals formed the higher and middle brackets of colonial society; they were prosperous and there was no question of any threat to life and life's basic necessities. They resented the British government's demand that they share the cost of the common war against the French just as in recent times America's European allies resented the United States' request that they shoulder a fair share, financially or in terms of manpower, in the defense of the Western world; and the resentment of the colonists became inflamed when the British government tried to enforce its will just as European resentment has become inflamed at any sign of the United States trying to impose its will. Whatever we may think of the merits of democracy, or of the principle of "no taxation without representation," revolution in the name of such principles is a far cry from the revolutions of the feudal peasants or slaves (not to mention the Warsaw Jews). The bottom of the colonial world was made up of Indians and Negro slaves. Had it been their revolution, the outcome would not have been the Federal Union of 1789; they would have driven the white settlers from the continent. The American Revolution probably actually worsened the lot of the Indians because the British Crown had followed a policy of protecting the natives, to a degree, against settler expansion—a policy that is listed in the Declaration of Independence among the grievances of the settlers against the rule of George III.

Another example is provided by the growing disaffection of various nationalities in the Austro-Hungarian Empire, a disaffection which paralyzed the Habsburg state for decades and which led to open disloyalty when Austria-Hungary tried to stem or reverse the tide and to re-establish her prestige by arms; and which led to revolution when Austria-Hungary was defeated. Members of these nationalities did not suffer any discrimination as such.[a] Austrians of Czech or Italian nationality who were loyal to the Austrian state could and did rise to the highest posts. The Habsburg monarchy, like all monarchies prior to the decision of the houses of Savoy and Hohenzollern to ride the tide of Italian and German nationalism, was indifferent to a man's national background and hostile to the concept of nationality as a politically relevant characteristic. But in the nineteenth century, the idea of nationalism, born and nursed in Western Europe, came to the Austrian dominions: a new mystique of nationhood, a common identification with a group characterized by a mixture, in locally varying proportion, of such common elements as extraction, language, culture, and historical memories or myths.[b] The Austrian citi-

---

[a] This statement, though roughly correct, is in need of some qualification, however. It is actually fairly correct only for the Austrian half of the dual monarchy; the Hungarian oligarchy practiced some oppressive measures against the "nationalities," i.e., the non-Magyars, in particular a policy of Magyarization. Also, the Ruthenians in Austria could complain of oppression, not at the hands of the Vienna government but at those of the Polish majority in Galicia.

[b] Nationality, in other ages, had little significance. The tenth-century Byzantine Bishop Gennadius noted that though he spoke the same language as the ancient Hellenes, he did not consider himself a Hellene because he did not *believe* as the Hellenes did; when asked what he thought himself to be, his answer would have to be: a Christian.

In the age of monarchic absolutism, loyalty was owed to the sovereign and nationality was of no political significance. Wallenstein's army in the Thirty Year War was recruited from all nationalities of Europe. Prince Eugene of Savoy, of Italian and French extraction, offered his services first to Louis XIV

zen of Czech or Italian "nationality" no longer wanted to be
an Austrian, regardless of the advantages, financial or otherwise. The Italians dreamed of a united Italy, kingdom or
republic, which they would join; the Czechs, geographically
less favored, thought at first of a revival of the ancient Kingdom of Bohemia (including, of course, the parts inhabited
by Germans) as a part of the Habsburg Crown, later of a
Czech, and finally of a Czechoslovak, republic. The Habsburg state was confronted with the aspirations of the various
groups that had awakened to national consciousness. It could
not satisfy them without disintegrating, and it could not find
a viable compromise because these aspirations were mutually
conflicting, and what might have been satisfactory to one national group was unacceptable to another.

The grievance of these nationalities, then, was the frustration of their national aspirations. The fact that the Austrian government did not give in to them—could not give in
to them without committing suicide—was experienced as oppression. What often happens in such cases is that the groups
whose ambitions have been frustrated take to civil disobedience, sabotage, or open violence and that the government,
usually after a time of hesitation and forbearance, resorts to
repressive measures. Then the opposition has a bill of particulars for its charge of oppression.

If Hitler had won the war in Europe, many Americans of German descent—say, in Wisconsin or Missouri—
might have discovered that they were really Germans and
demanded their "right of self-determination." People of
Spanish, French, and other extractions might suddenly have

---

and, upon rejection, to the emperor in Vienna; he later became Imperial
Commander in the Wars of the Spanish Succession, waging war against France.
Nobody thought it blameworthy that his services had been offered to both
princes.

When the great German philosopher Arthur Schopenhauer was born in
Danzig, this city belonged to the Kingdom of Poland. There is no sign that
Germans at the time considered it oppressive or disgraceful for Germans to be
subjects of the King of Poland. Goethe looked with considerable misgivings at
the first signs of German nationalism and kept aloof from the enthusiasm of
the Wars of Liberation against Napoleon.

"awakened" to national consciousness and followed this lead. The fulfillment of these aspirations would have meant the disintegration of the Union. If, then, the U.S. government, representing the desires of those who wished to preserve the United States as they had known it, had resisted these demands, the various newly awakened national groups would probably have complained of oppression,[c] according to the French proverb: *cet animal est très méchant, quand on l'attaque, il se défend.* We see in Canada today how national sentiment is growing among the French Canadians, some of whom demand autonomy within the Dominion if not total independence: if the Dominion government resists what may lead to the disintegration of the state, the French Canadians, too, will consider themselves oppressed.

When Adolf Hitler rose to power in Germany in 1933, the Austrian Nazis, carried by the prestige of the victory in Germany, swelled virtually overnight from a scarcely noticed "lunatic fringe" group to about 40 per cent of the population; they expected soon to take over the government and to carry out their dream, the *Anschluss* with Germany. But the Austrian government, under Dollfuss and Schuschnigg, decided to resist Nazification, and since democratic institutions function adequately only if all people play the game according to the rules, i.e., subordinate their various special interests to the preservation of the game itself, and since democracy becomes self-defeating once a sizable part of the population does not do so, the government abolished these institutions (or, perhaps, seized the opportunity of abolishing them) and set up an authoritarian regime that could not be overthrown from within. The Austrian Nazis, frustrated and infuriated, had recourse to open terrorism; they planted bombs. The Austrian government thereupon put known Nazi activists in preventive custody, and when bombs had

[c] In such a predicament, the majority of the American people would presumably have been spared the moral opprobrium of liberal Western opinion to which others in the same straits have been subjected, because then such a body of opinion would most likely no longer have existed.

been planted, Nazis were forced to pick them up. The Nazis considered themselves victims of tyranny.

In the United States, scientists and other intellectuals sometimes express bitter disaffection: e.g., that intellectuals do not have the status that is due them; that they are subject to abuse. This deplorable state of affairs is sometimes contrasted with the favorable position allegedly enjoyed by scientists and intellectuals in other countries; it is sometimes in the Soviet Union, and sometimes in Western Europe, that the malcontents believe it possible to find the proper appreciation of the intellect.

Yet repeated opinion polls do not support these allegations; rather, they suggest that the practitioners of academic professions, and scientists in particular, rank high in the estimation of the American public. In a recent investigation conducted by the National Opinion Research Center of the University of Chicago, scientists ranked third, second only to Supreme Court justices and physicians, ahead of governors, cabinet members, and Congressmen; college professors in general tied with the two last-named groups. All were far ahead of corporation board members, bankers, and owners of large factories.[5]

There is no reason to question the sincerity of disaffected scientists and intellectuals. They consider themselves oppressed because, in their estimate, they are the elite of the nation and should be so recognized; anything short of this registers as oppression.

In cases such as these, opposition sentiment crystallizes not among those lowest in the pecking order but among groups which are quite high, or even very high on the social ladder but whose ambitions have been frustrated. Eventually, as J. D. B. Miller put it, "*any group which is not itself the government may feel that it is suffering some inferiority, and may be induced to challenge the existing regime.*"[6]

These facts were already seen by Alexis de Tocqueville who wrote in a letter to a friend: "What is it that in general leads men to trouble the state? On one side, *the desire to at-*

tain power: on the other, *the difficulty of creating a happy existence for himself by ordinary means.*"⁷ Essentially the same idea was expressed by Aristotle:

> ... civil strife is caused not only by inequality of property, but also by inequality of honors, though the two motives operate in opposite ways—the masses are discontented if possessions are unequally distributed, the upper classes if honors are equally distributed, bringing it about that
>
> Noble and base in equal honor stand.
>
> Nor do men wrong for the sake of bare necessities only—the sort of wrongdoing for which Phaleas thinks that equality of substance is a cure—preventing highway robbery by removing the motive of cold or hunger; men also do wrong to gain pleasure and to satisfy desire. For if they have a desire above the bare necessities of existence, they will transgress to cure this desire ... clearly the greatest transgressions spring from a desire for superfluities, not for bare necessities.⁸
>
> [And again, even more pointedly:] ... when inferior, people enter on strife in order that they may be equal, and when equal, in order that they may be greater.⁹

In the present climate of opinion, it is widely taken for granted that only "the difficulty of creating a happy existence for oneself by ordinary means" but not "the desire to attain power," in de Tocqueville's words, has kindled a revolutionary movement; at least this is taken for granted if the movement is hostile to business. The very fact of protest and revolt is then taken as evidence that there has been oppression. In this way, modern Western men have time and again put the halo of sainthood on the heads of ambitious and ruthless men.

This discussion of the variety of conditions which may constitute frustration would be incomplete, however, if it were not added that surfeit and hunger for stimulation—boredom —can give rise to a sense of want similar to the frustration of desires and can be nearly as upsetting, at least for those who have never experienced much of the other. Arthur Schopenhauer suggested in the middle of the nineteenth century that there are two obstacles to human happiness, viz., pain and boredom, and that the two are antagonistic to each other so that the more one gets away from the one, the more one is in danger of falling prey to the other. All life thus appears, in some degree, to be an oscillation between pain and boredom.[10]

The antagonism between the two is due, according to Schopenhauer, to an external and an internal factor. The external reason rests in the fact that frustration of desires creates pain while their satiation leads to boredom. The inner reason for their antagonism lies in the fact that a low sensitivity to stimuli—or, as we would say in psychoanalytic terminology, a high stimulus barrier—which protects men from pain also hands them over to boredom and may make them desirous of strong external stimulation, while a low stimulus barrier which protects them against boredom leaves them open to pain.

Schopenhauer emphasized that the lower classes suffer from pain while the upper classes suffer from boredom, which they try to escape in a hunt for new stimuli. Society has become much more affluent since his days, and more and more people have been transferred from the ranks of those suffering from pain and frustration to the ranks of those suffering from surfeit and boredom. The malaise seems to be rampant today in Western societies, and if people are in the habit of blaming their unhappiness on society, this too may give rise to revolutionary sentiment.

THE QUESTION OF FRUSTRATION TOLERANCE

We know that tolerance of physical pain varies greatly. A modern student of pain, the surgeon René Leriche, reports on a man with so little tolerance that the hypodermic needle caused him great distress; his father, an officer in the Franco-Prussian War of 1870, had refused any anesthetic for the amputation of an arm.[11]

Tolerance for other kinds of frustration varies no less; what is hardly noticed by some is hardly bearable to others.

Some intellectuals have complained about the pressures of American life which are supposed to make creative work difficult, if not impossible. The noted novelist Norman Mailer, for instance, spoke of "the slow deadening of the best of our possibilities" in a "tyranny one breathed but could not define."[12]

Whatever these pressures may consist of, they are bound to be minor compared to the pressures under which men of past ages have produced with overflowing creativity. Galileo worked under the shadow of death at the stake. Kepler had to petition his imperial employer repeatedly and humbly for salary arrears accumulated over years; his family, meanwhile, suffered from hunger and disease. To add to his woes, his aged mother was accused of witchcraft and Kepler spent more than a year of his life and much of his meager funds in her defense. In this distressing picture, it seems hardly worth mentioning that he could do his astronomical research only as a sideline after his official duties as an astrologer. The situation of scientists and scholars improved in the nineteenth century; they were no longer threatened by torture or execution, but many still lived and worked under conditions of grinding poverty and uncontrollable disease, such as tuberculosis.

Pressures such as these did not stifle the creativity of these men (though they probably diminished their output; Kepler once wrote in a letter that he "could produce more, yet the times are unfavorable"[13]). But the "pressures" of contemporary society apparently do. It sounds like Dr. Leriche's story of father and son.

THE FLUIDITY OF CIRCUMSTANCES

Frustration leads to action in the outside world only if conditions are not taken for granted, as part of divine or otherwise immutable order like the climate or the mortality of man, but are believed to be subject to change. The untouchables of India did not act against the heavy burden which the caste system put on their shoulders because for them it was part of an eternal cosmic order.

What makes people aware of the fact that their condition is not immutable is either critical thought, of which the Sophists in fifth-century Greece provide the first well-documented example, or contact with people who live under different conditions; or the combination of both. Both influences undermine tradition. Both have immensely increased in effectiveness through the spread of education and communication. The printed word, radio, television, the movies propagate new ideas and make people familiar with the living conditions of other social groups or in other countries. S. I. Hayakawa has plausibly argued that television has been a major factor in revolutionizing the American Negro community by familiarizing Negro youth with the amenities of life in white America.[14]

THE BIRTH OF GRIEVANCE

Intense frustrations which are not considered inevitable will lead to action except in the aged, the sick, the handicapped, and the dispirited. But these actions do not take the form of attempts at changing the social order unless the latter is considered wholly or predominantly responsible for one's distress so that remedy must be sought in the change of this order.

Countless millions have lived in poverty, have been aware of it, have suffered from it, and have not considered it unalterable, but have nevertheless not thought of turning against the social order because they believed that prosperity was largely a matter of hard work, sustained effort, and education. This is sometimes contemptuously called a Horatio Alger philosophy and believed to be characteristic of the American scene in the nineteenth century. Yet this idea is both older and far more widespread. Goethe had his Faust say: "To the able this world is not mute."[15] Actions that grow out of this philosophy aim at personal advancement rather than at overturning the social order.

THE ROLE OF VIOLENCE

Revolution is a violent process, in any case, during the struggle for power—I would not call it revolution otherwise—and often, particularly in modern times, also after the seizure of power, when human institutions and human life are being remolded according to the ideas of the revolutionaries in power.

Some of this is unavoidable. All government is based on a mixture, in varying proportions, of force and consent, and the more there is of the latter, the less need is there for the former. Regimes which have been long established and in which the ethos of the community is internalized, inculcated in the individual standards of conduct, may get along with no more than Force in Being, or indeed Force in the Background, scarcely visible to the naked eye. In Great Britain in the twentieth century, violence has practically disappeared, and force has been held in reserve for extraordinary challenges which so far have not materialized.

However, revolutionary regimes which aim at a far-reaching remodeling of affairs—and often at utopian goals that cannot be realized at all—do things and make demands that cannot be fulfilled by widespread consent; many people remain in outright opposition, and even in those who approve of the principles involved, the reluctant flesh must be constantly chastised. Thus, a revolutionary regime depends far more on violence for the attainment of its ends than do old established ones.

But it must be asked whether this is the whole story; whether revolutionary violence always stays strictly within the limits of what is necessary for the achievement of the political ends. And beyond that, one must ask the more general question whether the promotion of human welfare is the only goal, as is claimed by the revolutionaries, or whether the ends do not already contain some elements of malice, at least to some.

CONSTRUCTIVE OR DESTRUCTIVE EMPHASIS

The realization of new ideas often requires the destruction of something old. Slums may have to be razed before modern, healthy dwellings can be built in their place. However, destruction is *not always* required; there is often empty space available on which architects can build new homes without demolishing old ones. Destruction may be a prerequisite of construction far less often than is claimed by revolutionaries, and the argument may sometimes hide the fact that one has more taste, or more talent, for the job of destruction than for that of construction.

Concern for mass poverty is a case in point. Poverty can be relieved either by an increase in production or by a redistribution of the existing social product or, of course, by both. The two are interrelated, but their interrelation is not simple. Sometimes, redistribution may be a spur to production; at other times, it may be a hindrance. If the emotional emphasis is on improving the lot of the poor, redistribution will be resorted to only if it is likely to increase the social product or at least not likely to impair it; but if the emphasis is on expropriating the rich, that road will be chosen without much regard for its impact on production or with no regard for any adverse influence on it. The revolutionaries seem to come from the second rather than the first kind of people.

Lenin was without rival in revolutionary organization and propaganda, in the strategy of civil war and the arts of building absolute power. Yet Lenin's prerevolutionary writings show little evidence of serious thought about the way the future society would actually work. All that he deemed necessary was to smash, uproot, and utterly destroy capitalism;

once that was done, everything would fall in its place and turn out well. We see here a group of men reaching out for total power, with complete self-confidence, and with scarcely a thought about what they will do with that power beyond the annihilation of the existing order. When the first crisis turned up, Lenin searched in vain for guidance in Marx's writings; what followed was improvisation.

Castro has shown great ability in the arts of revolutionary warfare, military and psychological; in seizing power and making it absolute; and in supporting, materially and morally, sister movements in Latin America. Yet the material benefits his regime has so far bestowed upon the poor seem to be limited to the distribution of consumers' goods formerly in the possession of the upper and middle classes, and including in particular durable consumers' goods such as villas and beach establishments. Walter Rathenau once said that during revolutions one can always loot the bakeries; today the accumulation of consumers' goods, inherited from previous regimes, goes far beyond bread alone. Thus redistribution can temporarily give to the poorest a measure of affluence and make them into staunch supporters of the regime, but it does not contribute to a lasting improvement of their living conditions. The latter is a matter of production; and in this respect, reports from Cuba, though conflicting and inconclusive, contain little evidence of genuine progress and some indications of retrogression.

To sum it up: *construction and destruction are the two forms, or outlets, of activity*[d] and *the more one has of the one, the less there is of the other.*

VIOLENCE: AN INEVITABLE PRICE OR A NEED IN ITSELF?

The violence of revolutions is, in the eyes of some, a prerequisite of revolutionary achievements; in the eyes of others, it has little or no part in whatever positive achievements the

---

[d] They are closely related, though, and it is often a moot question whether a certain activity should be looked upon as predominantly constructive or predominantly destructive.

revolution may bring about; in fact, violence may even detract from them.

The violence of the French Revolution was, in the view of its defenders, necessary for one reason or another. It was, for instance, necessary to behead a king in order to break the hold of absolutism over the minds of men; the Germans, who never had that experience, remained submissive to instituted authority until recent times, with disastrous consequences.

On the other side, it is pointed out that all the lasting achievements of the Revolution had already been secured before the Terror began and that the most important of them, the abolishment of feudal privileges, was in principle decided by the King's order that the Three Estates should meet in joint session rather than in three separate bodies a few weeks before the storming of the Bastille, the first violent revolutionary act. It has also been pointed out that other countries, for instance, Great Britain and the United States, achieved similar results without widespread violence; that the Revolution left a deep split between the Left and the Right in French society, an unhealed wound that festers in each crisis (e.g., in the debacle of 1940); and that the violence of the Revolution finally led to the Thermidor and to the Napoleonic dictatorship with its wars of conquest—two decades of war in which the youth of France perished on the battlefields of Europe to no visible good to anybody but the war lords.

The same question presents itself with regard to the Russian Revolution. The Red Terror was necessary, it is argued on one side, to hold the counterrevolution down. The other side may reply that we have meanwhile seen a Communist regime established in Yugoslavia, with no comparable terror and yet no counterrevolution. But the defender of violence need not concede the point; he can reply that at the time of the Communist victory in Yugoslavia the prestige of Communist power had already been established and that the Yugoslavs could dispense with terror precisely because the Russians had applied it; moreover, that the Yugoslavs, in 1945, were not alone in the world but were backed up by Russia, and the presence of the Soviet army was a sufficient deterrent to counterrevolutionary ambitions. As always, the historical record is inconclusive and open to more than one interpretation.

Let us consider a circumscribed economic issue in which assets and liabilities can be more easily assessed. Europe was profoundly shocked when the Russian Bolsheviks announced the confiscation of all means of production *without compensation*. The European world had, of course, expected that socialists would nationalize the means of production; but it was always taken for granted that owners would be paid some compensation. The principle that there should be no retroactive law was deeply ingrained in European consciousness. The property owners had acquired their holdings in accordance with the laws and moral concepts of their time; if a new morality emerged which took a different view of the rights and wrongs of property, it was expected to start from then on and not retroactively stamp yesterday's right into a wrong.

For the Communists, however, expropriation without compensation was a fundamental point, a *shibboleth* that permitted no discussion. The fact that the people had been robbed for so long by the capitalists, they felt, was no reason why the people should continue to pay them tribute indefinitely. Moreover, compensation paid to capitalists would be an intolerable burden for the workers' state and go a long way toward canceling out the benefits that socialism was to bestow on the workers. Finally, such payments might provide the capitalists with the means to prepare for a counterrevolution.

Leaving out the emotional part about robbery, the question of the economic burden for the socialist state deserves closer scrutiny. Actually, the burden of compensation need not have been heavy. Compensation could have been based, tionalized properties. Nobody expected compensation in such cases to cover the full value of the properties, including consideration of their future earning capacity. Even where "capitalist" states have exercised the right of eminent domain and expropriated land or other facilities, the compensation paid was, at least on the continent of Europe, based on low estimates, and this was more or less accepted as one of the facts of life.

Furthermore, the government need not have paid compensation in cash but could have offered low-interest-bearing, nonnegotiable bonds. Moreover, through a progressive income tax, accepted as just in our time, the state could have taken back with one hand a sizable part of what it had given with the other; inheritance duties, likewise accepted as just, would have cut the government's indebtedness considerably each time the bonds changed hands. Finally, the secular inflationist trend, the steady devaluation of money, would have further lightened the burden for the socialist state, by expropriating the bond owners slowly and imperceptibly. If all these factors are taken into account, it turns out that compensation which would have appeared reasonable at the time need not have cost the socialist government in the end much more than about 5 per cent of the real value of the nationalized properties. In return for this outlay, the socialist state would have derived considerable benefits; the legal continuity would not have been destroyed;[e] the former owners—unless driven out by terror—would have cooperated in large numbers in the operation of the economy (as they did later in China) instead of fleeing and leaving the country depleted of competent managers for years.

Similarly, a settlement of the prewar Russian government loans to which titles were held by the Western, mostly French, public, a settlement which would have been possible at small cost, thanks to the depreciation of the franc to a

---

[e] This the Communists would not have considered as beneficial; but did their insistence on completely eradicating the existing political, social, and legal order—with the significant exception of the institution of the family—flow from any intrinsic need of a socialist or Communist order, or from an inner need for violence?

fraction of its prewar value, would have led to a restoration of the credit of the Soviet state in the international markets. The various five-year plans need not have been financed entirely out of current earnings and the Soviet people might have been spared many of the hardships they suffered during the rapid industrialization—and with it perhaps the mass persecutions which still are, and may continue to be, the skeleton in the Communist closet.

Moreover, such an agreement on Russia's prewar indebtedness would quickly have led to the recognition of the Soviet government by Great Britain, France, and the United States, and with it to a diplomatic detente and a measure of international cooperation between these countries which might have prevented the rise of German expansionism in the 1930s, or at least have restrained it at an early stage.

In the light of such possibilities one must ask: were acts such as expropriation of domestic and foreign owners without compensation really necessary to the attainment of socialism—or was the socialist idea a rationalization for the needs of truculent men to satisfy their fury and their hatred?

IDEALISM, VIOLENCE, AND CRUELTY

Throughout most of history, powerful men have not felt the need to justify themselves for acts of violence or cruelty. The Greeks offered no excuses for the sack of Troy, the slaying of her men, and the enslavement of her women; that was their obvious right as victors. Henry VIII offered no excuses for the execution, with appalling cruelty, of scores of thousands of men who had stood in the way of his greed; that was his obvious right as sovereign.

At other times, however, and particularly in the last two centuries, since the secularization of the Christian message, those who committed acts of violence or atrocities have justified them as necessary for the achievement of some later Good, comparable to deplorable but unavoidable casualties in a rescue operation and hence to be accepted by all but the squeamish and the neurotic. Perhaps this is so. On the other hand, the human mind has an inveterate ability to deceive itself about its motives. Thus, it may also be that an inner need for violent expression or cruelty influenced and colored the judgment of what was necessary for the task at hand and what was not. The motives may actually have been mixed—a composite of the pursuit of desirable goals that seemed to require violence and a need for violence itself—and only the former appeared in consciousness; or it may have been that the desirable goal was but an ideological fig-leaf, or alibi, for the latter. On this subject Freud once said:

> When we read of the atrocities of the past,[†] it sometimes seems as though the idealistic motives served only as an excuse for the destructive appetites; and sometimes—in the case, for instance, of the cruelties of the Inquisition—it seems as though the idealistic motives had pushed themselves forward in consciousness, while the destructive ones lent them an unconscious reinforcement. Both may be true.[16]

As will be seen from this quotation, Freud made no allowance for atrocities being committed only for the sake of good ends, without any ulterior motives; he distinguished only between mixed motivation and rationalization pure and simple. If for the sake of theoretical completeness we admit the possibility of purely idealistic motivation of cruelties, we should set up clear criteria according to which one should examine such claims. If acts of violence have been carried out disinterestedly, as it were, for the sake of overriding necessities, those who have ordered or executed them would be in the role of a good surgeon who may have to inflict pain on the patient for the patient's own good, and who would behave accordingly: he would do it with regret and be very careful not to do more than necessary; he would certainly not enjoy doing it.

If one sifts the behavior of great leaders of wars and revolutions according to these criteria, one will rarely, if ever,

---

† Freud wrote these words during one of the more quiet times in the history of Western societies (1932).

encounter these conditions. The writings of Lenin, for instance, are filled to the brim with the manifestations of a savage hatred of the bourgeoisie. Two episodes, out of many that are reliably reported, may illustrate the point.

At the time of the Red Terror, Maxim Gorky, an old revolutionary and a close friend of Lenin's, repeatedly intervened with Lenin on behalf of men or women who had been condemned to death. Lenin, according to Gorky, once said on such an occasion: "Don't you see you are wasting your time on *mere trifles?* You are compromising yourself in the eyes of your comrades, the workers."[17] Lenin referred here to mass death sentences as "mere trifles"; this suggests, at the very least, callousness and indifference to the suffering of the victims.

Bertrand Russell traveled to the Soviet Union in 1920. He came as a friend, prejudiced in her favor: "I went to Russia a Communist." Lenin told him in an interview, among other things, how the Soviet government brought class warfare into the villages and aroused the poor peasants to violence against the relatively more prosperous villagers: "He described the division between rich and poor peasants, and the government propaganda among the latter against the former, leading to acts of violence which he seemed to find amusing."[18]

Here we have the positive enjoyment of the sufferings inflicted on others. If it was only objective necessity, a bitter duty, why was Lenin amused? The greater prosperity of the "rich" was no crime, in terms of the existing laws, and no evil, in terms of the moral precepts prevailing at that time (and in all preceding time). In fact, it was probably often due to qualities which had heretofore been considered praiseworthy, viz., industry and thrift. But even if the rich peasants had committed crimes, or done evil, what kind of mind is *amused* by the agony that he inflicts on sinners?

The inclination to violence varies greatly in different persons, ages, milieus, and clusters of circumstances; the consideration of these relationships lies outside the scope of this essay.

THE DECLINE OF FEAR

Government, as we have seen, rests on a combination of fear and voluntary obedience; the latter is based mainly on loyalty. As long as a government inspires sufficient loyalty in an inner core, and sufficient fear universally, revolutionary action is effectively deterred. The disappearance or substantial weakening of both is therefore a prerequisite of revolution.

Fear may disappear for a variety of reasons. The decline in fear need not always be due to a decline in the government's coercive power or its reputation for power and determination; fear may vanish while the government is still all-powerful. This was the case in the rising of the last survivors of the Warsaw ghetto. The greatest part of former inmates had been deported to unknown destinations without offering any resistance since resistance against the overwhelming armed might and unshakable determination of the Nazi state was utterly futile. But word had finally spread through the ghetto that the destination of the deportees was the grave, and that all of them were doomed. As soon as they realized that nobody had any chance of survival, they lost all fear—"So farewell Hope and with Hope farewell fear" (Milton)—and rose to determine at least the conditions of their death and to exact a price for it.

However, this is an extremely rare situation. Ordinarily, people lose fear because the government has lost, or appears to have lost, its coercive power or seems unwilling to use it, or has lost *prestige*, which is the presumption of victory based on the memory of past victories.

Revolutions have thus often occurred *after defeat in war*. The first Russian revolution followed defeat in the Russo-Japanese War, the second, the reverses and enormous casualties in two and a half years of war with the Central Powers. The revolutionary unrest in Italy after the First World War, culminating in the seizure of the factories and leading to a chronic paralysis of government and eventually to the violent Fascist countermovement, followed the defeats which Italy had suffered in the War; Italy was formally among the victors, but by virtue of the successes of her allies rather than of her own military prowess, and the prevailing mood was that of a humiliated country. The Czech people had given little support to the Austro-Hungarian war effort and some troops had wilfully surrendered to the Russians, but revolution broke out only after it had become clear that Austria-Hungary was defeated and that the victors had underwritten an independent Czechoslovak Republic. When Marshall Foch, after the War, was warned of Communist ideas spreading among French soldiers, he replied contemptuously: "Bolshevism is a disease of the defeated armies."

In the Western hemisphere, resentment of the "Colossus of the North" is widespread and of old standing. But anti-Americanism assumed a revolutionary potential only after the United States, beleaguered by Communism and therefore in need of friends as never before, had become dependent on Latin goodwill; and particularly after the American mainland had become vulnerable to intercontinental rockets, so that the United States could no longer, as an *ultima ratio,* impose its will in the Western hemisphere except at great peril to itself, and after Fidel Castro had brought this new fact into the open by demonstrating to an astonished Latin world that the United States had no effective answer to his daily calculated insults.

THE DECLINE OF LOYALTY

In voluntary obedience, we should distinguish between love, confidence, and loyalty, and also whether its object is a person (e.g., a king, or a leader) or a system (e.g., a dynasty, or a party) or, in the case of loyalty, an idea which is part and parcel of a man's conscience (e.g., the common good, freedom or socialism). These types, of course, are ideal, or marginal, types and rarely appear in pure culture; reality is usually mixed. The German Nazis, for instance, loved the Germany of their dreams, were loyal to the idea of German greatness, and had confidence in Adolf Hitler as the man to realize it; but very many had also, or above all, a sense of loyalty to him personally. In the case of the Communists, the loyalty to the idea of Communism is mixed with the loyalty to the Party which is deemed to be the only effective tool for its realization (with not infrequent conflicts between loyalty to the idea and loyalty to the Party); personal loyalty to the leader plays a lesser role.

The greater the role of the person of the leader in the total structure of voluntary obedience, the more do things depend on his actions and his destiny. His death (and, particularly in shaky conditions, even his temporary absence) may mean disintegration and almost invariably means a crisis. Confidence in, and loyalty to, a leader wane if he fails in his function as a leader; all army manuals recognize the role of the officer in maintaining morale.

Loyalties are most lasting if they are attached to a system rather than to a person; in the former case the leader is merely a transient incarnation of a more enduring entity. Loyalty can then outlive the failure of a temporary administrator of a lasting estate because the failure need not weigh too heavily against the memory of past achievements and victories. The Emperor of Austria could lose four wars with France in quick succession from 1796 to 1809 and see his capital occupied twice by French troops without any weakening in the loyalty of his subjects. Napoleon, on the other hand, felt that one lost war would spell his undoing. When his fortunes were declining and the Allies offered him peace terms involving moderate sacrifices, he rejected them. In his conversations with Coulaincourt, who acted as go-between, he reflected bitterly on the fact that the heirs of ancient thrones —the Emperor of Austria, for instance, or the King of Prussia—could surrender one province after another without jeopardizing their crowns, while he, a soldier of fortune whose throne rested solely on his own victories, would not survive the loss of a single one of the French dominions.

FRAMEWORK FOR A FUTURE THEORY

There is a close relation between the *domestic authority* of a
leader or a system and the *international power* of the state in relation to other states. These basic facts are observable in the animal kingdom. C. R. Carpenter measured the territorial range of
a group of macaques on Santiago Island, i.e., the range over
which the group members freely moved. One group not only had
its own exclusive territorial range but its members also roamed
freely over the territory of the other macaque groups on the
island. Carpenter then removed the dominant male from this
group; the result was that *the territorial range of the group
shrank* and that they no longer trespassed upon the territory of
others. Apparently, the top animal, which had bullied the others
in the group, had also intimidated the animals in other groups
and so enlarged the territory of the entire group.[19]

These observations, incidentally, may help to explain the concept of "national interest" which British writers, and to an even
larger extent American writers, found so hard to understand in
the period when British and American security was almost effortlessly secured by sea power. Carpenter's observations also go a
long way toward explaining how Hitler rose to power in Germany. Britons and Americans have often wondered in amazement
why the Germans submitted to a bully like Hitler and many have
attributed it to submissiveness in the German character. But the
Germans who turned to Hitler were anything but submissive people. They did not *submit* to Hitler; they *chose* him as their leader
because they were intensely and arrogantly nationalistic and they
expected, not entirely without reason, that Hitler would subdue
Europe and would lay their neighbors prostrate at their feet.

The same attitude was expressed in seventeenth-century England by Andrew Marvell:

> I freely declare I am for old Noll;
> Though his government does a tyrant's resemble,
> He made England great and her enemies tremble.

A remarkable modern example of loyalty outlasting defeat is the behavior of the Japanese people toward the Emperor at the time of the Japanese surrender, unconditional
except for the preservation of the imperial system (1945).
The Japanese people did not cease being loyal to the Emperor; many people were reported to have bowed in the di-

rection of the Imperial Palace and asked for forgiveness because their exertions had been insufficient for victory.

The Hapsburgs could still lose wars and provinces in 1859 and 1866 without any peril to the dynasty. But in 1918 the monarchical idea was sufficiently weakened so that defeat and dismemberment of the state necessitated abdication.[g]

Allegiance to an idea declines either if the system which incorporates the idea conspicuously fails in terms of its own promises; or, particularly with the young, if a seductive leader succeeds in ousting the old superego and putting himself in its place; or if a new idea, with an appeal to one part of a person's conscience, takes hold of an unrecognized inner contradiction, trying to make it an open conflict and to dislodge opposing tendencies. These processes become socially potent once such an idea has infiltrated the inner ring of the power system and perhaps even the rulers themselves, weakening the determination of the latter and the loyalty of the former.

In the last prerevolutionary stages, the governments frequently become oppressive, for as their basis of loyalty narrows, they must increasingly take recourse to force if they are not to abdicate. The picture is usually that of *alternating attempts at reconciliation and repressive measures.* Examples abound, as in the latter days of the Bourbon, the Romanov, and the Habsburg monarchies, the pre-*Anschluss* regime in the first Austrian republic or the pre-Castro regime in Cuba. The regime that is being overthrown is therefore often, to a greater or lesser degree, authoritarian.

---

[g] It was perhaps some vague sense of this situation which prevented the monarchies in World War I from coming to terms with their adversaries at some sacrifice once the initial campaigns had failed to bring them victory, as their predecessors had done in comparable situations. The degeneration of the First World War from a "continuation of politics with other means" (Clausewitz) into an endless and increasingly futile massacre was therefore perhaps a consequence of the modern instability of monarchical regimes. Once they had gone to war and had not triumphed immediately according to their schedule, they could find no safe exit, and their adversaries lacked the wisdom or the forbearance to build bridges of retreat for them.

The gist of these processes has been described by a modern historian, the late Sir Lewis Namier:

> Discontent with government there always is; still, even when grievous and well-founded, it seldom engenders revolution till the moral bases of government have rotted away: which are the feelings of community between the masses and their rulers, and in the rulers a consciousness of their right and capacity to rule. *Revolutions are usually preceded by periods of high intellectual achievement and travail, of critical analysis and doubt, of unrest among the educated classes, and of guilt-consciousness in the rulers;* so it was in France in 1789, in Europe in 1848 and in Russia in 1917. If such corrosion of the moral and mental bases of government coincides with a period of social upheaval, and the conviction spreads even among the rulers themselves, that the ramshackle building cannot last, government disintegrates and revolution ensues.[20]

THE ROLE OF LEADERSHIP

In addition to all these "objective" conditions, there probably remains room for leadership and a place for pure chance.

It is impossible to appraise their influence exactly, as events can be interpreted in more than one way. Sometimes one gains the impression that the forces operating in one direction were so strong, and the supply of leaders so ample, that the absence of a particular personality would have made little difference. Given the conditions of late fifteenth-century Europe, it is hard to believe that America would have long remained undiscovered if Columbus had died in his childhood. Similarly, the Russian revolution of March, 1917 does not seem to have depended on any particular individual. The October Revolution was different; time and again Lenin was the only one in the Party councils who saw the opportunities for radical action, and one wonders whether the Bolsheviks would have seized power without him.

It can be maintained that the supply of leaders is in itself a function of the interplay of social forces; this is undoubtedly correct in the cases of ample supply. But we have here to do with probability considerations, and such considerations never explain the *individual* case. The appearance of a large number of artists in a certain area at one time probably has a cultural significance, but the appearance of an isolated painter of genius hardly has. The hypothesis is therefore irrelevant in the case of unique figures, not duplicated in their time and place. This kind of leadership remains an independent factor, accidental from the point of view of the sociopolitical struggle.

The picture is further complicated by the fact that the factors discussed are not independent variables; they influence each other and they are all influenced by the feedback from the revolutionary development. Interdependence of variables and feedback are the typical complications of social theory; market prices are a function of supply and demand, but supply and demand are themselves functions of prices. The study of these dependent relationships goes beyond the sketch intended in this chapter, but it is a prerequisite of any comprehensive theory.

THE POLITICAL OUTCOME OF REVOLUTIONS

The social, economic, and cultural consequences of revolutions vary greatly, but the resulting political structures seem to have one important characteristic in common. Bertrand de Jouvenel remarked in this connection:

Before the rapids, there was the rule of a Charles I, a Louis XVI, a Nicholas II.[h] After them, that of a Cromwell, a

---

[h] Jouvenel based his generalizations on the experience of the great revolutions of modern Europe, viz., the English, the French, and the Russian. He did not consider in this context the American Revolution, presumably because the American Revolution merely emancipated the American colonies from metropolitan control but left their social structure virtually intact. To Europeans, the

Napoleon, a Stalin. Such are the masters to whom the people that rose against Stuart or Bourbon or Romanov "tyranny" find themselves subjected next.

The phenomenon is as startling as the usual interpretation of it is misconceived. How sad, it is said, that the revolution strayed from its natural course, that the anti-social extravagancies of liberty called for a constraining force to discipline them, that these extravagancies caused so widespread a ruin that there had to be a man to reconstruct! If this or that mistake had but been avoided! Ingenuity is freely expended in unearthing the exact moment at which licentiousness set in, in isolating the act that made the revolution sin, in naming the criminal.

O pectora caeca! What a misunderstanding is here of the revolutionary phenomenon! The Cromwells and Stalins are no fortuitous consequence, no accidental happening, of the revolutionary tempest. Rather they are its predestined goal, towards which the entire upheaval was moving inevitably; the cycle began with the *downfall of an inadequate Power* only to close with the *consolidation of a more absolute Power*.[21]

Two decades have passed since these words were written, and in the meantime we have seen more successful revolutions, particularly in China and Cuba. Jouvenel's description seems to fit them well enough. They both have led to the establishment of a "more absolute Power." There is in all these revolutions approximately the same relationship between the system that had been overthrown and the system that took its place. The dictatorship of Cromwell was to the Stuart monarchy about what the rule of Robespierre or Napoleon was to the Bourbon monarchy in the days of Louis XVI, what the so-called "dictatorship of the proletariat" is to the later days of Czarism, or the Communist rule in China to the Kuomintang regime, or the rule of Castro to that of

---

concept of revolution is shaped by the violent experiences of European history and the American Revolution is therefore not seen as a revolution at all; it is usually referred to not as the American Revolution but as the American War of Independence.

Batista. In all these instances, *the systems overthrown were authoritarian systems; the systems which took their place were totalitarian.*

This result is not surprising; it follows from the very nature of a successful revolution, as discussed in these pages. If it is true that successful revolutions take place when an old set of beliefs is waning and a new set of beliefs has grown within the society, we must expect just this kind of relationship.

The ruling men, or the ideas in the name of which they ruled, no longer commanded wide loyalty. The rulers themselves ceased to believe fully in their right or their mission to rule and so were not able to apply the kind of force which might still have coerced not only the people's hands but also their minds. The attacks of the revolutionaries, on the other hand, did not allow the rulers to let freedom prevail but drove them to apply coercive measures in self-defense. These two factors together make for *authoritarianism.* In contrast, the revolutionaries fanatically believed in their mission and in the future of their cause; otherwise they would not have prevailed. Once in power, they seek to impose their beliefs —which, to them, are simply Truths—upon the people as naturally and, in a way, innocently as our medical schools or law schools request the students to learn the accepted doctrines. The result of these conditions is *totalitarianism.*

Successful revolutions, it thus appears, *are likely to replace an authoritarian regime with a totalitarian one.*

15

The Modern Revolution and
Its Relation to War

Revolutions can be classified according to the degree of change they seek, i.e., according to the range of their ambitions. On the one end of the spectrum are those which aim at a change of government personnel or at the redress of specific grievances; on the other end are those that aspire at a total reconstruction of society or even at the creation of a new type of man.

The "American Revolution" must be placed close to the first extreme. Originally, the rebels merely rejected "taxation without representation" and asked for the restoration of what they considered the rights of Englishmen violated by George III; eventually, they demanded self-government and independence from London. On the extreme other end of the spectrum must be placed the various chiliastic, or millenarian, movements such as that of the Anabaptists; this type occurred particularly frequently from the end of the eighteenth century on.

The French Revolution searched for a completely new order of society—in Robespierre's words, for "the empire of wisdom, justice, and virtue."[1] The Russian, Chinese, and Cuban revolutions had equally all-encompassing aspirations;

263

and so have the budding revolutionary movements on college campuses throughout the Western world, from Caracas
to Oxford, from Athens to Berkeley. They all aim at the rebuilding of society in accordance with a preconceived pattern—preconceived in very general outlines but not thought
through to the problems of actual implementation.

These patterns of the "good society" are derived neither
in Aristotelian fashion from observation of political conditions which have actually occurred in historical reality nor,
in Platonic fashion, from some theory about the nature of
man; they are derived from ideas about the *rights of man,*
i.e., from *moral aspirations,* without any investigation of
their empirical feasibility or costs.

The ideas in question are usually abstractly defined. In
the French Revolution, for instance, men spoke of liberty,
equality, and fraternity, without a clear notion of what the
people should be free to do, in what respects they should be
equal, how liberty was to be reconciled with equality, what
fraternity consists in, and how people should be made to behave as brothers all the time.

In the contemporary world, the demand is raised for
equality of Negroes with Caucasians in countries which have
hitherto lived under white domination, and for the equality
of Africans with Europeans and Americans on a world scale;
there is no clear picture of how the masses of unskilled or
semiskilled workers and even "unemployables" of an industrial civilization could be transformed, in short order, into
prosperous burghers and professionals, or how Guinea or
Tanzania could be transformed, overnight, into something
like Holland; whether this is possible at all, or if it is possible, what the enterprise entails and what its consequences
—physiological, psychological, social, and political—would
be. It is for this reason that Matthew Arnold credited the
Jacobins with a "love of abstractions" in the statement which
serves as a motto of Part II of this study.

Since the French Revolution, then, we have seen three
main political groups in action. There are, first, those who

wish to maintain the *status quo*; among them were the Bourbon monarchy in France, the Holy Alliance of the European powers after the Napoleonic Wars, the Habsburg monarchy throughout the century from the Congress of Vienna to the debacle in 1918; or at present there are the regimes of Spain and Portugal, and the traditional white regimes or power structures in the American South, in South Africa, and in Rhodesia.

On the other side are the revolutionary movements from Robespierre and Babeuf to Louis Blanc and Marx to Lenin, Mao Tse-tung and Castro.

In the middle, uneasily perched, are those who reject both the maintenance of the *status quo* and the integral revolution but who seek gradual progress, permitting step-by-step adjustments between the demands of a new order deductively conceived or pragmatically suggested, and the resistance of historical realities. To this group belonged the Orléans monarchy in nineteenth-century France; to it belongs the United States in the contemporary world.

In times in which conservatism holds sway, the gradualists are aligned with the revolutionaries, as was the case in the later years of Czarist rule and in the later years of Batista in Cuba. In times when a revolution is advancing, the gradualists become aligned, reluctantly and ambivalently, with the *status quo* conservatives. At the present moment, when the revolution carries immense momentum, conservatives and gradualists appear to be aligned against the integral radicals.

We then see on the one side those who have a vested interest in the complete or partial preservation of the old. They include by no means only the rich; there are also all those who have already carved out a place in life for themselves and who are afraid to lose in the change; and also those who, though actually belonging to the lower social echelons, have come to love their world—their broken-down shacks or slum apartments, for instance. The investments of their "vested" interests are not financial but purely libidinal. In this group will usually be found many elderly people for whom adjustment to a new order of things is particularly difficult and may no longer be possible.

On this side are also all those who, on account of temperament or experience, suspect that established realities reflect the unconscious experience of mankind and who do not have confidence in man's ability to foresee all the complex interrelations of things to make large-scale planning auspicious; they have a high estimate of the role of the unforeseeable, and thus incalculable, in human affairs. And there are those who distrust rapid change, fear its upsetting consequences, and dislike violence.

On the other side are those who either have no vested interest at all—e.g., youths who have not yet put down their roots—or whose vested interests are not threatened because their positions seem to be immune to change—e.g., scientists and teachers; and those whose personal interest lies precisely in change because they see, or fancy, themselves as the rulers in the coming order of things. And there are those who, because of temperament or lack of experience, have complete faith in human foresight and the unlimited possibility of rational management of all matters; they do not believe in the existence of, or do not greatly fear, the unforeseeable and incalculable. Furthermore, there are those who thrive on change; the faster the better. Finally, there are those who are indifferent to violence, and those who love it.

This modern revolutionary movement is a revolution in favor of what is conceived as progress—progress in the scientific-technological sense of rational management, and in the sense of liberty or, far more frequently, of equality. It is a revolution in the name and under the banner, though not necessarily in the service, of the very aspirations which are now holding sway over most of the world.

This fact gives particular strength to modern revolutions because it weakens the forces of conservation and those of gradualism by dividing their camps and, more important, by dividing the mind of each person in their ranks.

But the onward march of the revolution and the very

weakness of the forces of the *status quo* and of gradualism simultaneously stimulate the emergence of counterrevolutionary movements—the so-called radical Right—which use revolutionary enthusiasm and revolutionary violence in the service of the old gods (and often intensify them). Situations have arisen and may arise again in which the traditional defenders of the *status quo* and the gradualists are ground down between the pressures from the revolutionary Left and the counterrevolutionary Right, and in which the alternatives narrow down to a choice between revolution and counterrevolution.

THE PLANNED REVOLUTION AND THE REVOLUTIONARY TECHNIQUE

As the goal of revolution changes from the change of government and the redress of specific grievances to the reshaping of society or of man according to an image derived from moral aspirations, so does the character of revolution change from spontaneous explosions to consciously planned and centrally steered enterprises. The French Revolution can still be viewed as an essentially spontaneous outbreak if we do not call the playing with ideas in salon conversations a conscious preparation; "It is the historical truth," said Metternich, "that in the years preceding the Revolution, *nobody* foresaw the Revolution *as such*."[2] The Cuban and the Vietnamese revolutions, on the other hand, have been consciously prepared and steered by an elite of revolutionary activists. Jacob Burckhardt saw this difference and attempted to condemn planned revolutions without disavowing spontaneous ones: "A revolution is justified only when it rises unconsciously from the soil rather than being conjured up" (1842).[3]

Revolutionaries have studied the record of the French Revolution, which in a mere ten years had run the whole gamut from the transformation of an absolutistic regime into a constitutional monarchy, through the Jacobin Terror, the reaction of the Thermidor (which crushed Babeuf's communist rebellion) to the Bonapartist military dictatorship; and they also studied the record of the various revolutions of 1848. They wanted to find out how power had been wrested away from victorious revolutions and so learn how to avoid a similar contingency in the future.

Bakunin—perhaps with the collaboration of Nechaev—wrote the "Revolutionary Catechism" in which rules of conduct were laid down for the professional revolutionary. The revolutionary totally rejects existing society in all its aspects and aims not at its reform but at its destruction. He is characterized by total dedication to his goal—by total subordination of both the normal desires of men and ordinary morality, i.e., of morality of the Decalogue and of the Golden Rule, to the revolutionary goal. His tactics are total duplicity.

Bakuninism was defeated by Marxism in the Russian Social Democratic movement; but this was one of the cases in which the victor was gradually absorbed by the vanquished. In a process comparable to what in psychoanalytic theory is called the return of the repressed, Lenin, a Marxist, adopted, in fact, the Bakuninist strategy and created the Bolshevist Party, not as a mass party, but as an elite cadre of professional revolutionaries, *l'armée de métier*[4] of the Revolution. He greatly enriched the art of revolutionary warfare.

Lenin's contributions include, in the area of physical force, the conscious concentration on the nerve centers of the enemy—that is, in the case of Russia in 1917, the garrisons of Petrograd and Moscow; and, in the area of propaganda, the principle that revolutions are won "with the slogan of the day." The revolutionaries do not present their real program to the people in an attempt to persuade them of its merits; rather they pretend to fight for what the people want (or would want if they dared); once power has been won and fortified beyond the possibility of challenge, they can safely disregard the promises made in the struggle for power and carry out their real intentions. Thus, the Bolshevists agitated for the distribution of land among the peasants and encouraged landless peasants to seize it themselves in direct action. Yet, they had no intention whatever to create, or to tolerate, a system of small peasant ownership; once they held unchallengeable power, they would take the land back again. Similarly, Castro rose to power with the support of the middle class, pretending to fight for the restitution of a democratic constitution; on his triumphal entry into Havana, he looked amused at the crowds of middle-class enthusiasts who had no inkling of what was in store for them.

Another major contribution of Lenin to the theory and technique of revolution was the building up of the one-party totalitarian state, modeled after the Byzantine-Russian combination of absolute physical power with the priest's control of conscience, but vastly streamlined in efficiency; and the absolute priority to be given to the building up of total power over any other governmental concern.

Later revolutionaries, e.g., Mao Tse-tung, General Giap, Ernesto "Che" Guevara, have dug deeper into the pre-Marxian, Bakuninist, heritage and have developed guerrilla war into a fine art.

The basic principles of revolutionary warfare have been stated in simple words by Bertrand de Jouvenel:

> A group quite incapable of mustering an electoral majority can be quite capable of mobilizing a marching crowd at a strategic time and place and to endow it with such impetus as to place the committee [a term in Jouvenel's theory which for practical purposes means the government] between the alternative of shooting or fleeing.

This is his description of terrorist strategy:

> It requires only a small number of adepts willing to commit acts of violence to place the committee in a position of extreme embarrassment. Especially if the terrorist blows are dealt at random, it will almost invariably happen that reactions will fly wide of the mark and affect the innocent. *Goading the authorities into hurting the innocent bystanders is essential to terrorist strategy.* Its efficiency lies mainly in evoking blind anger and blundering retorts.... A course of terrorism can be guaranteed to call forth from the authorities reactions

which displease public opinion and worry consciences within the government itself. Any innocent who happens to be hurt by repressive actions benefits the guilty, to whom compassion extends. *The trick of combining the manners of gangsters with the moral benefits of martyrdom* has been developed throughout the twentieth century.[5]

The deadly power of guerrilla warfare has become clear in this generation. Guerrilla warfare becomes possible if a relatively small number of revolutionaries are ready, in the service of their cause, to accept every hardship, to inflict torture and death on countless innocents, and to brave it themselves. The fundamental principle is outlined in the above-quoted lines. Random acts of terror are committed all over the country; minor officials are shot; bombs explode in stores, cafes, and other public places. The frightened population looks to the government for protection and restoration of order. If the government fails to protect the ordinary law-abiding citizens, it loses its authority. But the suppression of anonymous terror is a staggering task. Many ordinary crimes, committed by unaided individuals, are never cleared up even though the police can count on the cooperation of the populace. The guerrillas have effective means of dissuading the people from cooperating with the authorities; if those who have conveyed information are killed or mutilated, others will think twice before talking. As in the case of the Mafia murders in Sicily, the ordinary person questioned by the police has seen nothing and heard nothing.

If, then, the authorities want to suppress the guerrilla operations, they can resort only to mass arrests of suspects and near-suspects, in the hope that the terrorists will be among them; and in order to make the people talk, they would have to apply pressures commensurate with those the guerrillas have used to intimidate them into silence, and so neutralize the fear of the guerrillas with an equal fear of the authorities. But mass arrests of innocents will alienate wide sections of the population; people want to be protected, but they do not want to be molested in the process. Mass arrests, and even more police torture, will give the regime the reputation of a tyranny. Aid from revolutionary governments abroad will become bolder and liberal opinion all over the world will rise in protest against the tyranny of the government.[a]

It has often been argued that guerrilla warfare is possible only if its goals are approved by "the people"—which may mean either a substantial segment of the population, or a substantial segment of articulate opinion. In a less sweeping way, this claim has been put forth in the form that guerrilla war needs a cause.

The guerrilla wars fought by revolutionary movements in our times certainly have had a cause which had a strong appeal for some people and a measure of appeal for many others; moral exhortation and physical coercion have been interwoven in the actions of the guerrillas as they are in brainwashing and in totalitarian practices in general. But the role of the ideological factor need not always be great.

As has been pointed out earlier, all government is based on a mixture of force and consent, and the more there is of consent, the less need there is for force; or, conversely, the less consent there is, the more force is needed. Guerrillas are a kind of "private," or subterranean, government; they can operate easily if they are carried by a wave of popular consent; but if they are prepared to proceed with great ruthlessness, they can operate with minimal consent.

What is necessary, of course, is that the guerrillas themselves believe in the merit of their cause.

This is, of course, only the barest skeleton of the principles on which has been built one of the most elaborate and sophis-

---

[a] This statement is in need of some qualifications, however. There was no sympathy for the terror acts of Germans in South Tyrol protesting against Italian police for making mass arrests and no demand for an investigation of alleged police torture. The reason, of course, was that the people involved were German nationalists and thus suspected to have Nazi sympathies; but even if they had not been subject to this suspicion, the very fact that they were Germans would have brought the Nazi association into play and discredited their cause. Actually, the Germans of South Tyrol have as good or as bad a cause as any national group demanding its independence from alien rule.

ticated of strategies—a strategy which aims at the disruption of government and at wearing down its will through unceasing pressure.

Guerrilla warfare confronts a government with the alternative of ruling despotically or abdicating. No way out of this desperate dilemma has so far been found.

The most effective weapon against revolutionary warfare so far devised seems to be the infiltration of the revolutionary movement by agents of the regime, i.e., the application of the techniques of subversion against the subversive movement itself. Governments have scored some successes in this way; the Czarist Ochrana was able to infiltrate the revolutionary movements to a remarkable degree—a fact which must be taken into account in evaluating Stalin's suspicion of virtually everybody in his environment. In other places, however, this method has not been developed very far.

It is crucial for the viability of free societies to find an effective answer to the strategy of terror; if they do not succeed in this, only totalitarian or severely authoritarian societies will be able to exist.

Conservatives in Western countries call for repressive measures, but apparently have not faced up to the question to what degree repression is compatible with the functioning of a free society. Liberals, on the other hand, seem to believe that guerrilla war could be prevented—or even terminated once it has broken out—if the government would only provide "justice for all," but they do not consider the fact that there exists no human community in which there are no malcontents.

WAR AND REVOLUTION

Revolutions, i.e., internal wars, have been intertwined with international wars throughout history. In the Peloponnesian War the military operations between Athens and Sparta were intimately connected with civil wars in various Greek cities. The Spanish Civil War of the 1930s became a kind of trial run for the clash between Germany and the Soviet Union. An inspection of the interrelationship between war and revolution in the last two hundred years seems to reveal a definite pattern.

The violent events of the French Revolution ended in military dictatorship. Napoleon put an end to the Revolution, effectively united the nation behind the idea of national glory, and led it into a sixteen-year period of wars of conquest.

As a consequence of these events, the princes of Europe became willing to subordinate their rivalries to the common defense against a common danger, and so to hold the peace among themselves. For a generation Europe was ruled by men like Metternich and Talleyrand—men who had been deeply impressed by the violence both of the Revolution itself and of its aftermath of constant warfare, and who were determined to prevent a recurrence. They attempted to maintain the *status quo* under an ideology of legitimacy; this, of course, implied that governments had to surrender any aspirations to bring about major changes in the existing power relationships.

The system lasted for about a generation. Around 1840, the presence of revolutionary sentiment, socialist and nationalist, became clearly visible, particularly among the intellectuals. Revolutions broke out in several places in 1848, but they were quickly defeated. In France, an electorate, consisting exclusively of the propertied classes and frightened by the Leftist trend which the revolution had assumed, elected another Bonaparte as head of state. In Central Europe, the uprisings were put down by armed might: by the Prussian army in Germany, by Radetzky in Northern Italy, Windischgrätz and Jellachich in Vienna, Paskevich in Hungary.

The speedy defeat of these revolutions had an unexpected result; it convinced many of the rulers of Europe that they had been frightened by a mere specter and that they need no longer restrain their competitive ambitions. The solidarity of the Divine Right kings in the Metternich era was quickly forgotten and intra-European rivalries again came to the fore. When the Frankfort Parliament offered the King of Prussia a German Imperial Crown, a Prussian Junker, Otto von Bismarck, spoke in strong words against the acceptance of this crown from the revolution; yet, some years later, the same Bismarck, as Prussian Prime Minister, carried out a policy which expropriated the ancient House of Hanover, ousted the House of Habsburg, the senior German dynasty, from the German scene, and founded the second German Empire in an alliance with nationalism.

The subsequent decades saw the rise of both socialist and nationalist sentiment. The conservative states, particularly the Austro-Hungarian, Turkish, and Russian empires, were increasingly pressed against the wall: Austria-Hungary reeling from one provisional budget to the next; Russia wavering between police oppression and attempts at reform; Turkey at first muddling along in the ruts of traditional Oriental despotism and then, under the Young Turks, making an attempt at violent self-assertion.

The first World War broke out over a strong Austro-Hungarian response to subversion. The Habsburg monarchy had struggled for decades against subversive movements, nationalist and socialist, which could not be appeased and which, moreover, were mutually irreconcilable. There was increasing doubt among loyalists and even among the rulers themselves whether the ancient state could long survive; demoralization had set in. Yet, the rulers were at all times in possession of a powerful instrument of war, surpassed in strength only by the armies of Germany, France, and Russia.

Some of the subversive movements of Austria derived moral support from independent national states across the border: the Ruthenians from Russia, the Italians from Italy, the Serbs from Serbia. This situation created a temptation for the frustrated Austrian rulers to use the one effective weapon in their possession—the army—and to strike at one of the weaker of these foreign powers, Italy or Serbia, in the hope of thereby stamping out the domestic subversion.

The assassination at Sarajevo showed that the subversive movement of the Serbs in the Habsburg monarchy had received from abroad not only moral but also material support; arms had been smuggled in from Serbia. The Austrian rulers chose war against Serbia. A decisive defeat of Serbia would demonstrate to the Austrian Serbs—and to other discontented Slavs as well—that the Habsburg state was here to stay and that they had better adjust themselves to this fact and look for the fulfillment of their—appropriately modified—aspirations within the framework of the monarchy.

The Austrians, of course, could not have embarked on a venture so loaded with the danger of war with Russia, had they not been assured of German backing. The Germans, in fact, not merely endorsed the Austrian enterprise but actually pressed the Austrians to pursue an uncompromising course.

Why did German leaders decide on such a policy and do so with such apparent lightheartedness and irresponsibility? It seems to me that most historians have not sufficiently questioned the motives of this behavior or have been satisfied with such glib answers as "Prussian militarism"—as if militarism as such would explain the willingness to face a European war in general, and in particular to engage in a war in the defense of the Habsburg state, which they knew to be half moribund.

A good part of the answer, it seems to me, can be found in a hypothesis advanced by Elie Halévy.[6] Halévy suggested that the German leaders were motivated, consciously or unconsciously, by fear of a revolution and by the idea of uniting the nation through a national war. They hoped to strengthen their own prestige and to secure their power by what was confidently expected to be a short and victorious war.

The German Social Democratic Party had been steadily gaining votes in every election and had become the largest party in the German Reichstag. Its programs and speeches were belligerent, replete with revolutionary fervor. With the benefit of hindsight, it may seem incredible that the German Social Democrats, who proved so tame when power finally fell into their hands in 1918, should have been so greatly feared. But this tameness was not evident in 1914; moreover, it was characteristic only of half the movement because the post-War Social Democrats were the product of a split in which the radicals had broken away.

Halévy's interpretation is strongly supported by another consideration: viewed in this way, the action of the German leaders in 1914 would merely have been a repetition of the eminently successful policies of Bismarck in the 1860s. For Bismarck, too, took the reins at a time when revolution was feared by many. The Prince Regent (who later became the first German Kaiser) was persuaded to call on this "bloody reactionary," as Friedrich Wilhelm IV had called him, as a kind of last resort; but he did it with little hope.

Yet, Bismarck tamed the revolution. A wave of enthusiasm swept through the country when the Franco-Prussian War, gently engineered by Bismarck, broke out in 1870 and the other German states followed Prussian leadership, ultimately to the Kaiser proclamation in Versailles a few months and many victorious battles later. The Liberals who had been so feared split into the National Liberals, who supported the new Empire, and the traditional Liberals, who proved impotent. The specter of the revolution evaporated into nothing and the regime was re-established, unchallengeable for another half century. It is not astonishing that the grandsons, consciously or unconsciously, tried to repeat the successful coup of the grandfathers.

Seen in this perspective, World War I appears to have been due to an attempt, by the rulers of Austria-Hungary and Germany and their loyal subjects who felt threatened by revolution—the Austrians primarily by nationalist revolutions, the Germans by a sociopolitical one—to rescue and fortify their position by using the one, immensely powerful weapon in their hand—their armies. But this step implied *turning a threatening disruption of civil authority,* a threat in the face of which they felt weak, *into an external war* which they felt confident they could win.

The contemporary world situation shows many of the same characteristics. Revolutionary techniques have immensely improved in effectiveness; the strategies by which a small group of determined men—a professional army of civil war —can undermine the government of large states and prevent it from functioning can now be taught, and are being taught, in academies of civil war, just as international warfare has been taught in the traditional military academies for centuries.

A *status quo* power attacked by methods of revolutionary warfare which aim at the destruction of civil order is at a grave disadvantage; at the same time, it is in possession of a powerful war machine. There naturally rises the temptation to use the weapon in its hand and to strike at the foreign power which gives moral and sometimes also material support to the revolutionary movement and thus to transform an internal war which is slowly eroding its strength into an external one which it feels it might win.

The state of Israel, once established, became a *status quo* power; its aims are preservation rather than further expansion. The Egyptians sent trained terrorists across unguarded parts of the frontier who killed farmers and destroyed property. This kind of terrorism is disruptive of ordinary life and is extremely difficult to control, with the possible exception of savagely punishing terrorists who are caught—a method that the *status quo* power could not apply without outraging international opinion and a major part of domestic opinion as well. The Israelis struck with their army against Egypt. This was universally condemned as an act of aggression.

A similar situation developed between India and Pakistan. India had succeeded in incorporating Kashmir with the assistance of the Hindu Maharaja of the predominantly Moslem state; she was now the *status quo* power in this area. The

Pakistanis, frustrated in their aspirations, sent trained terrorists into the country to disrupt civil life; the Indians re-
taliated by sending their army across the border, thus again
transforming an internal war into an external one, because
the Indian government saw more chance of prevailing in the
latter than in the former.

The United States was confronted with a similar situation
in South Vietnam. A revolutionary movement, morally and
materially backed up by the government of North Vietnam,
had already succeeded by ruthless large-scale terrorism in
disrupting the functioning of the government in South Vietnam. The United States government was strongly tempted to
strike at North Vietnam as the source of this support. At the
time of this writing, the President has proceeded along this
line to the extent of bombing communications in North
Vietnam but has resisted further extension, for instance, to
the major industrial installations. There have been several reasons for this action, but among them one should not overlook
the fact that the military organization of a traditional state is
better equipped for external than for internal war.

The existence of nuclear weapons in the hands of a potential adversary or his backers has, of course, put severe restraints on the pursuit of this course of action. As a consequence, there has been a shift in the power equations to the
detriment of the *status quo* powers, which rely mainly on
traditional military establishments, and in favor of revolutionary powers. This does not mean, however, that this
course of action has thereby been completely deterred; there
may be instances in which the *status quo* power deems the
danger of escalation to a nuclear level to be slight. It all depends on the *quantitative relation* between two opposing
pressures: the requirements of defense against the attack of
the revolutionaries and the danger of nuclear involvement,
viz., on the *quantitative relation between two fears*.

These examples might suggest that the instigation or support of internal war in the country of an antagonist is an effective weapon that can be equally applied by all revisionist

powers against all *status quo* powers. But this is not the case. Internal war is an extremely effective weapon against free countries and a rather effective one against mildly authoritarian ones; but totalitarian countries are practically immune to it. Internal war, *once started,* is an immensely powerful instrument; a free state cannot suppress it at all because it would have to resort to oppressive measures, and even authoritarian and totalitarian states sometimes find it difficult to do so unless they are able and willing to resort to savage measures such as the deportation of whole populations. But *in order to start revolutionary warfare,* there must be a tight, if originally small, *political organization.* This is easy to build up in a free state and not too difficult in an authoritarian one, but it is virtually impossible in a totalitarian system where all nuclei of potential opposition have been destroyed, the population has been effectively atomized, and tight supervision on the level of apartment, factory, and office makes it all but impossible for like-minded people to find each other.

Internal warfare is therefore the weapon *par excellence* in the hand of a revolutionary totalitarian power against free or authoritarian ones. Guerrilla warfare presents the most serious test of the *viability of free institutions.*

CONCLUSION

Revolutions, in modern times, have increasingly aimed not merely at the change of a regime or at the redress of specific grievances but at a total reshaping of all life according to a plan—or, rather, a dimly conceived scheme derived from moral aspirations, i.e., at the realization of a vision of a perfect society. They have therefore been increasingly planned, carried out, and administered by an elite cadre of full-time revolutionaries while revolutions which rise more or less spontaneously from an anonymous multitude tend to disappear. Because of the magnitude of the ambitions of the planners, these revolutions have inevitably been totalitarian.

We thus see in modern times a worldwide revolutionary movement set against the forces of conservation and the forces of gradualism. More recently, these revolutionary movements have enjoyed the support, moral or material, of great revolutionary Powers.

Revolution—internal war—has often been intimately related to, and intertwined with, external, or international war. This relation has assumed in modern times a more specific significance.

The *status quo* powers have mostly been either free or authoritarian states and, as such, highly vulnerable to subversion and revolutionary warfare, to which totalitarian systems are practically immune. Revolutionary warfare is therefore a potent weapon in the hands of revolutionary movements and of totalitarian powers.

Status quo powers, on the other hand, are, like all sovereign states, in possession of military establishments.

When *status quo* powers have been attacked by revolutionary warfare against which they are more or less helpless, they have usually tried to combat it with the help of the military forces at their disposal. In the case of revolutionary movements backed by sovereign powers across the border, this implies the transformation of a purely internal war into an external one.

The latter tendency has been severely restrained by the existence of nuclear arms and the fear of nuclear "escalation"—a fact which has altered the power relations in favor of the revolutionaries and the revolutionary totalitarian Powers; but it has not been completely checked and neutralized by this fear. *Status quo* powers are searching for ways of bringing their external war potential to bear on the situation while minimizing the danger of nuclear involvement.

Revolutionary powers deeming it their right to encourage internal war in other countries consider it a crime when the latter turn these internal wars to external ones. Both revolutionary movements and revolutionary Powers seek to transform all external wars in which free states are involved into internal ones.

We may be reminded of a remark by Paul Valéry: "Opposite opinions about war stem simply from the uncertainty of an era—our own—about the following question: *what kind of human groups should make war on each other?* Should it be races, classes, nations, or other groupings as yet not discovered?"[7] These melancholy words—or are they facetious?—seem to picture well enough the currents in the contemporary world.

III

The World Crisis of the Mid-Twentieth Century

The history of the world is ... a continuous struggle between sense and senselessness, always waged and never fully decided.

—Friedrich Meinecke[1]

16

The Predicament of the
Developed Countries

*... it is apparently our fate to be facing a "golden age"
in the power of sorcerers who are totally blind to the
meaning of the human adventure.*

—JACQUES ELLUL[1]

I have so far tried to distill typical patterns from the record
of history. It is time to tie the various strains together, with
special focus on the world problems in the mid-twentieth
century.

It is "the nature of man to transcend nature";[2] hence, man
has since time immemorial changed his environment and
disturbed the balance of nature. Yet, throughout most of his
life on earth, he has done this piecemeal and very slowly.
After each interference the old equilibrium either has re-
asserted itself, with painful human losses, or man's innovations could be integrated into a new equilibrium. The whole
process was so slow that it was virtually unnoticed; the world,
for all practical purposes, seemed to be stable or round. It
was the essence of wisdom that man should strive to live and
die *in comformity with nature* and in accord with her
rhythm.

In modern times, however, Western men have embarked
on the *systematic conquest of nature*. There has been an
ever-accelerating process of *rationalization,* i.e., of substituting rational plan for the automatisms of biological mecha-

nism and social custom (tradition). This process has led to enormous successes in alloplastic adjustment, to an increasing control of external nature.

At the same time, moral impulses have worked toward breaking down ancient privileges and, later, restricting or breaking down new privileges which have been created in the very process of emancipation and rationalization.

Both developments together have made it possible that populations have multiplied, human life expectancy has doubled in less than a century, pain and backbreaking labor have been all but abolished, and steady further advances along this road can confidently be expected. These benefits have been distributed not only among the few but also among the many. The modern development, it may be said, has *enlarged the area of Life* and has forced the Empire of Death to contract.

But this process has also had some other, undesirable, consequences which seem to become less tractable as time goes on.

Every successful interference with nature leads to several new challenges, as was the case with the mythical Hydra who grew ten heads for every one that was cut off. This means, at the least, that stability and equilibrium are no longer possible. Men must now be continuously on the move—and at an ever-accelerating pace. There is "escalation" in the war with Nature and Culture. As the process accelerates, it is increasingly questionable how long it will be possible to deal satisfactorily with the emerging challenges.

As the modern process continues, these challenges multiply and the margin of error diminishes; more and more, man is in a situation in which a slight mistake can have the most dire consequence. As is so often the case, the higher forms of life are also the more vulnerable ones.

The modern development has probably passed beyond the point of no return; men would not be able to stop it without major catastrophe even if they desired to do so. They have to keep moving and to do so at an ever-accelerating speed. It is perhaps the bitterest irony of human history that at the very moment when man's power over nature surpasses the most exuberant dreams, he is losing the power over his own destiny and is becoming the puppet of his own creations.

But this may be reaching out into a still distant future. At this moment in time, the following liabilities of the modern process are particularly conspicuous:

1. A widespread *anomie* or spiritual malaise; more and more people feel the lack of meaningful goals in life.

2. The psychological difficulties created by a state of constant change even though the change may bring important improvements. Frustrations so caused lead to *discontent* and restlessness and give rise to the search for *scapegoats*.

3. The constant rationalist challenge of everything existing means, in the political sphere, the steady undermining of the ethos that holds the community together. That, in a time of widespread discontent, may mean permanent revolution; and since permanent revolution is not indefinitely tolerable, it may mean totalitarianism. Thus, in more old-fashioned but still quite valid terms, the political trend seems to be toward *anarchy or despotism*.

Ad. 1. In times of stationary cultures governed by traditional wisdom, there were simple answers to the question of the meaning of life. In the world of Hinduism, for instance, it was to fulfill the duty of one's caste and so to acquire the prospect of a more favorable reincarnation. In the European world of yesterday, it was to lead a "clean" life, to earn one's daily bread in obedience to the word of God, and to raise one's children in the fear of His law. Those who had done so were respected by their neighbors regardless of their economic or social position and they could feel that their lives had been worthwhile.

These answers are no longer satisfactory to moderns. But at the very time when the traditional answers fail to put the mind to rest, the demand for an answer is becoming more widespread and more pressing. For in earlier generations, most people had their hands full just to provide for themselves and their families, and as long as the struggle for survival is hard, the question of the meaning of life seems remote. To moderns, with overfed stomachs and with ample leisure, however, the question is real and urgent and the metaphysical needs are keenly felt.

For these metaphysical needs, the modern world offers the Gospel of Progress. Human life, it is held, acquires purpose and dignity from making a contribution to the ascent of the human race to ever greater, unimaginable, heights.

This answer is quite satisfactory at an early stage of progress when men just begin to emancipate themselves from an age-old crust of custom and myth and from the prohibitions of thought imposed by traditional beliefs, and when the intoxicating vision of limitless expanding horizons opens before them. In these circumstances the pioneers must have experienced immense exhilaration.

Such must have been the experience of Columbus when he reached land on his westward journey—land which he thought to be India—and so believed himself to have proved that the earth was really round. It must have been the experience of Pasteur when his surmises proved correct in an extremely critical moment and he was able to save a child who had been attacked by a rabid dog and seemed fated for a horrible death. Such must have been the experience of Freud when he realized that consciousness, which since Descartes had been believed to encompass all psychic life, was but a small part of it, while a major part of active psychic life was inaccessible to the naked eye, like the submerged parts of an iceberg, but could be made subject to systematic exploration.

Such experiences still exist where men venture out on uncharted paths, but they become rarer as the land becomes more built up. Old masters' paintings may still be discovered by a discerning connoisseur in a small-town antique shop, but it does not happen very often.

Except for the exhilaration of genuine pioneering, the question is bound to be asked: Where will it all lead? What is the end of it all? Is man in the world in order to run and keep running? Edward Bernstein said at the turn of the century with regard to the socialist movement: "The goal means nothing, the movement means everything to me." But that, too, was said at a fairly early stage; I doubt whether contemporary trade union leaders would find this idea equally inspiring.

The absence of meaningful goals may lead to a sense of disorientation. In some persons, it may lead to a desperate *quest for ideals,* which then are often accepted without too much discrimination of what is offered. In others, it may lead to a kind of *nihilism* that prides itself on being free of illusions, to a "flirting with Nothingness as though it were Brigitte Bardot," as Jean Rigaux called it;[3] in still others, it may lead to a *cynical realism,* the unashamed pursuit of self-interest as the only thing worthwhile.

When the spiritual malaise goes hand in hand with a passive attitude toward the world and the expectation that all answers will be provided from the outside, there results the now much-discussed phenomenon of alienation from society.

What in a minority appears as spiritual malaise presents itself in a majority as the question of *leisure*-time occupation. There has been much disappointment in some quarters about the fact that the masses have not used their newly won free time to perform classical music and to discuss Plato or, better still, to create comparable works themselves, but instead have indulged in the sensual pleasures of suburban living, in driving their cars to the "playgrounds of the nation," or in looking at canned entertainment on television. "The famous leap from the realm of necessity into the realm of freedom," complained the old socialist Ignazio Silone, "turns out ever more clearly to be a leap into the realm of laziness."[4]

Others have been more bitterly critical, blaming their disappointment on the greed of the "mass media" and the entertainment trade, or on that all-purpose scapegoat, "our society."

A number of authors give the question of leisure occupation high priority among the challenges of the time. Dennis Gabor considers the danger of nuclear war, overpopulation, and leisure the three great problems of our age.[5]

Ad. 2. The following are examples of problems created by rapid change.

(a) A condition of *open-ended* progress and a climate of opinion which considers everything possible if only inertia and vested interest can be defeated are likely to sharpen the sensibilities and to *increase the consciousness and impatience of suffering faster than remedies can be provided* even by the most progressive society. Given these conditions, desire is always a step ahead of satisfaction. Thus, people who enjoy far greater creature comforts than previous generations are actually more discontented then the latter were.

(b) In the area of moral aspirations, the goal has been set: either a "free" society, in the libertarian tradition; or a "just" society, in the egalitarian tradition; or the "good" society, in a more or less vague combination of both.

Experience has shown that the libertarian society, in which human beings are subject to few restraints in their dealings with each other, is a place of great inequalities of wealth and status; and only a small minority of people in the West (and only a minuscule few in other lands) uphold it as their ideal.

Equality, on the other hand, is not fully realizable. It could be maintained through voluntary cooperation only if nobody ever took advantage of a possibility to secure for himself a disproportionate share of rare goods, of power or of honor, i.e., if people purged themselves of all selfishness. But this is a utopian expectation. Enforced compliance, on the other hand, requires a new hierarchy of supervisors who can hardly be expected not to abuse their powers.

Thus, the movement toward equality does not seem to bring the goal much nearer. "You can chase unequal distributions out of one field after another, they will reappear in new fields."[6]

Moreover, inequalities, however small, in a society that

proclaims equality as its guiding principle, are more wounding than far greater inequalities in societies which openly uphold a hierarchical order.[7]

The goal of the just, or good, society is thus receding from our grasp like the hare in the mechanical race. The result is a state of *growing frustration*.

(c) Man's adaptive capacity is very great and it can probably be greatly increased by appropriate training, for instance, by an education designed to bring about *not adjustment to* particular conditions but a *maximum of adaptability*. With due allowance for all such possibilities, however, the adaptive capacity of man does not yet seem to be unlimited.

In a recent study of extremely alienated youth in America, Kenneth Keniston suggested that rapid social change may be among its causes.[8] I cannot judge the validity of this explanation in this particular case, but I see no reason to doubt that rapid change proceeding beyond a certain speed constitutes a severe strain, and that some people are likely to break under it.

(d) When this adjustment takes place, however, its results are not necessarily always desirable.

Modern society requires a high degree of mobility. People must change their place of abode and their habits of working and thinking quickly and repeatedly. This puts a penalty on any firmly shaped attitude and puts a premium on a high degree of flexibility and fluidity.

In the area of human relationships, such conditions are not favorable to the development of stable and deep relationships; rather they facilitate the extensive and superficial relationships which can be easily established and easily dissolved. Love, after all, is a commitment, and that means a loss of adaptability. He who loves one person has lost, or greatly diminished, his ability quickly to change over to another person.

The late Kurt Lewin, one of the protagonists of Gestalt psychology, was a German Jew who migrated to the United

States in the Hitler era. Like many immigrants, he was greatly impressed by the differences between the old and the new milieu and, as a scientist and a thinker, he tried to translate his bewilderment into insight and understanding. Among other things, he compared social relationships in the United States and in (pre-Hitler) Germany. He found

> . . . the average "social distance" between persons in the United States . . . to be smaller . . . in regard to more peripheral layers of the person. The more intimate "central" regions of personality seem to be at least as separated between different persons, and at least as difficult to get access to as among Germans. . . . Compared with Germans, Americans seem to make quicker progress toward friendly relations in the beginning, and with many more persons.
>
> [But these relationships do not often reach down to the deeper layers of the personality:] Yet, this development often stops at a certain point, and the quickly acquired friends will, after years of relatively close relations, say good-bye as easily as after a few weeks of acquaintance. . . . Several facts seem to indicate that the *most intimate* region . . . is generally less accessible in the [American] type than in the [German] type. . . . The most central regions are defined as the more intimate, personal regions. In these regions, the individual usually is more sensitive than in the peripheral.[9]

Thus, Lewin saw, on the one hand, American relationships, numerous and developing very quickly to a point of easygoing friendliness and ready mutual assistance in the management of the externals of life but rarely reaching great depth; and on the other hand, relationships in his old country, few in number and developing very slowly but sometimes reaching down to the depth of existence and not infrequently ending in tragedy.

While the greater ease of forming human relationships and their wider spread may impress us as a gain, the difficulty of reaching greater depth may appear as a loss.

What Lewin described seems to me to be of more general significance: it is the difference between human relationships in a society already far advanced along the road toward modernity, under conditions of great mobility, and human relationships in societies rising slowly from a stationary, semi-feudal mold—societies in which the old world still lives on and refuses to die. The Europe of today has probably moved much closer to the American—i.e., the modern—pattern than was the case at the time of Lewin's observations.

Nineteenth-century literature is full of stories which describe the tragedy of lovers whose union was prevented by external obstacles such as social conventions. This kind of motif seems impossible today; it does not strike us as tragic at all. We do not believe in "elective affinities"[10] sufficiently exclusive to rule out happiness with any other partner. Yet, the nightly embrace of Peter Ibbetson and his beloved in their dreams seemed tragic and moving only two generations ago.

One may indeed wonder whether deep and lasting relationships do not belong to stationary social conditions (or social conditions which change but little during a single lifetime) and have perhaps no place in furiously progressive societies in which everything must remain on a high level of adaptability.

(e) If and to the degree that mobility means that all can rise to the top according to their merits, unimpeded by fetters of caste, class, or tradition, the stage is set for an open competition in which, in the nature of things, only a few can reach the top while most people must be losers. The more society approaches the ideal of meritocracy, the more is it assured that the majority will know the *bitter taste of defeat* and humiliation. Thus, despite all body comforts guaranteed by society, most people "lead lives of quiet desperation," licking their narcissistic wounds.

Ad. 3. A progressive age is a time of great intellectual travail in which everything that exists is immediately questioned and challenged and the spirit of innovation reigns supreme.

The challenge may or may not extend to the fundamental principles, the ethos on which the existence and the functioning of the community rests. Socrates questioned everything, but he stopped short of the loyalty to his city, which he accepted as basic; the Sophists—if we can credit Plato's report —recognized no such limits.

Alexis de Tocqueville described democracies as being constantly given to innovations in secondary matters while holding the basis of the political setup inviolate:

> I do not assert that men living in democratic communities are naturally stationary; I think, on the contrary, that a perpetual stir prevails in the bosom of these societies, and that rest is unknown there; but I think that men bestir themselves within certain limits beyond which they hardly ever go. They are forever varying, altering, and restoring secondary matters; but they carefully abstain from touching what is fundamental. *They love change but they dread revolutions.*[11]

This is still true to a considerable degree (and contributes to the impression of conservatism which a country like the United States makes upon the world, in spite of its being in a state of perpetual flux); but the challenge increasingly extends to the basic ethos as well, though the letter of the Constitution is preserved and even held sacred. The new is, in fact, presented as a realization of the old, fundamental, values.

Be that as it may: the rising spirit of rationalist critique will not forever stop at closed doors and leave the ethos of the community unquestioned. *The door is thus opened to revolution—and to counterrevolution.*

In this aspect there is an important difference between free (or mildly authoritarian) societies, on the one hand, and totalitarian or severely authoritarian ones, on the other; more will be said on this in the next chapter.

CONCLUSION

Some people are confident that men will always be able to deal successfully with new challenges. Some, particularly in the younger age groups, face up to the future not only with sober confidence but with enthusiasm. It need not detract from an appreciation of the virility of their posture if one wonders whether they always grasp the full extent of the challenge.

What happens on the political level does not put these doubts to rest. We see, time and again, "experienced old hands" or New Frontiersmen descending upon, say, Washington or London, feeling their oats, confident that they have, if not necessarily all the right answers, at least the right approach to find these answers; and time and again, they have after a few years either merged into an anonymous bureaucracy or returned, with some ruffled feathers, to a privileged sanctuary in business, law, or academic life.

It is all as Michelangelo has shown in his statues of the Morning and the Evening (*crepusculo*) in the Medici Chapel in Florence: the Morning, a man of titanic physique, rising to conquer new worlds; the *crepusculo* sinking back in defeat, his body still imposing, a monument of past glory, but his muscles limp and the vigor all gone.

Perhaps, men will somehow triumph over all these and other difficulties. They will probably be able to do so for some time to come, but one wonders whether they will be able to do so indefinitely; *whether one can neglect indefinitely a part of man's totality*; or whether there will come a time in which the cost of advancing modern civilization will clearly outweigh any further benefits. The latter possibility was envisaged by T. S. Eliot:

> ... the indefinite elaboration of scientific discovery and invention, and of political and social machinery, may reach a point at which there will be an irresistible revulsion of humanity and a readiness to accept the most primitive hardships rather than carry any longer the burden of modern civilization.[12]

17

The Predicament of the
Western Democracies

In the preceding chapter I tried to enumerate some of the perils and liabilities of modernization. They apply, albeit in different degrees, to all societies which are fairly advanced along this road, viz., to the West, Japan, and the Soviet Union.

But the West also faces perils more specifically its own.

First, as the seat of democracy, the West is *wide open to subversion*. Freedom unleashes energies for both Good and Evil. Free societies reap benefits in the form of creative initiative of all kinds, intellectual, economic, and otherwise, but they are also subject to constant challenge to their institutions and their fundamental ethos, whereas totalitarian societies can nip all opposition in the bud, in the name of an absolute Truth which they claim to possess.[a]

The viability of free societies, therefore, depends on the ratio between the benefits of freedom and the dangers of freedom; and this not only in the long run but constantly because totalitarianism can transform a transient advantage into a practically irrevocable reality. Hence, free societies are at bay. Their increasing inner diversity tends toward anarchy, and behind anarchy looms despotism either as the do-

[a] Totalitarianism, in the modern context, can be seen as an attempt to put an end to spontaneous, centrifugal change without putting an end to change itself, i.e., to substitute centrally guided change for change brought about by the activities of countless individuals and groups.

mestic consequence of disintegration or through the triumph of an external totalitarian enemy.

Second, the West faces a *worldwide anti-Western movement* which is assuming revolutionary proportions.

The West gave birth to the idea of continuing progress. It set in motion the process of demythification and rationalization and produced a self-perpetuating science of nature and its continuous application to technology and medicine, the products of which are widely available through the expansion and rationalization of industry and commerce. On the moral side, it gave birth to the ideas of liberty and equality.

Since the West is the place where the challenge to tradition first developed and finally became institutionalized as part of its culture, the West is also the birthplace of revolution in the modern sense.

This revolution has now become worldwide, and in the process of expansion it has assumed an anti-Western stance which threatens the welfare and ultimately the political existence of the nations of the more advanced West. For precisely because the Western nations have been the pioneers and still are the protagonists of modern progress, they are now the wealthiest nations on earth; they can do many things of which others can only dream. Reshuffling of the sociopolitical order on an international scale, therefore, inevitably threatens the position, the way of life, and the prosperity of the Western nations.

For these reasons the West is forced into the position of the conservative power which opposes the sociopolitical revolution in the world. *The pressures of self-preservation are set against ideological inclinations* and the desire of many, particularly in the United States, to be not only in the forefront of modernization but also in the forefront of political revolution.

Revolutions have changed their character in recent times and Americans have been slow in noticing the change. Revolution once meant "the liberation of society from outworn political and spiritual fetters"; but in recent decades it has come to mean "the reshaping of society by a dictatorial regime in control of a centralized state apparatus and an all-pervading party organization."[1]

Americans call the emancipation of the American colonies from the mother country the "American Revolution." Revolution, in this context, means a single act through which an arbitrary government is replaced by a constitutional government, or government by laws, that is periodically answerable to an electorate. Once this goal has been reached, revolution, in this older sense, has been fully consummated.

In the Communist world and in the world of Latins, Asians, and Africans, however, revolution means a process of indefinite duration in which the existing social structure and culture are destroyed and replaced according to a plan; and this process is directed by an elite equipped with unlimited power and unencumbered by law or moral restrictions.

It was in the former sense that the word "revolution" acquired prestige in the Western world, and particularly in the United States, and the prestige so acquired seems to have adhered to the word even though its substance has changed. If a different kind of whiskey were sold in bottles carrying the name of a popular brand, the substitution would be detected in no time; but it seems to take several generations before people notice that a different idea is being sold under a reputable old name.

Although twentieth-century revolutions have little in common with the "American Revolution," the use of the same word has seduced many Americans into believing that the revolutionary movements of our time are similar in nature to those of the American colonies in the eighteenth century; they have assumed that a Nkrumah or a Castro is some kind of twentieth-century incarnation of Washington or Jefferson, and that Americans, by opposing these men, would betray their country's "revolutionary" tradition and become latter-day loyalists. The United States has therefore aided these modern movements, at least in their beginnings, to the detriment of her interests, both material and moral.

Some people think that American foreign policy was at fault, not in supporting revolutionary movements abroad but in not supporting them enough. They feel that if the United States had only sympathetically understood the revolutionary aspirations of other peoples, all would have been well. They overlook the fact that revolution as it has been understood by revolutionaries in Russia or China, Indonesia or Cuba, Algeria, Venezuela, or Chile, is diametrically opposed to all American tradition; that all American experience militates against the assumption that these revolutions can deliver the goods they promise; and that these revolutions directly threaten American self-preservative interests. These critics believe, against all modern experience, that preachers of violent revolution can be appeased by such concessions as the United States could make without destroying herself.

During the French Revolution, a royal prince, Philip, Duke of Orléans, resigned his title, assumed the name of Philip Egalité and joined the Revolution. He even voted for the execution of Louis XVI. All this did not save his life because what he had been was more conspicuous than what he pretended to be; his head fell under the guillotine. The various American attempts at appeasing Afro-Asian nationalism appear to me like attempts at playing Philip Egalité on a world scale; and they seem to me to hold no greater promise of salvation.

The worldwide anti-Western movement will in what follows be discussed under three headings: the hostility of the Communist (or other left-totalitarian) Powers, the resentment of the third world, and the censure of the moralists at home.

THE COMMUNIST HOSTILITY

Communist hostility against the West is an outgrowth of the Marxian theory of history reinforced by some native anti-Western traditions. According to the Marxian vision, history is the scene of a relentless class war to be transcended only by the establishment of a classless, Communist, society; and the West represents the capitalist bourgeoisie on an international scale.

This attitude was manifest in the first days of the Soviet regime. When the United States Ambassador contacted the Soviet authorities, an official bulletin reported the event as a visit from "a representative of American big capital."

However, some people believe that the hostility of the Communist world is purely reactive, a response to hostile acts or suspicious behavior on the part of the West, such as, for instance, the Western intervention in the Russian civil war; the long years of nonrecognition of Soviet Russia; the belated consideration, by Great Britain, of a stop-Hitler front that would include Soviet Russia, and the lack of enthusiasm in its execution once the attempt was made; the Western insistence, in San Francisco, on including Argentina in the United Nations; or the nonrecognition of Communist China by the United States, and other acts of a similar nature.

These explanations are based on a highly incomplete picture of events. A complete picture would have to include not only hostile acts of the West but also acts prejudicial to Western interests which preceded them. The intervention, for instance, was preceded by acts of this kind. Great quantities of arms which had been manufactured in the West, from scarce metal supplies, and transported in Allied ships, with great losses, through submarine-infested waters, were stored along the harbor of Archangel. The Soviet authorities had begun to move this material into the interior at the time of Brest Litovsk and there was apprehension lest it fall into the hands of the Germans and be returned to the Allies from the mouths of German cannons. It was a particularly menacing aspect of the Russian withdrawal from the Alliance which left the Western nations alone vis-à-vis the German onslaught. The original aims of the Western intervention were to prevent these arms and ammunition from falling into German hands and bringing death to Allied soldiers; and to bring about a government in Russia that would recognize the Alliance and continue the war. It is unthinkable that the West would have intervened in Russia if the Soviet government had stayed in the war against Germany, whatever its domestic policies might have been.

To give a complete picture one would also have to enumerate the friendly actions of the West such as the liberation of the Soviet Union from the German stranglehold after the Allied victory over Germany; the extensive help offered by private American citizens, with government approval, during the Great Famine; the British and American warnings of the impending German attack in 1941; and the great and probably decisive aid during the War in 1941-1945. It may well be argued that these actions were motivated by the selfish interests of the Western powers. This is true, but it is true only if we assume that the Western nations were prevented by moral sentiments from pursuing their interests with complete ruthlessness; for had they been without such inhibitions, they could have found other, equally effective, ways of safeguarding their interests.

But all these considerations are actually unnecessary because it must be clear to any student of Leninist thought that Communist hostility to the "capitalist" West is simply a consequence of its ideology, i.e., of its convictions. As the Marxist-Leninist sees it, history is the scene of a relentless class struggle which lasts until Communism has seized power and has liquidated the "capitalist classes," thus ushering in an entirely new era of history. Until this happens, all governments that are not Communistic are enemies by definition; even a coalition government in which the Communists hold the leading posts (e.g., the Czechoslovak government immediately after World War II) is still considered capitalistic. There is no way in which "capitalist," i.e., non-Communist, governments can permanently escape Communist hostility—except by always carrying out the policies demanded by the Communists and so eventually destroying themselves.

Inasmuch as Westerners have understood at all that Communism does not permit compromise except as a temporary expedient, they have often believed that ideological Communism of this kind has come to an end. There have been three periods so far in which this belief was nearly universal in "enlightened" Western opinion.

The first was the time of the New Economic Policy (N.E.P.). It was then widely assumed that Lenin had convinced himself that the Communist ideas were impractical, and that he was willing, or forced, to introduce some kind of market economy. No attention was paid to the fact that Lenin himself had said in no uncertain terms that the new economic policy was a temporary emergency measure and changed nothing in Communist goals.

The second period of illusion followed the victory of Stalin over Trotsky and lasted until the end of the Second World War. It was then widely assumed in the West that the goal of world revolution had been dropped and permanently replaced by the goal of "socialism in one country," i.e., that the Soviet Union was concerned exclusively with the construction of her own society, demanding from the rest of the world nothing but peace and security. As far as international relations were concerned, Russia seemed to have become a state among states, not fundamentally different from others. No attention was paid to the fact that, according to the official Russian version at the time, "socialism in one country" was merely a policy appropriate to the current phase of history, i.e., to the temporary reconsolidation of Western "capitalism."

The third period began with Khrushchev's policy of "peaceful coexistence." It has led to a degree of detente, particularly in Europe, which few expected at the turn of the decade. It is now widely assumed, at the time of this writing, that this time at last the Russian Communists have turned the corner, that talk of world revolution has become ceremonial oratory, and that the Soviet Union has become a state among states, exclusively concerned with her national interest.

Yet it is too early to judge whether the new turn will prove to be durable. Moreover, the Soviet leaders still claim it as their right to encourage subversion within the Western sphere of interest and to support "wars of liberation." And the leaders of Communist China are still in the grip of a pristine messianism.

Eventually, of course, one can expect that if "capitalism" and "socialism," or "democracy" and the "dictatorship of the proletariat," cannot eliminate each other, they will learn to coexist just as Christians and Moslems, or Catholics and Protestants, or Crown and Parliament have learned, after long and bitter struggle, to exist side by side.

It seems to be a universal phenomenon of nature that antagonistic forms of life which cannot eliminate each other eventually reach a biological equilibrium in which both can survive.[b] But even if the stage of coexistence between Western pluralism and Communism is reached, we should not expect Communism to denounce its universalist aspirations any more than Catholicism ever gave up its claim to be the only true religion; all we can expect is that Communists will not press their claim in day-to-day actions. For a Communist Party that completely discounted ideology and became purely pragmatic would thereby lose its power and raison d'être and commit suicide. Ideologically committed institutions can go a long way toward making tactical compromises, but they cannot give up the core of their belief and continue to exist. The Roman Catholic Church has made many compromises in the past; she appears to be prepared to make many more compromises at present. But the Church can never give up, for instance, the belief in the divinity of Christ, for in so doing she would cease to be the Catholic

[b] This is the case, for instance, in the relation between man and nocuous microorganisms. The introduction of such organisms into a population not previously exposed to them leads to disastrous epidemics. Yet, after a few generations the illness loses its virulence and a stage is reached in which both host and parasite survive. We assume that this is probably due to the fact that the human organisms most susceptible to the illness and the most virulent invaders are both eliminated through the epidemic itself, leaving only less susceptible humans and less virulent microorganisms as survivors and that the respective mutants have superior survival value.

Church and become a Unitarian association; there would then be no more need for the Church.

The Communist claim of a monopoly of power is based on the belief that the Communist Party, and the Communist Party alone, can make policy in a "scientific" manner because it alone is in possession of the scientific knowledge of the laws of history. In the eyes of a Communist, the Communist Party differs from all other parties, just as the medicine practiced by a scientifically trained physician differs from the exhortations and administrations of the tribal medicine man. The power of the Communist Party rests therefore on the claim of the Marxist ideology to be the true science of history; without the latter, it would be a party like any other party, groping its way, muddling through, and blundering—sooner or later to be overthrown.[c]

An ethos such as this may be eroded in time—usually a very long time—but an institution born in fanatical belief and having acquired tremendous power will not be inclined to discard the doctrine that has led it to such heights merely on the ground of incongruous facts.

The Communist hostility toward the West is dangerous on account of two circumstances, viz., the existence of pro-Communist forces in the West and in the Third World, and the nature of totalitarianism.

The first is the fact that the great Communist states, the Soviet Union and Communist China, are not only powerful nation-states, with all the perquisites of national sovereignty, but also centers of an international revolutionary movement. This double role enables Communism to attack its opponents in a kind of pincer movement, one claw being the power of the Russian or Chinese states, the other consisting of the internal pressure of pro-Russian or pro-Chinese forces within Western countries. The power of the Communist state can move against a Western country, while pro-Communist forces

---

[c] The unceremonious fall of Ben Bella in Algeria shows how easily in a purely pragmatic totalitarianism a regime can be changed by a palace revolution.

within impede the defense; or Communists within a Western country can prepare or initiate a revolution, while Soviet or Chinese military pressure prevents the authorities from acting against it. The latter was the case, for instance, in Czechoslovakia when the Communists rose against the democratic republic while President Benes was effectively deterred from suppressing the revolt by fear of Red Army intervention. The former was the case, for instance, when, during World War II, Communist sympathizers in the United States (of whom only a small number were actual members of the Communist Party) obscured the fact that the Soviet Union, while a temporary ally against Hitler, was nevertheless an opponent in the long run, and thus prevented American foreign policy from being adapted according to this fact.

The condition in which a country has an ally within the population of its adversary is not altogether new. At the time of the Peloponnesian War, there were aristocratic, or Spartan, parties in the cities of the Athenian coalition, and democratic, or Athenian, parties in the cities of the Spartan alliance. There was a Spartan party in Athens itself though not, visibly at least, an Athenian party in Sparta. Philip II of Spain was not only the external enemy of Elizabethan England but also the hope of English Catholics; had the Armada succeeded, they would have rallied to the invaders. The armies of the French Revolution had the support of the liberals in the countries they were fighting; President Wilson appealed to the German people over the head of their government, and his appeal may have weakened German fighting morale and so contributed to Allied victory.

The Communist pincer operation is therefore far from unique, but the game has perhaps never before been played so effectively.

The second factor that makes Communism a grave danger to the West lies in the rules of the game which are inherent in any struggle between free and totalitarian societies: every victory of the free society is provisional, subject to revision every day, while every totalitarian victory is irrevocable for a long time, probably for generations.

Communist or other totalitarian revolutionaries have tried to obtain power by legal or illegal means and have been defeated in their bids in many countries, for instance, in France or Italy, in Chile or Venezuela. They remain in a position to renew their bids for power at any moment they deem propitious; but when a revolutionary dictatorship, Communist or otherwise, has seized power, as in China or Cuba, it immediately proceeds to destroy all nuclei of potential resistance and to set up an effective system of supervising all activities of the citizens, measures which make the overthrow of the regime impossible until the time when the ruling elite itself disintegrates. The game between free and totalitarian societies is thus played under ground rules heavily loaded in favor of the latter. It is as if two chess teams were to engage in a permanent contest according to the rule that each time a player of team A loses a game he loses a point, while each time a player of club B loses a game he is disqualified from further participation. Unless the players of club B are so vastly superior to those of club A that there is no possibility of their ever losing a single game, it is only a matter of time until team A emerges as the victor because all members of team B will have been disqualified.

In the early days of the Communist world revolution, this condition was not adequately understood in the West; Western statesmen did not realize that a Communist seizure of power was, for all practical purposes, an irreversible event. At the present time, this fact is widely recognized, at least in the United States, and has led to frantic attempts to prevent Communist take-overs everywhere. This policy strains American resources to the utmost and is likely to create ill-will among third parties (e.g., Latin Americans) and to alienate other Western nations which do not feel immediately threatened. It may yet lead to situations in which the choice will be between two desperate alternatives: humiliating retreat and enlargement of military commitments with the dangers of escalation toward nuclear war. But whether un-recognized and accepted unaware, or recognized and resisted regardless of geopolitical possibilities—in either case the ground rules which make every Western success reversible and every Communist triumph irreversible have disastrous consequences. It is a factor of strength inherent in totalitar-ianism that it can use the freedom in democratic societies to its own advantage without having to reciprocate.

THE RESENTMENT OF THE THIRD WORLD

The hostility of the third, or underdeveloped, world seems to be more in the nature of resentment. It does not seem to make any difference whether a Western power has actually ruled over colonies, as have Great Britain, France, and other European nations (or, for that matter, Turkey and Japan), or has abstained from the competition for colonies, as the United States has done, with the exception of the aftermath of the Spanish-American War. On the contrary, anti-Ameri-can sentiment has so far expressed itself less in the Philip-pines, at one time under American rule,[d] than in Cuba, where United States intervention was brief and limited, far short of annexation, or in many countries of South America on whose soil no American soldier has ever set foot. Similar-ly, anti-British sentiment seems to be far weaker in India than in China, where Western rule never penetrated beyond coastal regions.

The sentiment does not seem to be the consequence of oppression or of iniquities endured, grave in proportion to the gravity of the preceding injustices; rather it seems to be due to humiliation experienced in relations with the West. It is easier to attribute one's unfavorable position to unfair play on the part of others than to inquire into one's own shortcomings. Eric Williams, Prime Minister of Trinidad,

[d] This may well be changing now with the coming of age of men who have no memories of American rule and whose ideas and feelings are therefore ex-clusively determined by abstract ideas and fantasies, free from contamination by facts.

for instance, tried to prove that the Industrial Revolution in England was financed by the income from the slave trade. Thus, while Negroes did not inaugurate the Industrial Revolution, it was they who made it possible through their tribulations.[2]

This kind of resentment, though potent with germs of violence, does not stem from philosophical dogma, as does the antagonism of the Communists. It derives from ordinary human relations and is therefore subject to influence by human relations. In many cases the gulf is daily bridged by personal relations, while the objectivized hatred of the Communists rarely is.

Above all, the "underdeveloped" world is not homogeneous; it is split by countless antagonisms—tribal, ethnic, religious—which are often more intense than the resentment of the West. There is bitter conflict between Hindus and Pakistanis, between Malaysians and Indonesians, between Arabs and Negroes in the Sudan, between Hindus and Negroes in Guiana, between different African tribes. These inner antagonisms make a united front against the West unlikely; moreover, some countries or groups are not disinclined to call for Western help against their neighbors or against rebellions in their own ranks.

The so-called Negro revolution in the United States represents a special variant of the resentment of the third world. The Negro situation is the tragic heritage of the transportation of Africans to America to work as slaves on American plantations. Slavery is one of the many historical examples in which men have used other men exclusively as a means to their own ends, without any regard for their will and their unhappiness.[e] In the present climate of opinion, slavery is

---

[e] Our age condemns such practices unequivocally and considers them to be monstrous crimes. Yet, on closer inspection it turns out that it does so only when the master derives personal wealth from the procedure; it is quite lenient in the now common and hardly less cruel procedure of using others as building stones for ideological ends, where masters derive for themselves not privately owned goods but the satisfactions of unlimited power and of a virtually godlike position as the creators of future history. Unwavering in its condemnation of the crimes of greed, prevailing opinion is all-forgiving with regard to the crimes of self-aggrandizement.

commonly looked upon as a crime committed by whites against blacks. In fact, responsibility for it should rest equally on the African chieftains who sold these unfortunates to the slave traders, the European traders who bought and transported them under inhuman conditions, and the American planters who bought and used them; credit for their emancipation, on the other hand, can be claimed, essentially, by whites.

The course of events has followed the pattern described earlier in these pages. As long as the dominant group was united in purpose and unquestioningly convinced of its right to rule, the subjects accepted the situation as inevitable and, in some degree at least, incorporated the ethos of the ruling group. This is shown by the fact that light mulattos enjoyed a higher prestige in the Negro community than blacks.

When the whites began to doubt their right to be masters of the Negroes, the slaves were emancipated. From then on, there has been a constant interaction between guilt feelings and compassion among whites and upward pressures of Negroes. In accordance with de Tocqueville's analysis, a revolutionary situation was reached only when social differences had lessened considerably and a large, educated, Negro middle class had developed which did not have to worry about its daily bread and thus became primarily concerned about status.

There are many who believe that the Negro problem, the open wound in American society, can still be healed by giving full equality of human dignity and professional and social opportunity to American Negroes. This may turn out to be an illusion. Equality, presumably, means color blindness on the part of the whites. Color blindness already exists in many aspects of American life and, probably, will soon extend to all but one area; for some time now there has even been color consciousness in favor of Negroes in matters of employment and promotion in some places such as the Federal government, the great Northern universities, social agencies, and related institutions.

The area, however, in which color blindness is unlikely to become widespread in the foreseeable future is that of unselfconscious personal friendship and, in particular, marriage. Most white Americans are still unwilling to welcome Negroes as in-laws. The readiness to do so would be a surrender of ethnic identity which cannot be reasonably expected in an age of universal nationalism when far smaller differences, such as those between Germans and Poles, or Germans and Czechs, or Greeks and Turks, have proved intractable. Marriage taboos between, for instance, Gentiles and Jews have long outlived political, occupational, and social inequalities. But in the latter cases, the taboo was mutual; there was as much opposition to intermarriage among Jews as there was among Gentiles, and possibly more of it. In the above cases we are speaking of groups which have a strong common ethos and tradition; among the American Negroes, however, a special ethos and collective pride are still rare. The absence of a pre-American past as a source of collective pride, and of native institutions as a source of continuous moral support (as was the Church for the Irish, the Jewish community for the Jews, or family cohesion for the Chinese) marks the difference between the situation of the Afro-American and the situation of other ethnic groups which were at one time at the bottom of the social hierarchy, and gives the former its particular severity. Under such conditions, it is questionable whether equality that stops short of personal relations and the marriage bond will be satisfactory to Negroes.

Moreover, there is another important open question. Full equality of opportunity is *beneficial* to a group *only if its achievements grow as fast as barriers fall and doors are opened,* or at least follow it with but little delay. Thus, integrated schools will be beneficial to Negro children only if the distribution of achievement among them is about the same as among their Caucasian classmates; it would not be beneficial if it turns out that the majority of Negro children end up at the lower levels of the class. The opening of all doors of opportunity will be beneficial to Negroes only if they soon make an equal contribution to the significant aspects of Western civilization—science, technology, medicine, business organization. If this happens, all may yet be well and Negroes may be satisfied living as partners in our civilization even though it was not created by Africans. But if Negro achievements remain for a considerable time below the level of Caucasian achievements, the result could be disastrous. Their failures would lead to further self-doubt in the Negroes, and since human beings of all races have little inclination to look in themselves for the causes of their disappointments, the result may be violence.

THE CENSURE OF THE MORALISTS

There is in Western countries, above all in Great Britain and in the United States, a continuous barrage of moral criticism; "society" or the "Establishment" are denounced, debunked, and castigated, with a virulence reminiscent of a Jeremiah or a Savonarola. The particular frequency of these ideas in the English-speaking countries is probably due to the fact that the expectation of universal innocence, which underlies these criticisms, can be entertained only in countries which have enjoyed extraordinarily high security.

These critics may be called moralists in the sense that they have set themselves up as judges of the morals of others. There are moralists of the Right and moralists of the Left. The content of their criticism differs, the vituperativeness does not. A famous evangelist was recently reported to have said: "If God does not soon do something drastic to America, He will have to apologize to Sodom and Gomorrah."[3] A well-known left-wing writer stated: "Woe to the Germans silent under Hitler, woe to Americans silent today."[4]

There is an incessant outpouring of publications of this kind. Some of them claim the authority of "science"; all of them are replete with self-righteousness and moral indignation. Some are brought forth together with vigorous protests against allegedly overwhelming pressures toward conformity in American society, an accusation which, to my mind at least, seems invalidated by the very fact of these publications and the continuing prosperity of the authors. As one English observer recently put it: "Protesting against the uniformity of American life is one of the most prosperous intellectual industries of contemporary America."[5]

The targets of the Right are the sins against the Ten Commandments: the decline of religion, the divorce rate, the loss of respect for one's elders, juvenile delinquency, sexual licentiousness. The targets of the Left are the inequalities in Western societies, and such impairments of freedom as interfere with the activities of the Left. More recently, since the end of American isolation under the umbrella of the Pax Britannica and the consequent emergence of an American military establishment, real or alleged militarism has become another target.

By and large, one can say that morality, for the Right, means the utmost restriction or control of sensual desires, while for the Left morality means the guarantee of their utmost satisfaction for all. There was a time when the moralists of the Right were on the offensive: the days of Torquemada and Savonarola, of Calvin, of Cotton and Increase Mather. There are traces of this type of moralism in contemporary China. But in the Western world today, the moralists of the Right fight rearguard actions, while the moralists of the Left are engaged in a full-scale offensive.

The position of the moralists is basically similar in England and in the United States, with some local differences. What I shall say about American moralists applies with slight variations to their English opposite numbers as well.

A large part of the accusations of the moralists comes down to this: that the people are concerned primarily with advancing their own interests and those of the people close to them—as a rule, family and friends; i.e., that the average American is what the French call *l'homme moyen sensual,* the average sensual man—"the masses live for the satisfaction of desires," as Aristotle put it—and that he does not pay enough attention, in the eyes of Rightist criticism, to the law of God, or, in the eyes of Leftist criticism, to the service of his less fortunate fellow men. But this is hardly an exciting discovery; it might have been taken for granted all along.

A favorite device of the Western critic of Western culture is the attribution of common human traits to Western, or to American, civilization. Since the dawn of time, observers of human events and critics of human affairs have noticed certain characteristics of men, or at least of most men: their concentration on their own interests rather than on those of others, and on sensual satisfactions rather than on concerns of a higher order, their short-sightedness, their temptability, their vanity, and their self-righteousness. Aristotle spoke of the "inexhaustible depravity of men," Baudelaire of their "eternal and incorrigible barbarity." Hamlet enumerated in his monologue the many injustices such as "the insolence of office and the slights that quiet merit of the unworthy takes" as arguments for suicide. Such traits have been ascribed, in naturalistic terms, to man's animal nature, or, in Christian terms, to the corruption of human nature through original sin. Men with a scientific bent of mind have described them and have offered various explanations of them. Men with a moralist bent of mind have preached against them and have issued their exhortations and condemnations. But they all knew that these were *human* characteristics and *human* failings. More recently, however, the most vocal sector of the American intelligentsia insists that they are characteristics of *American* society, features of *American* culture.

Thus, if acts of violence have occurred—if a President has been assassinated; if some individuals have been killed in the course of passionate political strife; or if some criminals have shot down a whole family for the sake of a small amount of loot—we are told that violence looms below the surface of *American* culture. If official words do not always wholly dovetail with deeds, if actions are rationalized in moral terms and idealistic motives are put in the foreground while selfish ones are played down, we hear that hypocrisy is inherent in *American* culture.

The poet, Randall Jarrell, for instance, complained about what he believed to be the unfavorable situation of intellectuals in American society and stated: "If you are so smart, why aren't you rich? is the ground bass of our society—a grumbling and quite unanswerable criticism since the society's non-monetary values *are* directly convertible into money."[6] The ground bass of *our* society? Let us hear what an ancient writer, Aristotle, tells us about the criticism encountered by Thales, the first of the Ionian philosophers of nature:

> The people had contempt for Thales on account of his poverty which in their opinion showed how useless his philosophy was. But once, so the story goes, Thales foresaw on the basis of his astronomical studies that there would be a rich olive harvest and as he happened to have some available cash, he leased in the winter all available oil presses in Miletos and Chios; he could secure them cheaply as there was no higher bidder. When the harvest time came around, there was great demand and Thales sublet them at his terms, made much money and thus showed that philosophers could easily be rich if they put their minds to it, but this just did not happen to be his interest in life.[7]

The story is age-old. What is specifically Western and, in particular, American is only the fact that intellectuals are no longer really poor; quite a few of them are rather well-to-do.

Or, we are told by a reputable author that "our society . . . increasingly dissociates sexual performance from the wholeness of the self."[8] One is led to believe that in other societies, past or present, men have never cohabited for any other reason than the highest expression of a harmony of souls.

This implication is all the more misleading since a comparison of sexual life in "American society" and in European and even more in Asian countries will probably, on the whole, turn out to be favorable to the former: because the deepest degradation of sexual life, prostitution, has been reduced to marginal proportions, puberty is provided with an outlet through institutionalized dating, and bachelordom is very rare.

A sociologist from one of the country's most prestigious universities writes:

> Children have been chronically misused, abused and exploited in American society. . . . In recent years, Americans have developed a refined form of captivity and exploitation of their children as hostages in the adult war for status and prestige.[9]

No doubt, things which can be so classified—and worse things—have occurred in this country, as they have in other countries. Nobody has ever systematically investigated their relative frequency and severity in different "societies," but I doubt whether the American people would emerge from such investigation in a particularly unfavorable light. European observers of the American scene, both immigrants and visitors, have often noticed how child-centered American life is, and have commented on it, favorably or unfavorably, according to their attitudes.

The *habit of attributing common human failings to Western* civilization in general or to *American* civilization in particular goes hand in hand with the *refusal to give the latter any credit for its specific achievements.* Thus, Mr. Irving Howe, prominent writer on sociopolitical questions, says, with reference to somebody's remark about saving the West: "What is this 'West' that is to be saved? The Salk vaccine or Jim Crow, anesthesia or torture, Shakespeare or Spillane, the seven-hour day or child labor?"[10] Western civilization, as the reader must realize, is a very dubious thing.

The impression is achieved by *lumping together Western achievement with common human failings and sins:* the Salk vaccine (i.e., scientific medicine) is exclusively Western, while Jim Crow (i.e., caste distinctions) is found in all civilizations and in some (e.g., in Hindu civilization) extends much farther than in the West; anesthesia is on the whole a Western invention, while torture has occurred in all societies; Shakespeare (i.e., high-quality literature) belongs to high civilizations, Western and Eastern, while Spillane (i.e., low-quality literature) is ubiquitous; the seven-hour day (i.e., leisure due to high-level technology) is a specifically Western achievement, while child labor (i.e., the abuse of defenseless children) is recorded in all societies.[f] In this way, the achievement of the West is effectively obscured.

These examples can be multiplied from the daily publications of a vocal and influential minority. Alfred Kazin remarked recently:

> What Socrates attributed to the passions and Montaigne to human vanity, Dostoevski to spiritual servility and Kierkegaard to the fear of self-contradictions, we attribute to the American character, the American economic system, American nursery schools, American sexuality, American breast fetishism—and at a pinch, if we are of the right sort, Calvinism along the Southern frontier.[11]

If the Church Father who said the famous words: *intra faeces et urinas nascimur*,[g] had been a contemporary American intellectual, he would probably have qualified his statement with the words: "in American culture."

The incessant outpouring of this kind of literature, presented with an implicit claim of moral and intellectual superiority, has already succeeded in painting the picture of a civilization which, on the whole—and it is on the whole that things must be judged, as Winston Churchill has reminded us—has probably been the most humane among those that men have so far built as the home of wickedness.

The sins with which Americans are charged by moralists —selfishness, greed, lack of concern for others—are what Christian philosophy called the *sins of incontinence*. With

---

[f] It would, of course, be possible to pair the characteristic achievements of the West with its *equally characteristic shortcomings and defects* as I have earlier tried in the discussion of assets and liabilities of progress (Chapter 4). In this way, the question of the merits and demerits of the Western way of life in comparison with other forms of civilization can be raised. But the technique exemplified above makes any rational discussion of this question impossible.

[g] We are born between feces and urine.

regard to more severe failings—cruelty, perfidy—the American record compares rather favorably with the records of other lands; and even with regard to the sins of incontinence, a verdict—if a verdict there has to be—would have to take into account the long record of American generosity, not equalled anywhere else,[h] and the exceedingly short memory of the American people for iniquity suffered, i.e., their complete inability to hold a grudge against anybody for any length of time. It is therefore somewhat odd that Western moralists train their guns primarily on those who, while certainly sharing in the flaws of human nature, have, on the whole, sinned less than most others, and have made serious efforts at repairing many of the sins which they have actually committed.

While one part in the moralist's bill of particulars is thus composed of common human failings—original sin, in the Christian view, the instinctual nature of man and his less than complete socialization, in the naturalistic view—another part consists of the undesirable features which are the reverse side of the coin of modern progress. The latter aspect has been extensively treated in previous chapters.

One example may show how both charges can supplement each other so that one takes over where the other leaves off:

Americans are accused of being "status seekers." So of course they are; it is hard to see what else they could be. All men are status seekers—intellectuals, preachers or guerrilla fighters no less than athletes, officers or businessmen; only their areas of competition and their prizes vary. In a story presented in the form of an Indian legend,[12] Thomas Mann gave a delightful description of the ferocious struggle for status among the hermits in a forest, and the contempt with which one hermit looks on the bed of nails of another.

Max Weber saw society, in Reinhard Bendix's formulation, as "composed of a composite of positively or negatively privileged status groups that are engaged in efforts to preserve or to enhance

---

[h] Where but in the United States could it happen that the widow of a political assassin finds herself suddenly transferred into a state of relative affluence by the charitable contributions from the public?

their present 'style of life' by means of social distance and exclusiveness and by monopolization of economic opportunities."[13]

V. C. Wynne-Edwards, a prominent student of animal life, suggested that status differentiation characterizes not only all human society but animal society as well; *society came into being* when ruthless intraspecific rivalry became conventionalized into status competition: "the society is not more and not less than the organization necessary for the staging of conventional competition."[14]

In preliberal caste societies these strivings were kept within rigid confines of law and custom. But once caste barriers broke down and there was social mobility, the lid was off. It is consistent for men with a conservative, aristocratic philosophy like T. S. Eliot to despise the competitive melee, but it is absurd if the moralists of the Left demand ever more social mobility and then castigate "our society" for the ensuing scramble for better places.

The moralist may justify his paradoxical selectiveness in the choice of his target on the ground that he is fighting for the Right in his own habitat and all men of goodwill everywhere should do the same in theirs. But the constant denunciation, by Americans, of their "society," not accompanied and balanced by a proportionate denunciation of similar, or far greater, ills in other countries, inevitably creates the impression throughout the world that the United States is a particularly wicked place. The moralists do not seem to feel that they have any responsibility for having created this image.

But all this may still be relatively harmless. It might even be useful in the sense that all criticism, including unfair criticism, can stimulate self-criticism; there is always room for improvement. Perhaps, it may be argued, the inherent good of criticism more than compensates for the bad name that the moralists are giving America abroad.

It is less harmless, however, that many moralists, in their fight against the real or alleged sins of their society, adopt and idealize some other group or society and hold it up to their own. An early example of this kind of propaganda is provided by the Roman publicist and historian, Publius Cornelius Tacitus. He bitterly castigated Roman society of his time. He then wrote a book about the customs of the Germans in which he contrasted their alleged pristine purity and unflinching dedication to the common good with the vices of Rome. This book is a masterpiece of literature, but as history or anthropology it is misleading. The corruption which Tacitus attributed to Rome was probably real enough, but the virtues of the Teutonic tribes were pure imagination; whatever vices Rome was guilty of could be found among the Teutons in the same, and perhaps in greater, measure.

The historical consequences of Tacitus's pamphlet were disastrous. When nationalism reached Germany on its triumphal way across the globe, the Germans found in Tacitus the basis for their national myth: the strong, virtuous, and unsophisticated Germans confronting a rich but rotten, decaying, pseudo civilization. Tacitus's *Germania* was common reading in the German gymnasium and the educated strata of the nation were thus indoctrinated with this potentially poisonous Teutonic myth which derived special authority from the fact that it came from a foreigner. At first, France seemed to fit the role of the foul, oversophisticated center of vice;[15] later it was the Jews, and the myth, elaborated time and again in popular literature, probably had its share in giving German anti-Semitism its extreme viciousness.

Tacitus was not the last to idealize another group in the service of moral criticism of his own society. The practice becomes particularly dangerous when the object of idealization is an enemy of one's society; and it becomes paradoxical if the object of idealization displays to the nth degree the very traits for the minor manifestations of which one is castigating one's own society.

We thus see the paradoxical attitude of those who condone tyranny on the part of their country's enemies and condemn the slightest restriction of liberty at home without allowing for the fact that the latter may be defensive rather than offensive, i.e., that it may be but a reaction to the threat of the former. The intolerance toward minor restrictions of liberty at home is presumably based on uncompromising dedication to the ideal; the apology for its complete abandonment abroad, however, is presumably broadminded; one must not be ethnocentric and must understand an antagonist on his own terms. The moralists, of course, have never considered applying this principle to their domestic enemies.

Perhaps the puzzle permits of a rather simple solution. These are people who have always felt that "dissent" from everything official—except the officialdom of which they are themselves a part—is both their moral duty and the justification of their existence; they see themselves at war with the Establishment (or, rather, with the other partners of the Establishment). And as warring parties do, they are on the lookout for allies; the enemies of their country therefore become their natural allies, according to the principle: the enemies of my enemies are my friends. The greater the war hysteria, the less selective people are with regard to their allies.

There is no degree of cruelty or perfidy that would disqualify a man or a regime from being built up by Western moralists as a paradigm of virtue and an innocent victim of Western wickedness, and no degree of absurdity that would disqualify an argument from being used by moralists in the denunciation of their own society.

In this way there emerges a particular feature of Western society—inverted chauvinism. If the motto of chauvinism of the ordinary variety is: my country can do no wrong, the enemies of my country can do no right, the motto of inverted chauvinism seems to be: my country can do no right, the enemies of my country can do no wrong. Many people seem to derive from this a feeling of both intellectual and moral superiority. They feel intellectually superior because they never side with their government as, in their view, the herd of other-directed men is doing, and they feel morally superior because they act as judges of the mighty of their society.

Inverted chauvinism on the part of many Englishmen in the late 1920s and early 1930s substantially facilitated the renascence of a militant German nationalism by preventing the British governments from taking whatever modest measures they might have adopted to discourage it or to bolster English defenses. Malcolm Muggeridge described his experience in these years as a member of the editorial staff of the *Manchester Guardian:*

> It was Guardian doctrine . . . that our country was always in the wrong, and the vanquished necessarily in the right. This applied with particular force to the Germans who were, we insisted, being relentlessly ground down at the behest of the vainglorious French and their venal allies. It was to be hoped (we pontificated), it was greatly if not devoutly to be hoped, that wiser counsels would prevail, and men of good-will everywhere ensure that the great German people were readmitted to their rightful place in the comity of nations, among whom, otherwise, there could be neither peace, stability, nor true prosperity.[16]

This attitude changed only when it became clear that Hitler was *at once parochial* in his thinking *and expansionistic.* It seems that a nation can keep the support of Western moralists of the Left as long as it either holds to a defensive stance or pretext, no matter how parochial its outlook, or holds to a universalist philosophy, no matter how ambitious its expansionism. But it apparently cannot be both parochial and expansionistic at the same time and still keep the sympathies of the Left. Surviving Nazis may ponder that with some deception about their ultimate goals, they might have kept the good will of that powerful sector of Western public opinion for which the *Manchester Guardian* speaks, and so perhaps have conquered the world.

The Australian political scientist, Owen Harris, discussed what he called "Ways of Confusing Issues" common to ideologists. Among them he listed the application of a double standard, by many people in the West, in the assessment of the moral merits of the actions of Western governments on the one hand, and of their adversaries on the other. It is not only a matter of applying higher or lower standards; it is the method of selecting from the arsenal of partly conflicting moral principles for each case the one that permits the justification of the other side and the condemnation of one's own.[1]

The application of a double standard is, of course, nothing new; it always goes with bias. But, as Harris pointed out, it is more likely to mislead in the case of inverted chauvinism than it is in the ordinary garden variety of chauvinism:

> It is not only left-wing critics of the West who employ double standards; they also appear regularly in the arguments of its defenders. But this latter habit, however deplorable, and however much it deserves exposure, is hardly surprising, for people have always tended to give their own side the benefit of this way. *We are automatically on our guard against it* and make allowances for it. What is novel in the present situation is that people who insist that they are loyal to the West and what it stands for persist to operate the double standard in favor of communism.[17]

This attitude of a large sector of the nontotalitarian Left toward Communist totalitarianism was clearly illustrated in an article by the late Dr. Otto Bauer, leader of the Austrian Social Democrats (Austro-Marxists) and one of the founders of the so-called International Two-and-One-Half which in the period between the two World Wars held a middle position between the union-dominated, nonrevolutionary Second, and the Communist Third, International. The article was written in response to a parliamentary attack; the conservative Austrian Chancellor, Engelbert Dollfuss, had turned in a Committee meeting toward Bauer and had exclaimed: "You are a Bolshevik."

Bauer pointed out that he was not a Communist since it was his "conviction that socialism must not destroy the guarantees of individual intellectual freedom but must preserve this freedom, the most precious heritage of bourgeois revolutions, and carry it over into the socialist society of the future." He condemned the Russian rulers for forcing scholars to renounce their convictions

---

[1] At the very least, if no specific moral charges can be made, there is always the contradiction between the ideal of justice and the ideal of peace; for justice, however conceived, must be enforced against those who oppose it and its pursuit therefore jeopardizes peace, while it may be necessary for the sake of peace to settle for less than complete justice. It is thus always possible for the moralist to condemn his government: either for jeopardizing the peace, or for selling out on principle.

on the penalty of dismissal, arrest or exile and drew a clear dividing line at this point between himself and the Communists.

This having been said, however, Bauer emphasized his "indestructible hatred of capitalism ... of a social order which inevitably condemns in every decade millions of people to the most horrible misery, not because there is any dearth of goods but because it is not profitable to produce them." Therefore: "if the dictatorship of Russian Bolshevism would be forcibly overthrown, mankind would lose for a considerable time its faith in the possibility of another, higher, social order than capitalism, and the lifetime of capitalist barbarism would be prolonged." But he expected that if the Soviet dictatorship succeeded in the construction of socialism, dictatorship would become unnecessary and freedom would return.[18]

In short: Bauer was not a Bolshevik; he was opposed to Bolshevik tyranny, but *he hated capitalism far more.* Thus, when the chips were down, he had to side with the Soviets against the "capitalists."

This attitude seems to me to be typical of the stance of a large part of the nontotalitarian Left vis-à-vis Soviet power. In any serious conflict between the West and a Communist state these groups have, in effect, supported the latter, not because they were Communists—as many people on the Right had charged—*not because they liked Communism, but because they liked capitalism even less.* This is likely to remain so with all those who think of the Western market economy the way Otto Bauer did.

The extreme of these attitudes appears in the new radical Left. There we see men and women whose domestic policy is to step up revolutionary action against American society, which they consider profoundly evil—some, clearly, as evil beyond redemption; at the same time, their foreign policy is retreat before Communist pressure to whatever degree may be necessary to satisfy the Communists. The prevailing spirit is one of *unqualified condemnation of the use of force or threat of force in international relations and propagation of force in domestic affairs,* i.e., condemnation of international war and propagation of civil war.

This was the strategy recommended by Lenin during the First World War: to work for the defeat of one's own country and to turn the guns against one's own government. What these activists fail to see, or to consider, is that Lenin's policy put Russia at the mercy of Imperial Germany which would have reduced her to a colony (and with it have wrought havoc with all Communist plans), had the Western Allies not won the war against Germany within a few months and forced the Germans to disgorge their Russian prey. One wonders who would bail out a defeated America.

THE INTERACTION OF THE THREE OFFENSIVES

One may wonder which of these antagonisms is more dangerous than the others to the survival of Western societies. Those who pose this question overlook the fact that we are not dealing with independent threats, each autonomous in itself, but that each derives its nocuous potential from the existence of the others.

The Communist challenge would present no great danger to Western societies were it not for the fact that anticolonial resentment offers the Communists a chance to outflank and encircle the West and turn it into a beleaguered island, and for the further fact that a fifth column within Western societies could paralyze the defenders. If there were neither the reservoir of resentment in the third world nor the fury of the moralists at home, the only possible threat of Communist powers would be that of a frontal attack, a possibility which can be practically discounted as long as the West is militarily strong.

Similarly, anticolonial resentment would not jeopardize the security of the West were it not for the implicit threat that countries of the third world may become a base of operations for the Communist Powers, and for the internal dissensions within the Western camp; for in that case, the third world would lack the power to injure vital Western interests.

The steady gnawing of the moralists, finally, would constitute no great threat were it not for the existence of hostile forces abroad, both in the Communist and in the third world, standing in wait for the kill; without such external danger, it might even be beneficial because even the most patently unfair criticism may stimulate improvements.

There seems to me to be little reason to doubt that the West has the material and spiritual resources to deal with each of these challenges if it presented itself *alone*. Whether Western societies with their atmosphere of freedom and easygoing manners can survive[j] the simultaneous interacting onslaught from three quarters; whether they can survive a situation in which the metaphysical hostility of the Communist world finds in the resentment of the third world an opportunity for encircling the West, and in which every attack against Western interests is certain to be supported, with moral arguments, by a substantial part of articulate Western opinion—that is still hidden in the future.

THE DEMORALIZATION OF WESTERN SOCIETIES

While these offensives are going on, there are signs of disintegration of the ethos, or demoralization, at the core of free societies.

It has always been taken for granted by theoreticians as well as by constitution makers that the freedom of a citizen of a free country cannot mean his freedom to do as he pleases; there must be some forces of cohesion or else the system would explode. This cohesion was to be supplied by submission to legality—voluntary as far as possible, but submission in any case. There was a line dividing freedom under law from anarchy, and anarchy was believed to be a disastrous state of affairs that could not long endure and was likely to lead to despotism, hence to the end of freedom.

Freedom thus meant the right to oppose government policies with the spoken and printed word, to advocate the adoption of different policies or the election of different rulers;

[j] Survival, in this context, means *short-term* survival—perhaps for the next fifty years. But the above considerations have little to do with the long-term prospects of modern civilization which have been considered earlier in a different context (Chapters 7 and 16).

and the citizen had the right to win friends and influence people for this purpose. But it did not mean the right of the citizen to take the law into his own hands, i.e., to disobey laws of which he did not approve, or to organize people for the purpose of breaking the law.

Whenever a substantial number of citizens, particularly in the higher echelons of power, deem it their right to resort to unconstitutional means when they cannot fulfill their aspirations within the constitutional framework or cannot fulfill them fast enough—i.e., whenever the fulfillment of one's aspirations has precedence over the maintenance of constitutional process—then constitutional government has actually ceased to function and civil war has begun.

Moral philosophers have always upheld the right of the citizen, on the basis of natural law, to disobey *tyrannical* authority and to defend himself against arbitrary power. But this right was claimed only in those situations in which the rulers were clearly tyrants; and that meant, among other things, that they had left no room for the expression of opposition and no legal remedies for the redress of grievances. That citizens should have the right to disobey laws in a country in which governments are chosen at regular intervals by free elections, in which there is a constitution guaranteeing basic rights and an independent judiciary upholding the constitution, (or reinterpreting it in favor of the reform-minded), a free press, and trial by jury, has never been suggested by anybody except anarchists.

Yet, we see today that in Western countries, and particularly in the United States, civil disobedience is widely considered a legitimate political weapon within a democratic commonwealth if those disaffected feel that the legal machinery for the redress of grievances has not worked or has not worked fast enough. Moreover, even this view is still too conformist for the radicals of a younger generation. They seem to look upon civil disobedience not as a weapon of last resort, as *ultima ratio*—as force always has been under civilized conditions—but as the *first, or immediate,* reaction to any state of affairs which they consider unjust, or to any decision, however trivial, of the authorities of which they do not approve. Others go farther still and proclaim a right to resort to violence whenever the constitutional process has not worked to their satisfaction. The characteristic of the state, according to Max Weber, is a monopoly of legitimate violence; whenever violence is wielded by others and not looked upon as crime, the state has ceased to exist. It now appears that such attitudes are endorsed, or at least condoned and in any case abetted, by a sufficiently large part of the rulers to make it difficult or impossible to uphold the law.

As always when high principles are proclaimed, the question remains whether those who advocate the anarchic concept of freedom actually believe in it as a matter of their political philosophy or merely use it as a weapon in the political struggle, exploiting the uncertainty and the doubts in the minds of their adversaries in order to demoralize them.

Such questions can usually be answered with the help of a mental experiment. Are those who insist on the right of every citizen to disobey unjust laws, which in practice can only mean those laws which he deems unjust, are they willing to grant this right to their political adversaries—say, to conservatives who consider it unjust that the power of taxation should be used for a redistribution of income? Are they willing to concede them the right to withhold their taxes? If they do so, they are genuine anarchists; if they don't, they are merely engaged in psychological warfare.

Cyrus Sulzberger once asked: "At what point does an open society become a naked society?"[19] The most articulate sector of the Western intelligentsia seems to insist that society, or at any rate Western society, must be a naked society.

There seems to be a spectrum of opinion among the adherents of the new philosophy and their defenders within the Establishment. There is a core of activists who have no taste whatever for anarchy and are merely waging war against the political order with a view to destroying it and setting up their own order, which would be anything but anarchic; and there are their supporters and sympathizers who are themselves not full believers in the new ethos but merely demoralized ex-believers of the old one. The whole pattern corresponds to what I have earlier described as a situation with a revolutionary potential.

Of course, revolutionary pressures of the kind discussed in these pages and elite disintegration may stimulate the rise of a countermovement and the moderate or politically indifferent masses may seek shelter with a radical Right. In this case, not revolution but counterrevolution would be the order of the day. Free institutions would be doomed either way.

18

The Predicament of the Communist Countries

If the West is dedicated to progress, the Communist world is so with a vengeance. If Westerners find it difficult to believe that progress in terms of certain values exacts a price in terms of others, Communists would consider the very idea scandalous and obscene and would not grant it a hearing. They would dismiss it offhand as reactionary ideology, i.e., as a device by which a decaying class, doomed by history, condemned equally by science and by morality, tries to hang on to its privileges.

While the West sees scientific and technological progress as the consequence of the accumulation of knowledge and skills, and sees moral progress as the result of an unending struggle between enlightened, progressive forces and the forces of bigotry, the eternal yesterday, Communists see progress on both scores as the consequence of a universal law of all life and all nature, built into matter itself: the dialectic ascent. Those who oppose progress are thus not merely evil but also, in the long run, condemned to inevitable futility.

In its moral aspects, progress is seen in egalitarian terms; a society of equals is about to be established, a society in which all men put the interests of society, which are assumed to be always clear and about which there can be no ambiguity, above all self-concern. There is no room for liberty in this picture, as liberty would only be the liberty to go astray from the right path; but it will have its place in the indefinite future when it can safely be granted, i.e., *when all people will want only what they should want.*

Egalitarianism, however, is strangely mixed with an extreme elitism. The Party alone knows what has to be done because it alone is in possession of the scientific knowledge of the laws of history, and everyone must submit to its leadership like patients to the orders of their doctors. The members of this elite have developed an arrogance at least equal to any ever shown by a priesthood or a mandarinate.

Upon seizure of power, the Communists see it as their first task to establish a totalitarian system of complete control over body and mind of all citizens. This technique was novel when it was first applied in Russia; the world had long forgotten what totalitarianism was. Communism probably owed much of its success to the very novelty of its actions because it took its victims unawares. Since that time, the method has been well standardized. Once the totalitarian system has been built up, it can no longer be overthrown except through an erosion of belief within the ruling group itself. That is a slow process, requiring, probably, several generations.

THE TENSION BETWEEN THEORY AND EXPERIENCE

While the Communist system, once established, does not suffer from the instabilities that plague free, or partially free, societies, it is confronted with a problem of a quite different nature. Free societies are not fundamentally committed to particular political, economic, or social forms, or to a particular set of beliefs; their commitment is to the *procedures* by which government is constituted and political decisions are to be reached. Communist society, on the other hand, is committed to a large and detailed *body of doctrine,* which to Communists appear as virtually self-evident truth; moreover, the Communist claim of a monopoly of leadership rests on the exclusive possession of this doctrine, and this fact must substantially diminish the Communists' perspicacity for the flaws in their argument.

But this doctrine—Marxism-Leninism—is a highly distorted mirror of reality and constantly leads to conclusions which are not borne out by the facts. Hence, there is in Communism a *perpetual tension between theory and experience,* between dogma and reality. "The history of the Communist world movement," said Richard Löwenthal, "is the criticism of its ideology by reality."[1]

In this unending conflict, Communists have attempted various solutions. On some occasions, they have proved flexible and have adjusted or reinterpreted doctrine so as to be able to respond adequately to facts; on other occasions they have held on to doctrine, disregarding facts almost to the point of seeming psychotic; at times they have even used their power to make the facts comply with their theory. The persistent ideological discussions within the Communist world are largely attempts to find new points of compromise between the conflicting claims of dogma and experience.

The cleavage between theory and reality has existed almost from the first day of Communist rule. According to Marxist theory, the capitalist system is exploitation of man by man, pure and simple. All "value" is produced by the workers; businessmen fulfill no productive function whatever. They are merely parasites who, thanks to their ownership of the tools, can extract tribute from the producers. Their role is equivalent to that of medieval robber barons who closed rivers to merchantmen and extorted tribute for passage.

If this is so, the expropriation of the capitalists should lead to an immediate rise in the income of the workers. When the strongholds of the robber barons were broken, the merchantmen could pass without paying tribute, and their fortunes improved by exactly that amount. If capitalists can no longer extract tribute from workers for the use of the tools, the income of the workers should rise by the amount that had previously been withheld by the capitalist.

There remains the question how great the tribute has been.

Marx leaves little doubt about it. In one example he calculated the surplus value at 100 per cent: "The worker worked one half of the day for himself, the other half for the capitalist."[2] Other examples suggest an even greater exploitation.[3]

If the worker received only half of the product of his labors, the end of exploitation would double his income. This should happen not in an indefinite future, after many efforts at "socialist construction," but practically immediately, i.e., after the few months that it takes from the actual production of goods to the influx of payments from the sale of the goods.

But this is not what happened. The workers' income did not double; in fact, it even diminished for some time, as Lenin himself noted. Perhaps one might expect that Marxists asked themselves the question: where is the surplus value? The capitalists can no longer take it away, where is it hiding? Perhaps, some doubt in the correctness of the exploitation theory of capitalist enterprise may then have sprung up.

But the Communists did not, and could not, ask themselves any such question; unaware of the economic problem as a problem of choice between alternative employments of resources, they saw in the labor theory of value and the exploitation theory of business enterprise not a theory subject to empirical verification or falsification but an *a priori* self-evident truth, somewhat the way we all look at the propositions of mathematics. If we put two dollar bills in our wallet in the morning, and add two other bills a little later, and at lunchtime find only three dollars there, we will not entertain the possibility that our arithmetic might be wrong and two and two might, perhaps, make three; we will assume either that we have somewhere spent a dollar, or that somebody else had taken it out, or that our memory of what we had put in originally was faulty. In a similar way, the Marxists could not conceive of the possibility that profit could be anything but the stolen product of labor; thus, if the surplus value was not there for distribution, it had to be due to some other circumstances such as sabotage, treason, civil war or whatever.

This is not to suggest that Communists are the only people in the contemporary world who hold on to doctrines in spite of adverse experience.

As far as democracies are concerned, the commitment to procedure is in itself rooted in deeply held convictions concerning the practicability and superiority of the democratic form of government. Americans, in particular, have held this doctrine in its pristine purity and have repeatedly made its introduction in other countries within the American orbit of influence a goal of foreign policy.

Yet, it should be clear on theoretical grounds alone that liberal democracy is a very difficult system to operate and that it presupposes specific conditions. Democracy is government by consent, with coercion kept at a minimum. This is possible only if people are willing to compromise; and this will be the case only if they feel that what they have in common is more important than what separates them. If this condition does not exist, the legal form of democracy merely institutionalizes a creeping civil war.

Actual experience with the introduction of democratic institutions into an uncongenial soil has borne out these statements. Latin American attempts at democracy have time and again been perverted or overthrown by dictatorships. Democracy in the Weimar Republic brought Hitler to power. The record of most new Asian and African states is similar. Yet, the American people do not seem willing to accept this fact.

The difference between the ideological commitment of a Communist and the ideological commitment of people in the Western world is thus a matter of degree. Above all, it is possible in free countries to challenge the ruling creed.

Discrepancies between theory and experience appear in all spheres of life. Theory sharpens the eye to the perception of some facts and blinds it to the perception of others; it will blind particularly when theories with a low content of truth are adhered to with passionate loyalty and fortified by strong prohibitions of thought.

Time and again in the history of Communism, the pressure of inconvenient realities has forced the rulers to make concessions at the expense of doctrine; and time and again doctrine has prevented them from perceiving facts accurately or from adapting to them. Agriculture is a prime example of this seesaw. On the basis of doctrine, one proceeds toward collectivization; when, in consequence thereof, agricultural production drops and the food supplies in the cities reach the danger point, the rulers make concessions to the peasants when the pressure is off, doctrine again takes over.

The power of doctrine over a sober view of reality can be seen in all areas. At the time of Hitler's rise to power, the large Communist Party of Germany, under the guidance of Stalin, considered it its main task to discredit and to fight the Social Democrats, the "social fascists" in the Communist parlance of the time. A parliamentary majority composed of Communists and Nazis forced the left-of-center government of Otto Braun in Prussia out of power. This majority, which could unite only for negation but not for cooperation, made parliamentary government in Germany unworkable, discredited it in the eyes of the people, and so prepared the way toward Presidential authoritarianism, which in turn facilitated, in the end, the rise of Hitler. It is questionable whether Hitler would have reached the top had the Left not been divided.

The Communist strategy was the outcome of the Marxist doctrine, further accentuated by Lenin, of the "homogeneous reactionary mass." Just as Lenin did not support a government of Mensheviks and Social Revolutionaries in 1917 but took an uncompromising maximalistic course, so did the German Communists in the totally different situation of Germany in 1932.

The utter destruction of the German Communist Party by the Nazis opened the eyes of the Communist leaders on this point; they then embarked on the policy of the "popular front," in a revision of the Leninist pattern.

Another example of the same kind is the decision of 1939 when Stalin preferred a pact with Hitler to participation, with England and France, in a stop-Hitler coalition. The Hitler-Stalin pact has been variously explained: sometimes it was seen as the consequence of Stalin's distrust of English and French intentions, a distrust aggravated perhaps by the ambiguous behavior of the Western powers during the Spanish Civil War, by their lack of enthusiasm for an alliance with Soviet Russia, and by their refusal to accept Soviet terms regarding the Baltic states and in other matters. At other times it was explained by a Russian desire to buy time so as to be able to complete her military preparations. Others have pointed at the attraction which, in spite of all enmity, one totalitarianism exercises upon another. There may be other reasons that have not yet been considered. Whatever the motives may have been, however, not enough attention has been paid to the fact that the policy of the Hitler-Stalin pact was quite consistent with Leninist doctrine, more so than the alternative policy of alliance with the West; it was shocking only to the liberal-minded. For the Marxist-Leninist, there was no important difference between England or France and Hitler Germany; they were just two competing camps of capitalist robbers. It was utterly incredible, on the basis of this doctrine, that England and France should enter into an alliance with the Soviet Union with any other purpose than to sell her down the river. In a view based on such an assumption, it may have appeared as a great triumph for Stalin's diplomacy to have succeeded in making the bandits fight each other instead of jointly falling on Russia. So greatly was Stalin impressed by this success that he told his Party only shortly before his death that they could repeat the performance: the next war was again to be a war between the capitalists.[4]

When, then, the unprovoked, treacherous German attack against the Soviet Union put an end to the Nazi-Soviet rapprochement, it did not put an end to the Communist belief in the fundamental sameness of "capitalism," which has its sturdy root in the Marxist-Leninist creed. All throughout the war, the Russians remained suspicious lest the war be "switched" and the Western countries turn around and join forces with Nazi Germany against the Soviet Union. The apprehensions, always latent, became most visible at certain moments, e.g., after the German attack when the Black Sea

Fleet was alerted to what could only have been an attack by the British Fleet, or at the time of Hess's flight to England, or toward the end of the war in Europe when Stalin notified Roosevelt that American commanders in Italy were negotiating, behind the President's back, with German commanders on a separate agreement which had already permitted the German generals to shift troops to the Russian front. Roosevelt was appalled and assured Stalin that no such negotiations were taking place, but Stalin insisted on the accuracy of his information.[5][a]

To us Westerners, it seems absurd that the men who ruled, for instance, England during the war—the Churchill Tories and the Labor Party—should have planned to turn around 180 degrees and ally themselves with Hitler; and even more

[a] There was an element of truth in Stalin's suspicions. American military leaders did not negotiate with German commanders, but the secret service —the OSS—which had all along cultivated contacts with dissident German groups, including potentially dissident groups within the Nazi hierarchy, was then in contact with a German group represented by SS General Karl Wolff who wanted Germany to surrender to the Western Allies alone in an attempt to keep the Russians out of Germany. These contacts were soon stopped by order from Washington.[6]

In private as well as in public life, extreme suspiciousness has almost always some real events to feed on; they are never lacking in the complexity and untidiness of human events. The prejudice lies in the onesided evaluation of evidence; some episodes which seem to bear out one's expectations are viewed through a magnifying glass, while all the rest is seen, if at all, through an inverted opera glass.

A similar case was the so-called "Copenhagen Complex" in Germany at the beginning of the century.[7] German leaders (including the Kaiser) were obsessed with the fear that the British might suddenly, without any declaration of war, attack the nascent German fleet and destroy it; such fears were ostensibly based on a faulty analogy with the British bombardment of Copenhagen and seizure of the Danish fleet during the Napoleonic wars. They could feed on occasional ambiguous statements and boasts made by officials like the First Sea Lord, Admiral Sir John Fisher, and the Civil Lord of the Admiralty, Arthur Lee; the latter had once said in a speech in his constituency that "the Royal Navy would get its blow in first before the other side had time even to read in the papers that war had been declared." Yet, an unprovoked British attack was never a real possibility; no British government of the time would have considered it and public opinion would not have countenanced it.

As Jonathan Steinberg has pointed out in his study of the Copenhagen Complex, the real basis for the German terror was the fact that the German leaders knew the vastness of their own ambition and therefore expected the British to react accordingly. I presume the same holds true of Russian suspicions at the time; the Russian leaders could not but assume that the West knew of the depth of their hostility and would react ruthlessly to thwart it.

absurd that if they had so willed, they could have turned British public opinion around at a moment's notice. But this is entirely plausible to a believer in Marxism-Leninism; for in his eyes, England, or any other "capitalist" country, was not ruled by men, with their convictions, prejudices, likes and dislikes, and ideals, their pride and vanities and their commitments, but by something impersonal called "the ruling class" which is conceived as pursuing, coldly and single-mindedly, an alleged class interest, totally unemcumbered by sentiments, morals, and loyalties, and in fingertip control of public opinion.

The weirdest example of the triumph of doctrine over observation is the Communist response to the extermination of the Jews under the Nazis. Marxism knows only class warfare, the struggle between owners and nonowners of the means of production, as the motor of history; racial or ethnic strife is a derivative of the class struggle or a diversionist maneuver of the capitalists. Marxists were therefore ill-equipped to understand Fascism in general and German National Socialism in particular; they saw it as a tool of the bourgeoisie in its struggle with the working class, an explanation which is only a half-truth in the case of Italian Fascism and altogether inadequate in the case of Nazism; it is entirely senseless when confronted with the phenomenon of Hitlerite anti-Semitism.

In the summer of 1932 when the danger of a Hitler regime already loomed large on the German horizon, I was once in a group of young, non-Communist Marxists. Conversation turned to a German playwright of Jewish extraction who, easily mobile by virtue of his profession, had just moved with his family from Berlin to Vienna to watch the course of events from a still safe distance; there was tremendous hilarity in the group over the fact that this man had taken the Nazi threats so seriously. How could one be so silly and not see that anti-Semitism was but a smokescreen and that, while poor Jews like all other poor would suffer grievously under "Fascism," wealthy Jews would be safe, and, indeed, profit handsomely?

These young people have certainly corrected their views

under the icy impact of experience. But in the Soviet Union, the paroxysmal Nazi anti-Semitism still does not exist because it has no place in the Marxist-Leninist universe of thought. Auschwitz was not a place for the "Final Solution" of the "Jewish Question" but a place where "Fascists" exterminated "people," Jews and non-Jews alike. When the Russian poet Yevgeny Yevtushenko wrote his poem "Babi Yar" in memory of the mass slaughter of Jews that had taken place in that locality, Nikita Khrushchev called him to task:

> The poem presents things as if only Jews were the victims of the fascist atrocities whereas, *of course,* many Russians, Ukrainians, and Soviet people of other nationalities were murdered by the Hitlerite butchers.[b] The poem reveals that its author *did not show political maturity and was ignorant of fact.*[8]

There was apparently no such thing as anti-Semitism in Nazi Germany. Khrushchev pointed out that when Field Marshall Paulus was captured with his staff, a Russian Jew who had served as an interpreter was captured with them. It all turned out according to pattern (to Khrushchev's satisfaction, in any case): the Jewish proletariat, like the proletariat of other nationalities, massacred; the Jewish bourgeoisie snugly in the camp of Hitler.

While there are examples of ideology prevailing over experience and common sense, there are other examples in which experience prevailed over ideology. The most important of them is, no doubt, the discarding of the Leninist doctrine of the unavoidability of war with the capitalist world. This revision was the consequence of the appearance of the absolute weapon, nuclear explosives.

[b] It is literally true that *many* non-Jews were liquidated in these camps, but only Jews and Gypsies were earmarked for *total destruction.* Thus, while other nationalities suffered grave losses, the end of the war found the bulk of these people alive, but there were only scattered Jewish survivors, and there would have been none had the war lasted but another year. Without doubt, the German occupation was hell for Poles, Ukrainians, and other Soviet people, but there were gradations in the Nazi hell and the difference between the higher echelons and the lowest among the damned was probably greater in terms of human misery than any difference between rich and poor.

Communist policy has thus followed a *zigzag course of shift-ing compromises* between a political theory to which Communists are tied by its superficial plausibility and by their interests, and the demands of adaptation to a non-Marxist reality. This kind of zigzag is likely to continue in the foreseeable future.

THE CREEPING CRISIS OF SOCIALIST ECONOMICS

There seems to be still another cloud on the Communist horizon: the regime may face a more or less chronic crisis of management. A crisis of agriculture there has always been. In some countries, the consequence of a Communist take-over was the substitution of agricultural deficits for previous agricultural surpluses; Russia, whose Ukrainian lands were in prerevolutionary times called the breadbasket of Europe, imported grains. The cause of the continuing crisis is the peasants' lack of enthusiasm for state farming and collective farming. The desire for personal property is not, as many Marxists seem to believe, a mere consequence of social institutions, fated to disappear together with them; it has more sturdy roots in human nature: in the desire for stable attachments, for continuity, for safety, for independence. The industrial worker sees clearly enough that a steel mill or a tractor factory cannot be divided up into a number of individually owned workshops; and men always accept the inevitable. The peasant, however, sees no such intrinsic necessity and suspects that his loathesome condition is due to the arbitrariness of power. He defends himself against it in the way slaves or forced laborers have always defended themselves, i.e., by working as little as they can get away with. Stalin broke the passive resistance of the countryside with appalling cruelty, but his successors do not seem willing or able to make this iron rule a permanent feature of Soviet society.

At the same time, the peasant gives all his loving care to the small plots that the government allows him to keep. These

tiny plots, a small fraction of the land, play a major role in
the food supply of the Soviet Union and Eastern European
countries.[9]

While inadequate food production is an old headache in
countries with socialized agriculture, a potentially more
dangerous new feature seems to be emerging in the more advanced socialist countries, viz., a crisis of industrial management. The difficulty of running a socialized industrial machine
without the possibility of calculating profit and loss in terms
of consumer satisfaction—a difficulty which has been voiced by
critics of socialism but which has not been understood by
Communist leaders—seems to be finally catching up with
Communist reality. When half a century ago von Mises saw
that the problem of socialism was the rational allocation of
primary resources which in "capitalism" is the function of the
market, he inferred that socialism was impossible.[10] This conclusion, of course, proved to be incorrect. Socialist economies
have existed and continue to exist; they are merely wasteful
and there is no reason to think that they are therefore impossible, at least as long as the people do not understand how
wasteful they are.

The more complex the industrial system, however, the
smaller the part of consumer goods and the greater the part of
capital goods is in the total output, the more difficult it becomes to rely on guessing for the evaluation of alternative
economic procedures, and the greater is the need for a rational system of comparison, i.e., the calculation of profits and
losses. Hence, there is increasing pressure in the Soviet Union
for the introduction of a system that would permit such calculation; and this means, in practice, a decentralization of
planning, with considerable freedom for the managers of
autonomous units to operate in a competitive market of goods
and labor. What this will in the long run mean for the power
monopoly of the Communist Party is impossible to foresee; it
is hardly likely to strengthen it.

19

The Predicament of the
Third World

The third, or "underdeveloped," world is only negatively characterized: it comprises all countries that are economically less developed and less affluent than the West, but they vary greatly both with regard to the stage of their economic development and their cultural traits. Some of them are fairly well advanced along the road of economic development, as far as, or perhaps farther than, some parts of Europe; others are, as Robert Sinai put it, pre-Hellenic or pre-Biblical.[1] The difference in prosperity and way of life between some Western and some underdeveloped countries is actually smaller than the differences within the third world itself; Uruguay is closer to Finland than to Haiti.

Yet, negatively defined as they are, they have negative attitudes in common. They all consider it imperative to have industrialization, particularly heavy industry which, in their circumstances, is more a source of power and prestige than of welfare. They consider themselves injured by the West, which has allegedly stunted their growth, and they believe that the West owes them something; and most of them expect fulfillment of their aspirations from their governments rather than from individual initiative.

This attitude is duplicated, on a smaller scale, by the attitude of certain relatively backward areas in the highly developed West, e.g., the Italian *Mezzogiorno* or French Canada; they, too, consider themselves "colonial." The differential that separates the *Mezzogiorno* from the industrially booming Italian North is much smaller than the differential between Milan and say, Tunisia, not to mention Yemen; and the differential between French and English Canada is much smaller still. Yet, difference there is; and the reaction is largely the same and the issue is inflammatory.

The case of French Canada is particularly illustrative. The French Canadians cannot claim that an alien government has deprived them of the possibility of working out their own destiny as Indians or Africans do. French Canadians have always had the right to vote on equal terms with English Canadians; the province of Quebec has been ruled by the French Canadians themselves. No external force has prevented them from building up French Canada into a great industrial complex or, for that matter, from spreading out into English Canada with their activities as Jewish businessmen and scientists have spread all over Europe, Armenian merchants of old over the Turkish Empire, or Americans over most of the accessible world. French Canadians see themselves as victims of discrimination; they may point to discriminatory employment practices of the great English Canadian concerns, but they do not seem to ask themselves how it came about that English Canadians were in a position to discriminate in the first place, i.e., why the large business concerns were operated mostly by English Canadians.

What happened was that the French Canadians, rooted in a conservative Catholic culture, had a more traditional way of life which was less favorable to the restless, enterprising spirit of economic development, while many more English Canadians had been inspired earlier with the spirit of modernity. That those more advanced in terms of alloplastic control of the environment and hence more powerful have then done what all holders of power in human history have done, i.e., have used it in a discriminatory fashion or, at least, in a fashion that seemed discriminatory to others, is quite likely; but this was the *consequence rather than the cause* of the differential in development.

The essence of economic development does not lie in the number of steel mills or airports. A steel mill may operate at a loss and thus, far from contributing to the general welfare, may actually detract from it; an airport may be used mainly by propagandists whose contribution to welfare is open to question. The essence of economic development is the *establishment of a chain reaction* of self-sustaining growth of the production machine measured in terms of people's preferences. In fissionable Uranium 235 or Plutonium, a chain reaction is established if the chance that a wandering neutron will free a neutron from another nucleus before leaving the fissionable material is greater than 1, however slightly; if it is smaller than 1, the reaction will die out. This is the simple characteristic of a *geometric* series. If the multiplicator which distinguishes one element of the series from the preceding one is smaller than 1, the sum has a finite value; if it is 1 or more, the sum is infinite.

The problem of development comes down to this: all relevant factors must operate and cooperate in such a way that a geometric series of the second type, a process of self-sustaining growth, ensues. Many an ambitious scheme in underdeveloped countries, whether inaugurated by local or foreign planners, led to disappointment because the multiplication factor was less than 1 and the spark, instead of kindling a larger fire, flickered out.

Biologists have learned more and more about the fact that organic life depends on highly intricate conditions; it cannot exist as long as one of them is lacking. In a similar manner, sustained growth is an intricate matter, depending on factors of nature such as available resources or conditions conducive to health, on the reactions of countless human beings, their habits of work or consumption, and on a favorable sociopolitical milieu such as, for instance, the existence of a large market.

One of these conditions is rooted in the ethos of the civili-

zation, the goals which people pursue in their lives—for instance, more wealth or more leisure—and on their habits.
The ethos of a community may be more or less favorable to
the requirements of an industrial civilization. Doctrines that
preach that the world is essentially evil and that wisdom lies
in withdrawal from it; or that human events are the manifestations of an inscrutable will of God and that happiness
lies only in unquestioning acceptance of the Divine Will;
or that the gentleman of leisure or the rentier occupy the
most desirable place in life—such doctrines are not favorable
to rapid industrial development.

The step from the prevailing ethos of a community to the
attitudes conducive to rapid growth may be greater or
smaller depending on whether or not the germs of the ideology of progress are alive in the existing body of tradition.
The step is relatively small for, say, French Canadians; there
have been great explorers, scientists, entrepreneurs and col-
onizers within the orbit of French Catholicism. It is large
for some of the really undeveloped countries.

Most leaders of the third world seem to desire only the
swift adoption of Western technology, either without awareness of the fact that these technological achievements have
grown in a particular cultural soil and cannot easily be trans-
planted to another soil, or, in any case, without much desire
to import anything Western except its technology.

The ensuing situation is very difficult. To adopt Western
technology, the countries of the third world would have to
adopt, in some degree at least, the Western ethos. This
means either discarding their own ethos and tradition, their
entire culture, in favor of an alien culture; or finding a viable compromise between the native tradition and the Western ethos, a compromise that would permit the development of Western technology out of some elements of the native tradition. The latter might be comparable to what
American winegrowers have been doing by grafting delicate
European vines on the sturdy but rather tasteless native variety.

The first course implies a total surrender of all collective pride; if it is adopted at all, it is likely to have stormy consequences. Today an attempt of this kind is being made in China where the great traditions of Chinese thought are consciously and contemptuously being thrown overboard. The ferocious nationalism of Communist China today may well be the necessary compensation for this surrender: if one's own traditions are worthless and an alien philosophy has to be embraced, one must at least be clearly the superior interpreter and defender of the adopted creed.

The second course, the compromise between native tradition and imported ethos, has so far been best realized by Japan. Yet, the Japanese solution, vastly superior though it seems in comparison with the present bungling efforts of others, is far from being fully satisfactory. Japanese society has shown severe stresses in consequence of the incompatibility of the ingredients of the mixture. Perhaps the period of unsound militaristic expansion which ended in the defeat of 1945 was ultimately due to stresses of this kind.

The desire for rapid economic development is further complicated by the anticapitalism of the ruling elites. While the resistance of uncongenial traditions makes economic development far more difficult than it was in the nineteenth-century Europe, other factors should make it much easier; the newcomers do not have to create out of nothing, they merely have to imitate and to adapt western inventions to local conditions. Moreover, the capital for the necessary investments does not have to come from surplus production or be squeezed out of the people through enforced underconsumption. Every year there are vast savings available in the Western countries, which seek safe and profitable investment opportunities. Western capital owners would be eager to invest in these new countries if they could expect a favorable return and feel safe from expropriation, partial or total, direct or indirect. But this the native elites do not want; they are mostly socialists of one or another variety.

It is sometimes argued that socialism is indispensable for

the development of the new countries because the Western "bourgeoisie," desirous to maintain a monopoly of wealth and industrial power, is no longer willing to finance the industrialization of other lands. This view is based on the Marxist doctrine which holds that people act according to class interests. In the real world, however, businessmen are motivated, as a rule, not by class interest but by the interest of their own parochial businesses. Class solidarity, like national solidarity or any other kind of group solidarity, comes into operation only in clear and pressing emergencies and gives way to more personal or parochial interests at other times. The theory is also at variance with the claim, made in the same ideological quarters, that "neo-colonialism," based on the desire of capitalists to exploit the resources of these countries, is a grave threat to their independence.

Others have argued that private business enterprise is unsuited to the economic development of the new countries, either because it would engage in projects which should not have high priority in terms of public interest and might actually be detrimental to it, or because business enterprise works too slowly to meet the urgent needs.

These contentions are based on the assumptions that government planners are motivated by the public good, which is always unambiguously clear and which they are competent to interpret, while businessmen are motivated by private profit, which is seen as essentially at variance with public interest. Nonsocialists may counter that the leaders' dedication to the public good becomes intricately interwoven with the striving toward power and self-aggrandizement and may at times be only a cover for the latter; and that it is impossible even for the wisest leaders to judge without the help of market mechanisms where the public good lies. Nonsocialists will further point out that, on the whole though not in every individual case, businessmen will make profits if they have been able to satisfy the wishes of the people, so that profits usually are indicators, if not of the public good in any absolute sense, at least of the people's own concept of it.

As far as the argument of inadequate speed is concerned, critics of the socialist position will point out that while it is possible for a government to mobilize national resources for any particular goal, it can do so only at the cost of neglecting other goals that may be as important, or more important, to the consumers; the superior power of government to deliver is thus based on its superior power to withhold.

These arguments pro and con are essentially the arguments that have been brought forth for generations in the discussion of the relative merits of a market economy and a command economy. They were advanced long before the issue of industrializing Asia or Africa turned up. I do not believe that any new aspect has been added to it—anything that is specifically African, Asian, or Latin American. The old battle is merely fought on new grounds.

In any case, the native elites of intellectuals in the third world are unwilling to share their new power with businessmen, foreign or native. They wish to remain free to spend national resources on prestige projects such as a splendid new capital city, or a streamlined airport in the midst of a Biblical landscape, or an atomic reactor in a land of wooden ploughs. They are more power oriented than welfare oriented, according to Nkrumah's famous slogan: seek ye first the political kingdom. Goals such as these can of course be achieved only by government action and not through private enterprise. But even where the production of goods of general demand is at issue, the present elites prefer any degree of waste to relaxing their hold on things.

We may wonder where the present unrest in the third world will lead. The wide diversity of the conditions in the countries involved suggests that the outcome may not be the same for all. Some of them will probably find their way into modern industrial civilization, through crises and violent upheavals of varying sharpness. Others may be less successful in this endeavor, at least as long as they are struggling along on their own.

Earlier in these pages, I quoted Bertrand de Jouvenel's formulation that revolutions substitute a strong for a weak authority; it seemed to me a correct description of their inherent trend. Applied to the global anticolonial revolution, this theory suggests that it may turn out to be the *replacement of the weakened authority of the West*—weakened through self-doubt—*by the strong hand of a new master,* whether Russian, Chinese, or new forces not yet on the scene. For the time being, the political independence of the new states is protected by big Power rivalry.

The sociopolitical picture that I have tried to sketch may appear to be very gloomy for all—for the West, for the Communists, and for the "third" world. The future need not be all that bad. The reason for this discrepancy is that I have considered only the *sociopolitical* scene: but there is more to life than public life; the two sources of power, physical force and ideas, do not make up the whole of history. There is still the anonymous mass of common people, trying to live their lives and build their nests, adjusting to currents and to storms as best they can, and forever building anew when the volcano has erupted and has destroyed their homes and gardens.

Notes

*The author wishes to thank the publishers
of the books and periodicals for permission
to quote from their publications.*

Part I

An Essay on Progress

1. Wolfram von den Steinen, *Das Zeitalter Goethes*. Bern: Francke Verlag, 1949, p. 150. Author's translation.

Chapter 1: Changing Views of Progress

1. Lucretius, *De rerum natura,* V, 1452-1457. Translated by Ronald Latham. Baltimore: Penguin, 1951 (italics added).
2. Sophocles, *Antigone,* 331-372. Translated by Elizabeth Wyckoff. *The Complete Greek Tragedies,* Vol. II, edited by David Grene and Richmond Lattimore. Chicago: University of Chicago Press, 1959.
3. See Christopher Dawson, *Medieval Essays*. New York: Shed & Ward, 1954, p. 140 f. For more detailed material, see George Sarton, *Introduction to the History of Science,* Vol. II. Carnegie Institution of Washington. Baltimore: Williams & Wilkins, 1931.
4. Dawson, *loc. cit.,* p. 145 f.
5. *Gratia naturam perficit, non sustulit.*
6. *Inferno,* 26, 107-120. Translated by Lawrence Grant White. New York: Pantheon Books, 1948.
7. *Ibid.,* 117-120.
8. Lorenzo Valla, *De libero arbitrio.* See *The Renaissance Philosophy of Man,* edited by Ernst Cassirer, Oskar Kristeller, and John Herman Randell, Jr. Chicago: University of Chicago Press, 1948, p. 156.
9. See Giorgio de Santillana, *The Crime of Galileo.* Chicago: University of Chicago Press, 1955, Chapter XVI.
10. Erich Przywara, *Religionsphilosophie katholischer Theologie. Handbuch der Philosophie,* Vol. II. München, Berlin: R. Oldenburg, 1927.

11. Condorcet, *Essquise d'un Tableau Historique de Progrès de l'Esprit Humain* (1795). English: *Sketch for a Historical Picture of the Progress of the Human Mind*. Translated by Jane Barraclough. New York: Noonday Press, 1955, p. 199 f.; italics added.

12. *Ibid.*, p. 201.

13. The source for the official Soviet interpretation of the principles of dialectic materialism has for a long time been the works of J. V. Stalin: *Principles of Leninism* (original Russian title: *Voprozy Leninizma*). English translation from the 11th Russian edition, Moscow, 1947.

More recent are two apparently authoritative textbooks: F. W. Konstantinow et al., editors, *Osnovy marksizma philosofii*. Moscow, 1958. German translation: *Grundlagen der marxistischen Philosophie*. Berlin (East): Dietz Verlag, 1961; and O. W. Kuusinen et al., editors, *Osnovy Marksizma-leninizma*. Moscow, 1958. German translation: *Grundlagen des Marxismus-Leninismus*. Berlin (East): Dietz Verlag, 1960. Both textbooks are the work of "collectives." They are indispensable for an understanding of Leninism.

There is, of course, an enormous Western literature on the subject, both descriptive and evaluative. One work may be mentioned as particularly useful: Kurt Marko, *Sic et Non: Kritisches Wörterbuch des Sowjetrussischen Marxismus-Leninismus der Gegenwart*. Wiesbaden: Otto Harassowitz, 1962. The author has extracted from authoritative Russian sources the meaning of the doctrine as applied to numerous political, sociological, and historical subjects and arranged the material in the form of a dictionary; it offers a quick orientation in contemporary Soviet thought on a variety of subjects.

14. V. Gordon Childe, *What Happened in History?* (1942). Baltimore: Penguin, 1954, p. 292.

15. J. V. Stalin, *Problems of Leninism*. Moscow, 1945, p. 557; italics added.

16. Newspaper report, quoted from memory.

17. M. Polanyi, The Magic of Marxism. *Bull. Atomic Scientists,* December, 1956. See also R. Waelder, *Psychoanalytic Avenues to Art*. New York: International Universities Press, 1965, p. 97 ff.

18. William Thomas, The Emergence of Ideas. *Times Literary Supplement,* April 7, 1966, p. 107.

19. F. M. Cornford, *The Unwritten Philosophy*. Cambridge: University Press, 1950.

20. Quoted from memory.

21. *Die Weltwoche,* December 26, 1963.

22. Denis de Rougemont, The End of Pessimism. In: *The Christian Opportunity.* New York: Holt, Rinehart & Winston, 1963, p. 158.

23. Raymond Aron, *The Century of Total War.* Boston: Beacon Press, 1955, p. 130.

24. The subject has been widely discussed. See, e.g., the remarks by Jeanne Hersch in *Colloques de Rheinfelden.* Paris: Calman-Lévy, 1962; also: I. Robert Sinai, *The Challenge of Modernisation.* London: Chatto & Windus, 1964. Some remarks by René Dubos on the introduction of science to underdeveloped countries are also relevant in this context. See *The Dreams of Reason: Science and Utopias.* New York: Columbia University Press, 1961, p. 155 f.

Chapter 2: The Modern Spirit

1. *Iliad,* 22, 210-213. *Translated by A. T. Murray.* Loeb Classical Library.

2. See, e.g., Basil Willey, *The Seventeenth Century Background.* (1934). New York: Doubleday Anchor Books, 1951. Foreword: The Rejection of Scholasticism. Also by the same author: *Darwin and Butler.* London: Chatto & Windus, 1960, p. 30 f.

3. F. M. Cornford, *Principia Sapientiae.* Cambridge: University Press, 1952, p. 6 f.

4. C. F. von Weizsäcker, *The World View of Physics.* Chicago: University of Chicago Press, 1952, p. 197.

5. S. Sambursky, *The Physical World of the Greeks.* London: Routledge & Kegan Paul, 1956.

6. Goethe, *Farbenlehre.* Polemischer Teil, 18; my translation.

7. *Georgics,* II, 490-492; my translation.

8. See, e.g., Henri Poincaré, *La Science et la Méthode* (1906). English translation by Francis Maitland. New York: Charles Scribner's Sons, 1916, p. 22.

9. *De rerum natura,* I, 62-71. Baltimore: Penguin, 1951; italics added.

10. See the discussion of Aristotelian dynamics by Stephen Toulmin, *Foresight and Understanding.* Bloomington: Indiana University Press, 1961.

11. Theodorius Dobzhansky, e.g., states that Darwin's *Origin of Species* "marks a turning point in the intellectual history of mankind" (*Man Evolving.* New Haven: Yale University Press, 1962, p. 1). Garrett Hardin calls modern science "the product of

two great revolutions in thought," viz., the Newtonian and the Darwinian, and finds that "the Darwinian revolution involved a far more profound re-assessment of the sense of the world" (*Nature and Man's Fate*. New York: Rinehart, 1959, p. 300 f.).

12. Albert Szent-Györgyi, The Promise of Medical Science. In: *Man and His Future*, edited by Gordon E. W. Wolstenholme. Boston: Little, Brown, 1963; London: J. & A. Churchill, 1964, p. 193 f.; italics added.

13. T. R. Bashow in *The New York Herald Tribune*, May 19, 1964.

14. Jean Rostand, *Bestiaire d'Amour*. London: Routledge & Kegan Paul, 1961, p. 126 f.

15. *Ibid.*, p. 126.

Chapter 3: The Moral Impulses

1. Quoted from memory.

2. *Summa Theologica*, Suppl. q, 94, art. 1.

3. D. P. Walker, *The Decline of Hell*. London: Routledge & Kegan Paul, 1964.

4. *Cautio criminales sive de processibus contra sagas liber*. Würzburg, 1635.

5. Robert Fedden, The Battle of Navarino. *History Today*, 11: 787, 1961.

6. *Institutiones*, I, 1. Loeb Classical Library.

7. *Politics*, 1280a. Translated by H. Rackham. Loeb Classical Library.

8. T. Schjelderup-Ebbe, Beiträge zur Sozialpsychologie des Haushuhns. *Zeitschr. f. Psychologie*, 88:225-252, 1922; Soziale Verhältnisse bei Vögeln. *Zeitschr. f. Psychologie*, 90:106-107, 1922; Weitere Beiträge zur Sozial- und Individualpsychologie des Haushuhns. *Zeitschr. f. Psychologie*, 92:60-87, 1923; and many subsequent publications. Schjelderup-Ebbe's discovery gave rise to a vast body of research into the social stratification in animals.

9. T. Schjelderup-Ebbe, Die Despotie im sozialen Leben der Vögel. In: Richard Thurnwald, *Forschungen der Völkerpsychologie und Soziologie*, 10:77-137, 1931; Despotism among Birds. *Scand. Scientific Review*, Vol. III, Nos. 3 and 4, pp. 10-82, 1935.

10. Denis de Rougemont, Christianity and World Problems. In : *The Christian Opportunity*. New York: Holt, Rinehart & Winston, 1963, p. 172; italics added.

11. R. Waelder. The Concept of Justice and the Quest for an Absolutely Just Society. Proceedings of the 28th Annual Judicial

NOTES   353

Conference of the United States, Atlantic City, September 8-10, 1965. *Federal Rules Decisions,* May, 1966. *Pennsylvania Law Review,* 115:1-11, 17-21, 1966.

12. *Maximen und Reflexionen,* 953.

13. George Santayana, *The Life of Reason,* Vol. II: *Reason in Society.* New York: Collier, 1962, p. 101.

Chapter 4: Assets and Liabilities of the Modern Movement

1. *Nan-hua Chen-ching,* XXIV, 2.

2. Romano Guardini, *The Death of Socrates.* New York: Meridian, 1945, p. 58.

3. C. H. Waddington. *The Ethical Animal.* London: George Allen & Unwin, 1960. New York: Atheneum, 1961, p. 15.

4. S. Ferenczi, The Phenomena of Hysterical Materialization (1919). In : *Further Contributions to the Theory and Technique of Psycho-Analysis.* London: Hogarth Press, 1950.

5. Attributed to Reinhold Niebuhr.

6. Rudyard Kipling. The Miracle of Purun Bhagat (1894). In: *The Jungle Books,* Vol. 2. New York: Doubleday & Co., 1949.

7. Arthur I. Waskow and Stanley L. Newman, *America in Hiding.* New York: Ballantine, 1962, p. 48.

8. Marcus Aurelius. *Ta eis heauton,* IV, 7; my translation.

9. Seneca. *Epistolae,* 123, 3; my translation.

10. Newspaper report quoted from memory.

11. Newspaper report quoted from memory.

12. Words from Shakespeare's *Richard II,* II, 1, 49.

13. René Dubos, *The Dreams of Reason: Science and Utopias.* New York: Columbia University Press, 1961, p. 57.

14. *Antigone,* 362-364. Translated by Elizabeth Wyckoff. Chicago: University of Chicago Press, 1959.

15. John Gardner, *Excellence: Can We Be Equal and Excel, Too?* New York: Harper & Row, 1961, p. 72.

16. Virginia Constitution.

17. Title of a book by Harold D. Lasswell, *Politics: Who Gets What, When, How?* New York: McGraw-Hill, 1936.

18. This was described as the prototype of leadership by the late Dr. Paul Federn (personal communication).

Chapter 5: The Conservative Criticism of Modernity

1. Ananda K. Coomaraswamy, Young India: In: *Indian Art and Culture.* New York: Noonday Press, 1957, p. 150.

2. George Santayana, *My Host the World*. New York: Charles Scribner's Sons; London: Cresset Press, 1953, p. 180 ff.

3. Paul Valéry, Our Destiny and Literature (1937). In: *The Collected Works of Paul Valéry*, edited by J. Mathews. New York: Pantheon Books, 1956, Vol. X, p. 167.

4. The phrase is taken from George F. Kennan, *Realities of American Foreign Policy*. Princeton: Princeton University Press, 1954.

5. Quoted from memory from one of the annual Surveys of the Royal Institute of International Affairs.

6. Stefan George, *Der Stern des Bundes* (1913). In: *Poems*, translated by Carol North Valhope and Ernest Morwitz. New York: Pantheon Books, 1943, p. 191.

7. *Der Stern des Bundes*. Berlin: George Bondi, p. 95.

8. T. S. Eliot, *The Waste Land*. New York: Boni & Liveright, 1922.

9. Quoted after W. Heisenberg, Das Naturbild der heutigen Physik. In: *Die Künste im technischen Zeitalter*. Darmstadt: Wissenschaftliche Buchgesellschaft, 1956.

10. Adolf Portmann. *Grenzen des Lebens*. Basel: Friedrich Reinhardt, 1943, p. 63 f.; my translation.

11. Reinhold Niebuhr, *An Interpretation of Christian Ethics*. New York: Harper & Row, 5th ed., 1935, p. 97 f.

12. Luis Diez del Corral, *The Rape of Europe*. London: George Allen & Unwin, 1959, p. 304.

Chapter 6: The Scapegoat Movements

1. *Die Weltwoche*, January 10, 1964. Retranslated from a German translation: "Wir beklagen uns über die Schuhe, aber schuld sind die Füsse."

2. J. D. B. Miller, *The Nature of Politics*. London: Gerald Duckworth, 1962, p. 158.

3. August Bebel, *Die Frau und der Sozialismus* (1883). Stuttgart: 1919, p. 444.

4. Leo Trotzki, *Literatur und Revolution* (Vienna, 1924, p. 189; Moscow, 1923). Quoted from Iring Fetscher: *Der Marxismus, seine Geschichte in Dokumenten*, Vol. III. München: R. Piper & Co., 1965, p. 462.

5. Ernest B. Haas, Toward Controlling International Change: A Personal Plea. *World Politics,* October, 1964, p. 9 f.

6. V. I. Lenin, *Pravda*, No. 113, May, 1913. German transla-

tion: *Über die nationale und koloniale nationale Frage.* Berlin (East): Dietz, 1960, p. 94; italics added.

7. Bertrand de Jouvenel, The Treatment of Capitalism by Continental Intellectuals. In: F. A. von Hayek, *Capitalism and the Historians.* Chicago: University of Chicago Press, 1954, p. 115.

8. Martin Offenbacher, *Konfession und soziale Schichtung: Eine Studie über die wirtschaftliche Lage der Katholiken und Protestanten in Baden.* Tübingen and Leipzig: Volkswirtschaftliche Abhandlungen der badischen Hochschulen, Vol. IV, Part III, 1901.

9. Charles Singer, Science and Judaism. In: *The Jews, Their History, Culture and Religion,* edited by Louis Finkelstein. New York: Harper Brothers, 1949, Vol. II, p. 1072; italics added.

10. Letter to Lewis Einstein, September 28, 1918. *The Holmes-Einstein Letters.* London: Macmillan, 1964; New York: St. Martin's Press, 1964, p. 171 f.; italics added.

11. Ludwig von Mises, *Socialism* (1922). New Haven: Yale University Press, 1951; Max Weber, *Wirtschaft und Gesellschaft.* Tübingen: J. C. B. Mohr (Paul Siebeck), 1925.

12. V. I. Lenin, *State and Revolution.* New York: Vanguard Press, 1929, p. 205.

13. Cp. Gregory Grossman, *Value and Plan: Economic Calculation in Eastern Europe.* Berkeley: University of California Press, 1960; L. V. Kantorovich, *The Best Use of Economic Resources.* Cambridge: Harvard University Press, 1965.

14. Cp. G. S. Brandon, *History, Time and Deity.* University of Manchester Press and New York: Barnes & Noble, 1965, p. 177 f.; Jesus and Politics. *History Today,* April, 1965, p. 283.

15. *Abdias.*

16. "Ressentiment der Zurückgebliebenen."

17. Hans Bernd Gisevius, *Adolf Hitler.* Munich: Ruetten & Loening, 1963, p. 449.

18. J. L. Talmon, *Political Messianism: The Romantic Phase.* New York: Frederick A. Praeger, 1960, p. 77 f.; italics added.

19. Francis E. Dart, The Rub of Culture. *Foreign Affairs,* Vol. XLI, January, 1963.

20. Cp. S. Freud, Formulations on the Two Principles of Mental Functioning (1911). *Standard Edition,* 12:213-226. London: Hogarth Press, 1958.

21. *Man and Superman,* Act III.

22. Francis E. Dart, *loc. cit.*

23. Charles L. Sanford, *The Quest for Paradise.* Urbana: University of Illinois Press, 1961, p. 37.

Chapter 7: Future Prospects of the Modern Development

1. In: H. Diels, *Die Fragmente der Vorsokratiker*. Berlin: Weidmannsche Buchhandlung, 1906-1910.

2. Karl Marx, *Kritik des Gothaer Programms,* IV, B. 3 (1875). (Studienausgabe der Wissenschaftlichen Buchgesellschaft, Vol. III, p. 1038.)

3. George S. Counts, Charles Beard, the Public Man. In: *Charles A. Beard: An Appraisal,* edited by Howard K. Beale. Lexington: University of Kentucky Press, 1954, p. 251 f.

4. S. Freud, Psychogenesis of a Case of Female Homosexuality (1920). *Standard Edition,* Vol. XVIII, p. 167 f. London: Hogarth Press, 1955.

5. Newspaper report, quoted from memory.

6. W. W. Rostow, *The Stages of Economic Growth: A Non-Communist Manifesto.* Cambridge: University Press, 1960, p. 166.

7. Quoted from memory.

8. Garrett Hardin, The Last Canute. *Scientific Monthly,* 63:203-208, 1946.

Part II

An Essay on Revolution

Chapter 8: The Power Structure

1. K. A. Varnhagen von Ense & Friedrich Schwarzenberg, *Europäische Zeitenwende, Tagebücher 1835-1860.* Munich: Albert Langen, George Muller, 1960, p. 208.

2. Cp. Eric Voegelin, Bakunin's Confession. *Journal of Politics,* 8:24-43, February, 1946.

3. *King Henry V,* IV, 1.

4. Ovid, *Metamorphoses,* I, 89-91.

5. Cp. the discussion of this subject in the fifth book of Aristotle's *Politics.*

6. *Annals,* 14:44.

7. Marchant, *Wit and Wisdom of Dean Inge.* No. 108.

8. Cp. R. Waelder, Authoritarianism and Totalitarianism: Psychological Comments on a Problem of Power. In: *Psychoanalysis and Culture,* edited by G. B. Wilbur and W. Muensterberger. New York: International Universities Press, 1951, pp. 185-195.

Chapter 9: The Influence of Physical Force upon the Mind or How Might Makes Right

1. Simone Weil, The Great Beast. In: Selected Essays. New York: Oxford University Press, 1962, p. 143.
2. Alexis de Tocqueville, Democracy in America. New York: Alfred A. Knopf, 1945, Vol. II, p. 11.
3. This is a somewhat simplified statement of facts and the reality is slightly more complex. The formulation is correct for the single encounter; but in prolonged contact a hypnotist may gradually condition a subject to obedience to commands at variance with the latter's former character.
4. Edgar H. Schein with Inge Schneier and Curtis H. Barker, Coercive Persuasion: A Socio-Psychological Analysis of the "Brainwashing" of American Civilian Prisoners by the Chinese Communists. New York: W. W. Norton & Co., 1961.
5. R. Waelder, Demoralization and Re-education. World Politics, 14:375-385, 1962.
6. Albert D. Biderman, in an Air Force report (1954) reproduced by the Senate Permanent Investigations Subcommittee and published in the author's March to Calumny: The Story of American POWs in the Korean War. London & New York: Macmillan Co., 1963, p. 144 f.
7. Wilhelm Röpke, The Solution of the German Problem. New York: G. P. Putnam's Sons, 1946, p. 38.
8. Ervin Sinko, Roman eines Romans. Köln: Verlag der Wissenschaft und Politik, 1962, p. 354 ff.

Chapter 10: Polemic Supplement: Underestimation of the Role of Violence

1. Christian Morgenstern, Galgenlieder. Translated by Max Knight. Berkeley: University of California Press, 1963.
2. S. L. Washburn and I. De Vore, The Social Life of Baboons. Scientific American, Vol. CCIV, June, 1961, p. 70.
3. Bertrand Russell, Which Way to Peace? London: Michael Joseph, 1936, pp. 139 and 137.
4. Speech at the opening session of the German Reichstag, March, 1933.
5. Thucydides, History of the Peloponnesian War, V, 91.
6. Jerome Frank, Atomic Arms and Pre-Atomic Man. Bulletin of the Atomic Scientist, Vol. XVII, November, 1961, p. 364.

7. *Die Weltwoche,* about 1962, quoted from memory.
8. Carl Benedikt Hase, ed. *Leonis Diaconi Caloënsis Libri Decem.* Bonn, 1828, pp. 87-91.

Chapter 11: The Influence of Ideas upon Force

1. *Theatrum Europaeum,* II, p. 198.
2. Max Lerner, *Ideas Are Weapons: The History and Uses of Ideas.* New York: Viking Press, 1939.
3. J. M. Keynes, *The General Theory of Employment, Interest, and Money.* New York: Harcourt, Brace & Co., 1926, p. 383.
4. *Das gesellschaftliche Sein bestimmt das gesellschaftliche Bewusstsein;* my translation.

Chapter 12: Utopianism

1. Seneca, *Epistolae morales,* 97, 1.
2. The term first used by President Clark Kerr of the University of California.
3. Seymour Martin Lipset. *Political Man.* Garden City: Doubleday & Co., 1960, p. 413.
4. Alexis de Tocqueville, *Democracy in America.* New York: Alfred A. Knopf, 1943, Vol. II, p. 30.
5. Michael Oakeshott, *Rationalism in Politics.* London: Methuen, 1960; New York: Basic Books, 1962, p. 185.
6. *Ibid.,* p. 194.
7. Dante, *Inferno,* 26, 107-120. Translated by Lawrence Grant White. New York: Pantheon Books, 1948.
8. Speech at the funeral of Neville Chamberlain.
9. Newspaper report at the time. Quoted from memory.
10. J. L. Talmon, *Political Messianism: The Romantic Phase.* New York: Frederick A. Praeger, 1960; Norman Cohn, *The Pursuit of the Millenium.* London: Secker & Warburg, 1957.
11. After the title of a book by Eric Johnston.
12. *Grundlagen des Marxismus-Leninismus.* Berlin (East): Dietz Verlag, 1960, p. 820; italics added.
13. Ovid, *Metamorphoses,* VII, 20.
14. Sayings of the Father. In: *The Union Prayer Book for Jewish Worship,* Part I. Cincinnati: Central Conference of the American Rabbis, 1944, p. 166.
15. Reinhold Niebuhr, *Of Empires and Nations.* New York: Scribners, 1956, p. 30 f.

16. Jean Rostand, *The Substance of Man*. Garden City: Doubleday & Co., 1962, p. 173.

17. Quoted after Carl J. Burckhardt, *Gestalten und Mächte*. Zurich: Manesse, 1961, p. 476.

18. *Epigramme*. Venedig 1790, No. 53; my translation.

Chapter 13: Three Current Views of Revolution

1. Werner Druckert, *Unehrliche Leute*. Bern: Francke, 1963.

2. Bertrand de Jouvenel, *Pure Theory of Politics*. New Haven: Yale University Press, 1963, p. 64; italics added.

3. H. R. Trevor-Roper, The Spanish Enlightenment. In: *Historical Essays*. London: Macmillan, 1957, p. 271.

4. George L. Blanksten, Fidel Castro and Latin America. In: *The Revolution in World Politics*, edited by Morton A. Kaplan. New York: John Wiley & Sons, 1962, p. 127.

5. Reported in the newspapers; quoted from memory.

6. Hugh Seton-Watson, *The Pattern of Communist Revolution* (1953). London: Methuen, rev. ed., 1960, p. 353.

7. Chalmers Johnson, *Revolution and the Social System* [The Hoover Institution on War, Revolution and Peace]. Stanford University, 1964, p. 12.

8. Alexis de Tocqueville, *Democracy in America*. New York: Alfred A. Knopf, 1945, Vol. II, p. 295; italics added.

9. Alexis de Tocqueville, *The Old Régime and the French Revolution*. New York: Doubleday Anchor, 1955, p. 176 f.; italics added.

10. *Ibid.*, p. 177.

11. Crane Brinton, *The Anatomy of Revolution*. New York: Prentice Hall, 1952, p. 264.

12. Friedrich Nietzsche, *Werke in drei Bänden*. Munich: Carl Hause, 1956, Vol. III, p. 637; my translation.

13. Joseph Hamburger, *James Mill and the Art of Revolution*. New Haven: Yale University Press, 1963.

14. Alexis de Tocqueville. *Recollections*. New York: Meridian Books, 3rd pr., 1965, p. 107.

Chapter 14: A General Framework for a Future Comprehensive Theory of Revolution

1. General theories of revolution have been developed during times of major revolutionary upheavals; i.e., particularly, at the time of the Greek city states and again since the French Revolu-

tion. In the first of these periods, Aristotle's theory in the fifth book of his *Politics* stands out as a magnificent achievement. We have experienced more than Aristotle could foresee, but his basic propositions still appear to be valid; more so than most of the currently popular theories. The literature since the French Revolution is, of course, immense, and some of the generalizations are hidden in historical treatises. In this second period of flowering of theories of revolution, Alexis de Tocqueville's work is outstanding. Among later comprehensive treatments of the subject are those by Vilfredo Pareto, Emil Lederer, Alfred Vierkandt, Pitirim Sorokin, Crane Brinton, Eugen Rosenstock-Huessy. Perhaps the most comprehensive treatment of the subject today can be found in Harry Eckstein, On the Etiology of Internal Wars (In: *History and Theory*, V 4: 133-163, 1965).

2. In the *Symposium*.

3. Speech delivered (in German) before a meeting of Swiss working class youths in Zurich on January 9, 1917. *Werke*, Vol. XXIII, Berlin, 1960, p. 261 f. (Fifth Russian edition of Lenin's works, Vol. XXX, Moscow, 1962, p. 328).

4. Cp. Hans Bernd Gisevius, *To the Bitter End*. Boston: Houghton Mifflin Co., 1947, on the difficulties encountered by the anti-Hitler conspirators in their search among oppositional officers for one who would accept the assignment of actually killing Hitler.

5. Robert W. Hodge, Paul M. Siegel, and Peter H. Rossi, Occupational Prestige in the United States, 1925-1963. *American Journal of Sociology*, 70:286-302, 1964.

6. J. D. B. Miller, *The Nature of Politics*. London: Gerald Duckworth & Co., 1962, p. 26; italics added.

7. Alexis de Tocqueville, Letter to Chabrol. See Charles Wilson Pierson, *Tocqueville in America*. New York: Doubleday Anchor, 1959, p. 87.

8. *Politics*, 1266 b/67 a. Translated by H. Rackham. Loeb Classical Library.

9. *Ibid.*, 1302.

10. Arthur Schopenhauer, *Aphorismen zur Lebensweisheit*, *Chapter II*.

11. Kenneth D. Keele, Pain: Past and Present. *Yale Review*, 1959, Autumn, pp. 43-50.

12. Norman Mailer, *The Presidential Papers*. New York: G. P. Putnam's Sons, 1963, p. 70.

13. Letter to Quietanus Remus, August 4, 1619. In: Carola Baumgardt, *Johannes Kepler, Life and Letters*. New York: Philosophical Library, 1951, p. 140 f.

14. S. I. Hayakawa, Communication: Interracial and International. *ETC.: A Review of General Semantics,* 20:395-410, 1964.

15. *Faust,* 11446. Translated by Walter Kaufmann. New York: Doubleday Anchor, 1961.

16. S. Freud, Why War? Letter to Albert Einstein (1932). *Standard Edition,* Vol. XXII, p. 210. London: Hogarth Press, 1964.

17. *Pravda,* January 21, 1937; italics added.

18. Bertrand Russell, *Bolshevism: Practice and Theory.* New York: Harcourt, Brace & Howe, 1920, p. 40.

19. C. R. Carpenter, Societies of Monkeys and Apes. In: *Biological Symposia,* Vol. VIII: *Levels of Integration in Biological and Social Systems,* edited by Jaques Cattell. Lancaster, Pa.: Jaques Cattell Press, 1942, p. 193 f.

20. L. B. Namier, 1848: Seed Plots of History. In: *Avenues of History.* London: Hamish Hamilton, 1952, p. 46; italics added.

21. Bertrand de Jouvenel, *On Power* (1945). Boston: Beacon Press, 1962, p. 216; italics added.

Chapter 15: The Modern Revolution and Its Relation to War

1. In his speech of June 7, 1794.

2. Letter to Alexander von Hübner, May 1, 1851.

3. Letter to Gottfried Kinkel, June 13, 1842.

4. An allusion to Charles de Gaulle's famous book, *Vers l'armée de métier.*

5. Bertrand de Jouvenel, *The Pure Theory of Politics.* New Haven: Yale University Press, 1963, p. 179 f.; italics added.

6. Elie Halévy, *The World Crisis of 1914-1918: An Interpretation.* Oxford: Clarendon Press, 1930.

7. Paul Valéry, On Political Parties (1931). *Collected Works,* Vol. X. New York: Pantheon Press, 1962, p. 249.

Part III

The World Crisis of the Mid-Twentieth Century

1. Letter to Siegfried A. Kähler, August 17, 1934. In: Friedrich Meinecke, *Ausgewählter Briefwechsel,* edited by Ludwig Dehio and Peter Classen. Stuttgart: K. F. Koehler, 1962; my translation.

This remark recalls Freud's vision of world events as a perpetual struggle between the two "giants" Eros and Thanatos, the Forces of Love and the Forces of Destruction.

Chapter 16: The Predicament of the Developed Countries

1. Jacques Ellul, *The Technological Society*. New York: Alfred A. Knopf, 1965, p. 435.
2. Denis de Rougemont, Christianity and World Problems. In: *The Christian Opportunity*. New York: Holt, Rinehart & Winston, 1963, p. 173.
3. *Die Weltwoche*, March 6, 1964.
4. Ignazio Silone, Vom Schrecken des Wohlfahrtsstaates. *Forum*, 8:318, 1961.
5. Dennis Gabor, *Inventing the Future*. London: Secker & Warburg, 1963; New York: Alfred A. Knopf, 1964.
6. Bertrand de Jouvenel, *Pure Theory of Politics*. New Haven: Yale University Press, 1963, p. 64. Cp. also the discussion of this subject by Alexis de Tocqueville in his *Democracy in America*, Part II, Book II, Chapter XIII: "Why the Americans Are so Restless in the Midst of Their Prosperity."
7. Cp. the previously quoted passage (Chapter 13) from Alexis de Tocqueville, *Democracy in America*, New York: Alfred A. Knopf, 1945, Vol. II, p. 295.
8. Kenneth Keniston, *The Uncommitted: Alienated Youth in American Society*. New York: Harcourt, Brace & World, 1966.
9. Kurt Lewin, Socio-Psychological Differences between the United States and Germany (1936). In: *Resolving Social Conflicts*. New York: Harper & Row, 1948, p. 18 ff.
10. Title of a novel by Goethe.
11. Alexis de Tocqueville, *Democracy in America*. New York: Alfred A. Knopf, 1945, Vol. II, p. 225; italics added.
12. T. S. Eliot, From Poe to Valéry (1948). In: *To Criticize the Critic*. New York: Farrar, Straus & Giroux, 1965, p. 42.

Chapter 17: The Predicament of the Western Democracies

1. George Lichtheim, *Marxism*. New York: Friedrich A. Praeger, 1963, p. 360.
2. Eric Williams, *Capitalism and Slavery*. New York: Russell & Russell, 1961.

3. Attributed to Billy Graham.

4. Allen Ginsberg, Back to the Wall. *Times Literary Supplement,* August 6, 1961.

5. The Land of Hope and Racial Crisis. *Times Literary Supplement,* August 13, 1964.

6. Randall Jarrell, A Sad Heart at the Supermarket. *Daedalus,* Spring, 1960, p. 363.

7. Aristotle, *Politics,* II, 1259 a.

8. Rabbi Eugene B. Borowitz of New York in *Commentary,* May, 1965, p. 10, summarizing an article by Dr. Leslie H. Farber in the November, 1964 issue of the same periodical.

9. Melvin Tumin, Shock Troops (Tennessee Division). *New York Times Book Review,* October 30, 1966.

10. Irving Howe, Madness, Vision, Stupidity. *The New Republic,* November 28, 1964, p. 23.

11. Alfred Kazin, The Bridge. *New York Review of Books,* July 15, 1965, p. 7.

12. The Transposed Heads (1940). In: *Stories of a Lifetime,* Vol. II. London: Mercury Books, 1961.

13. Reinhard Bendix, *Max Weber.* Garden City, N.Y.: Doubleday, 1960, p. 267.

14. V. C. Wynne-Edwards, Self-Regulatory Systems in Populations of Animals. *Science,* 147:1543-1548, 1965.

15. Cp., e.g., Lessing's *Minna von Barnhelm.*

16. Malcolm Muggeridge, Then and Now. *Encounter,* April, 1964, p. 31.

17. Owen Harris, Six Ways of Confusing Issues. *Foreign Affairs,* Vol. XL, p. 443, 1962; italics added.

18. *Arbeiter Zeitung,* October 23, 1932.

19. C. L. Sulzberger, A Problem First Posed by Pericles. *The New York Times,* May 13, 1961.

Chapter 18: The Predicament of the Communist Countries

1. Richard Löwenthal, *Chruschtschow und der Weltkommunismus.* Stuttgart: W. Kohlhammer, 1963, p. 9.

2. *Das Kapital,* Book I, Chapter VII, 2 (Karl Marx Ausgabe der Wissenschaftlichen Buchgesellschaft, Vol. LV, p. 228).

3. *Ibid.,* p. 229 f .

4. Speech at the Nineteenth Congress of the Communist Party. See Joseph V. Stalin, *Economic Problems of Socialism in the U.S.S.R.* New York: International Publishers, 1952, p. 27 ff.

5. Cp. James F. Byrnes, *Frankly Speaking*. New York: Harper & Brothers, 1952, p. 57 f.

6. Allen Dulles, *The Secret Surrender*. New York: Harper & Row, 1966.

7. Jonathan Steinberg, The Copenhagen Complex. *Journal of Contemporary History*, 1:23-46, 1966.

8. N. S. Khrushchev, The Great Strength of Soviet Literature and Art. *Soviet Booklet*, No. 108. London, March, 1963; italics added.

9. J. Newth, Soviet Agriculture: The Private Sector 1950-1959. *Soviet Studies*, October, 1961, April, 1962; Nancy Nimitz, The Lean Years. *Problems of Communism*, May-June, 1965; J. Karcz, The New Agricultural Program. *Soviet Studies*, October, 1965.

10. Ludwig von Mises, Die Gemeinwirtschaft (1913). *Socialism: An Economic and Sociological Analysis*, translated by J. Kahane. New Haven: Yale University Press, 1959.

Chapter 19: The Predicament of the Third World

1. I. Robert Sinai, *The Challenge of Modernisation*. London: Chatto & Windus, New York: W. W. Norton & Co., 1964.

Topical Contents

I

An Essay on Progress

III

The World Crisis of the Mid-Twentieth Century